1,000,000 Books

are available to read at

Forgotten Books

www.ForgottenBooks.com

Read online
Download PDF
Purchase in print

ISBN 978-1-334-23054-7
PIBN 10749998

This book is a reproduction of an important historical work. Forgotten Books uses state-of-the-art technology to digitally reconstruct the work, preserving the original format whilst repairing imperfections present in the aged copy. In rare cases, an imperfection in the original, such as a blemish or missing page, may be replicated in our edition. We do, however, repair the vast majority of imperfections successfully; any imperfections that remain are intentionally left to preserve the state of such historical works.

Forgotten Books is a registered trademark of FB &c Ltd.
Copyright © 2018 FB &c Ltd.
FB &c Ltd, Dalton House, 60 Windsor Avenue, London, SW19 2RR.
Company number 08720141. Registered in England and Wales.

For support please visit www.forgottenbooks.com

1 MONTH OF FREE READING

at
www.ForgottenBooks.com

By purchasing this book you are eligible for one month membership to ForgottenBooks.com, giving you unlimited access to our entire collection of over 1,000,000 titles via our web site and mobile apps.

To claim your free month visit: www.forgottenbooks.com/free749998

* Offer is valid for 45 days from date of purchase. Terms and conditions apply.

English
Français
Deutsche
Italiano
Español
Português

www.forgottenbooks.com

Mythology Photography **Fiction**
Fishing Christianity **Art** Cooking
Essays Buddhism Freemasonry
Medicine **Biology** Music **Ancient Egypt** Evolution Carpentry Physics
Dance Geology **Mathematics** Fitness
Shakespeare **Folklore** Yoga Marketing
Confidence Immortality Biographies
Poetry **Psychology** Witchcraft
Electronics Chemistry History **Law**
Accounting **Philosophy** Anthropology
Alchemy Drama Quantum Mechanics
Atheism Sexual Health **Ancient History**
Entrepreneurship Languages Sport
Paleontology Needlework Islam
Metaphysics Investment Archaeology
Parenting Statistics Criminology
Motivational

THE ARCHITECTURAL REVIEW

VOLUME XVI
JANUARY TO DECEMBER
1909

BOSTON
BATES & GUILD COMPANY
1909

INDEX

THE ARCHITECTURAL REVIEW

January to December, 1909

VOLUME XVI

INDEX TO ARTICLES AND EDITORIALS

Aërial Architecture, 81
American Domestic Architecture, Improvement of, 93
American Federation of Arts, 165
American Sculpture, An Open-Air Exhibition of, by Jens Jensen, 57
Amount of Information Received from Cement Manufacturers, 9
Amusement Architecture, by Frederic Thompson 85, 93
An Open-air Exhibition of American Sculpture, by Jens Jensen, 57
A "Skyscraper Schoolhouse", 53
A Suggestion to Lessen Fire Losses, 9
Architects' Disregard of Surroundings, 53
Architectural Forms Borrowed from Europe, 25
Architecture in Popular Magazines, 69, 153
Artistic Temperament, 25
Atelier System, 117
Berlin "Underground," The, by Julius Grundmann, 73
Beginners in Architecture, 141
Brown, Frank Chouteau, Exterior Plaster Construction, V, Metal and Concrete Framing, 133-138
Buckly, Julian A., Picturesque Country Buildings of Maryland, 1
Competitions, Conduct of, 37, 53, 69
Controversy in Regard to Location of Lincoln Memorial, 9

Current Periodicals 10, 26, 38, 54, 70, 82, 94, 118, 130, 142, 154, 166
Defects in Architectural Schooling, 117
Effect of Certain Tariffs on Incomes of Contractor and Architect, 81
Exterior Plaster Construction V, Metal and Concrete Framing, by Frank Chouteau Brown, 133-138
Filing of Magazines, 69
Ford, Geo. B. The Hotel Meurice, Paris, 121
Fowler, Lawrence Hall, "Montebello," 145
Garden Design in England, by Hon. Thos. H. Mawson, A. R. I. B. A., 41
Grundmann, Julius, The Berlin "Underground", 73
The Passage Kaufhaus, Berlin, 29
Half-Timber Buildings of Saxony, by C. A. Whittemore, 13
Hotel Meurice, Paris, The, by Geo. B. Ford, 121
How Early Architecture of This Country Can Be Preserved, 153
How the Standard of Architecture Can Be Raised, 81
Improvement of American Domestic Architecture, 93
In Memoriam of Mr. C. F. McKim, 129
Jensen, Jens, An Open-air Exhibition of American Sculpture, 57

Lack of Credit to Architects' Associates, 129
Lack of Simplicity in Dwelling Architecture, 141
Lincoln Memorial, Controversy in Regard to Location of, 9
McKim, C. F., In Memoriam of, 129
Magonigle, H. Van B. The Preparation of Working Drawings, 157
Mawson, Hon. Thos. H., A. R. I. B. A., Garden Design in England, 41
"Montebello" by Lawrence Hall Fowler, 145
Passage Kaufhaus, Berlin, The, by Julius Grundmann, 29
Picturesque Country Buildings of Maryland by Julian A. Buckly, 1
Popular Architecture, 93
Preparation of Working Drawings, The, by H. Van B. Magonigle, 157
Preservation of Early Architecture, 153
Rebuilding of Reggio, The, 25
Recent Work of York & Sawyer, 97
Relation between Senior and Junior Members of Architectural Clubs, 165
Residence of Bertram G. Goodhue, 75
Thompson, Frederic, Amusement Architecture, 85
"University Day" in University of Pennsylvania, 81
Whittemore, C. A., Half-timber Buildings of Saxony, 13

INDEX TO ILLUSTRATIONS

ACCORDING TO SUBJECT

Academies: West Point, N. Y., 155
American Sculpture: 57-59
Amusement Architecture: 85-90
Altars: Pittsburgh, Pa., Plate xv
Apartment Buildings: New York City, 91, 92
Banks: Albany, N. Y., 100, 103, 113, 115, Plates LXI, LXX; Babylon, L. I., 99; Baltimore, Md., 97, 103, 111, 114, Plate LXIX; Brooklyn, N. Y., 58; Cleveland, O., 130; Dudley, Eng., 144; London, Eng., 120; Montreal, Canada, 27, 110, 168; New Haven, Conn., 27; New Orleans, La., 155; New York City, 11, 26, 54, 103, 119; Pittsburgh, Pa., 131; Rochester, N. Y., Plates LIII-LX, 98, 103; Walsall, Eng., 144; Washington, D. C., 108, 109, 110, 112, 114, Plates LXIII-LXVIII

Baseball Pavilion: Philadelphia, Pa., 94
Bathrooms: New York City, Leow House, 92
Business Buildings: Berlin, Germany, 29-32; Chicago, Ill., 166; London, Eng., 28, 46, 72; New York City, 11
Chapels: New York City, 11; Normandy, 156
Churches: Bassett, Eng. (Modern English Churches), Plates XVII, XVIII; Blandford, Eng. (Modern English Churches), Plate X; Boerne, West Tex., 139, Plate LXXIX; Bologna, Italy, 142; Butler, Pa., Plates LXXII, LXXIII; Danbury, Conn., 94; Durham, Eng., 56; Edinburgh, Scotland, 28; Kensington, Eng., 28; Kent, Eng. (Modern English Churches), Plates XV, XVI; Kingsway, Eng., 168; McKeesport, Pa., 38; Montgomery,

Ala., 139, Plate LXXXVI; New London, Conn., Plate LXXVII; Notting Hill Gate, Eng. (Details), 55, 56; Paris, France, 28; Philadelphia, Pa., 142; Rochester, N. Y., 11; Staffordshire, Eng. (Modern English Churches), Plate IX; Stratford, E., Eng. (Modern English Churches), Plates XI-XIV; Somerville, Mass., 94; Worcestershire, Eng., 72; Yorkshire, Eng., 120
Club Buildings: Chicago, Ill., 71; Cleveland, O., 83; Greenwich, Conn., 95; London, Eng., 46, 71; Montreal, Canada, 120; New York City, 39; Norfolk, Va., 55, Plates LXXXIII, LXXXIV; Pittsburgh, Pa., 38; Washington, D. C., 70; White Plains, N. Y., Plates XLV, LII
College and University Buildings: Boston, Mass., Harvard Medical School, Ad-

ministration Building, Plate XXVIII; Boston College Competition, 60-65; Lake Forest, Ill., Lake Forest University, Dining-hall, 54; Norton, Mass., Wheaton Seminary, 7; Princeton, N. J., Princeton University, Stafford Little Hall and '79 Dormitory, 118
Dining-rooms: Auburn, Ala., Polytechnic Institute, 166; New York City, 39; Wiltshire, Eng., 7
Doors and Vestibules: Wiltshire, Eng., 7
Exterior Plaster Construction, 133-138
Fountain: Chicago, Ill., 58
Garage: Babylon, L. I., 99
Gardens: Chicago, Ill., 57-59; Cleveland, O., 167; Cornish, N. H., Plates XXXI, XXXIV; England, 41-52, Plates XXIX, XXX, XXXV, XXXVI; Paris, France, Plates XXXII, XXXIII

THE ARCHITECTURAL REVIEW

Gateways: Dedham, Mass., 10; Minneapolis, Minn. (Gateway Park), 10; Owings Mills, Md., 1; Trentham, M.I., 1
Government Buildings: Brooklyn, N. Y., Court-house, 82; Cardiff, Wales, County Hall, 40; Cleveland, O. U. S. Post-office, Custom-house and Court-house, 39; Denver, Col., U. S. Post-office and Court-house (Competitive Designs), 83; London, Eng., 12; County Hall, 84; New York City, Study for Court-house, 38; Accepted Design, 2d Battery Armory, 38; City Hall Interior, 118; Paris, France, 12; Simla, India, 12; Springfield, Mass., Accepted Design for Municipal Building, 26
Half-Timber Buildings of Saxony, 13-18
Hospitals: Boston, Mass., Competition for Peter B. Brigham Hospital, Plates I-XII; East Boston, Mass., Plates XCI-XCIV; New York City, 101; Southport, Eng., 168
Hotels: Paris, France, 40, 121-135, 154, Plates LXXI, LXXVIII.
Houses: Almont, Mass. 151; Ardsley, N. Y., 155; Auburn, N. Y., 35, 36, Plate XXVII; Baltimore, Md., 145-149; Barrington, Ill., 40; Berkshire, Eng. (Modern English Country Houses), Plates IX-XII; Berlin, Germany, 142; Birmingham, Ala., 95; Bovington, Eng., 96; Briarcliff Manor, N. Y., 68, Plates XLII, XLIII; Bronxville, N. Y., 26, 159; Brookline, Mass., 133, 138, 151, Plates LXXX-LXXXII;

Brooklyn, N. Y., 66, 67, Plates XXXVII-XLI, XLIV; Chestnut Hill, Pa., 95, 151; Cleveland, O., 131, 107; Clifton, Mass., 164; Cohasset, Mass., 10; Cynwyd, Pa., 87; Dallas, Tex., 83; Elan Valley, Eng., 156; Far Rockaway, N. Y., 55; Germantown, Pa., 10, 95; Glenridge, N. J., 154; Gloucestershire, Eng., 84; Grosse Pointe, Mich., 131; Hampshire, Eng. (Modern English Country Houses), Plate v; Hampstead, N., Eng., 84; Hollywood, Cal., 143; Islip, L. I., 143; Kenilworth, Ill., 55; Kennebunkport, Me., 40; Kent, Eng., 96; Kingston Hill, Eng., 168, La Crosse, Wis., 40; Lake Forest, Ill., 23, 24, 131, 167; Lansdowne, Pa., 143; Lenox, Mass., 39; Limpsfield, Surrey, Eng. (Modern English Country Houses), Plates XIII, XV; London, Eng., 77, 144; Los Angeles, Cal., 160, 161; Manchester, Mass., 164; Manchester, Vt., 164; Merion, Pa., 154; Milwaukee, Wis., 8, 132; Montclair, N. J., 131; Mountain Station, N. J., 131; New York City, 55, 75-79, 80, 83, 101, 130, Plates XLVI-LI; New London, Conn., 27; North Cornwall, Eng., 84; North Easton, Mass., 167; Northwood, Eng. (Modern English Country Houses), Plates VI, VII; Oceanic, N. J., 70; Peapack, N. J., 87; Radnor, Pa., 154; Richmond, Va., Plate LXXIV; Rockville, Conn., 162, Plates XCV, XCVI, CI, CII; Rochester, Eng., 28; Roehampton, Eng. (Modern English Country Houses), 105,

Plates XV, XVI; Rosemont, Pa., 95; St. Giles, Eng., 96; St. Paul, Minn., 27; Santa Monica, Cal., 70; Sea Gate, N. Y., 131; So. Manchester, Conn., 150; Somerset, Eng., 96; Summerville, Ga., 83; Surrey, Eng., 144 (Modern English Country Houses), Plate VIII; Toronto, Ont., 128; University Heights, N. Y., 131; Warwickshire, Eng., 156; Westchester, Pa., 167; Wiltshire, Eng. (Modern English Country Houses), 7, Plates I-IV; Winnetka, Ill., 167; Worcestershire, Eng., 132; York, Eng., 168.
Institutions: Washington, D. C., Plates LXXXVII-XCI
Lamp Standards: Banks, Albany, N. Y., Baltimore, Md., New York City, Washington, D. C., 102, 103
Libraries: Conway, Mass. (Detail), Plate XXI; London, Eng., 156
Mausoleums: Cleveland, O., 33, 34, Plates XXII-XXVI; Rondout, N. Y., 99, Plate LXII
Monuments and Memorials: Canton, O., 82; Vicksburg, Miss., 137, Plates LXXIV-LXXVI
Mural Decoration: Wilkes-Barre, Pa. (Court-house), 154
Museums: London, Eng. 120
Office Buildings: Aberdeen, Scotland, 84; Buffalo, N. Y., 99, 101; Hartford, Conn., 166; London, Eng., 168; New York City, 19-22, 94, 118, Plates XIII, XIV, XVI, XX; San Francisco, Cal. 155; Washington, D. C., 54

Picturesque Country Buildings of Maryland, 1-6
Private Libraries: New York City (Mr. Ferguson), 22; (Charles A. Platt) Plates XIX, XX; (J. P. Morgan), 26
Public Bathhouses: New York City, 106, 107
Public Buildings: Calcutta, India, 72
Pulpit: Manchester, Eng., 40
Restaurant: Berlin, Germany 31
Railroad Stations: Berlin, Germany (Underground), 73, 74; Birmingham, Ala. 118; London, Eng., 72; New Orleans, La., 26; Scranton, Pa., 21; Waterbury, Conn., 142
Schools: Berlin, Germany, 142; Chicago, Ill., 166; Dobbs Ferry, N. Y., 105; Englewood, N. J., 166; Middletown, Eng., 28; Mt. Vernon, N. Y., 140; New York City, 38; Norfolk, Va., Plates XCVII-C; Paris, France, 132; St. Louis, Mo., 155; Simsbury, Conn., 166; Washington, D. C., 98, 104, 167; Wimbledon, Eng., 120
Settlement House: New York City, 116
Stables: Mt. Kisco, N. Y., 70; West Point, N. Y., 155
Studios: New York City, 21, Plates XIII, XIV
Temples: Brooklyn, N. Y., 70; Oak Park, Ill., 10
Theaters: Boston, Mass., 166; New York City, 39; San Francisco, Cal., 70
Villas: Coblentz, Germany, 28; Seattle, Wash., 94

ACCORDING TO LOCATION

UNITED STATES

Albany, N. Y.: Banks, York & Sawyer, 100, 103, 113, 115, Plates LXI, LXX; Candelabra, Bank, York & Sawyer, 97; Lamp Standards, Bank, York & Sawyer, 102
Almont, Mass.: House, J. Lovell Little, Jr. 151
Ardsley, N. Y.: House, Oswald C. Hering, 155
Atlanta, Ga.: Building for Hon. Hoke Smith, Harry Leslie Walker, 118
Auburn, Ala.: Dining-hall and Dormitory, Polytechnic Inst., Warren & Welton, 166
Auburn, N. Y.: House, H. Van Buren Magonigle, 35, 36, Plate XXVII
Babylon, L. I.: Bank, York & Sawyer, 99; Garage, York & Sawyer, 99
Barrington, Ill.: House, Marshall & Fox, 40
Baltimore, Md.: Civic Development Plan, Carrère & Brunner, Architects, Frederick L. Olmstead, Landscape Architect, 143; Detail, Bank, York & Sawyer, 97, 103; House, 145-149; Lamp Standard, Bank, York & Sawyer, 102
Birmingham, Ala.: House, Warren & Welton, 95; Terminal Station, P. Thornton Marye, 118
Boerne, West Tex.: Church, Cram, Goodhue & Ferguson, 139, Plate LXXIX
Boston, Mass.: Administration Building, Harvard Medical School, Shepley, Rutan & Coolidge, Plate XXVIII; Boston College Competition, 60-65; Competition for Peter B. Brigham Hospital, Plates I-XII; Opera House, Wheelwright & Haven, 166
Briarcliff Manor, N. Y.: House, H. Van Buren Magonigle, 68, Plates XLII, XLIII
Bronxville, N. Y.: House, Delano & Aldrich, 159; House, Squires & Wynkoop, 26
Brookline, Mass.: House, Frank Chouteau Brown, 133, 138, Plates LXXX-LXXXI; House, J. Lovell Little, Jr., 151
Brooklyn, N. Y.: Bank, Mowbray & Uffinger, 38; Court-house, H. Van Buren Magonigle, Wilkinson & Magonigle, 82; House, James Brite, 66, 67, Plates XXXVII-XLI, XLIV; Luna Park, 85-87; Temple, Lord & Hewlett, 70
Buffalo, N. Y.: Office Building, York & Sawyer, 99, 101

Butler, Pa.: Church, John T. Comes, Plates LXXII, LXXIII
Canton, O.: McKinley Memorial, H. Van Buren Magonigle, 82
Chestnut Hill, Mass.: House, J. Lovell Little, Jr., 151
Chestnut Hill, Pa.: House, Charles Barton Keen, 95
Chicago, Ill.: American Sculpture, 57-59; Club Building, Pond & Pond, 71; Fountain, Mr. Crunelle, 57; House, Howard Van Doren Shaw, 83; Laboratory Building, Hill & Woltersdorf, 166; Rustic Figures, Mr. Crunelle, 57; Nellie V. Walker, 59; Schools, Dwight H. Perkins, 166
Cleveland, O.: Bank, J. Milton Dyer, Architect, Carl Bitter, Sculptor, 120; Club-house, Lehman & Schmitt, 83; Government Building, Arnold W. Brunner, 39; Hanna Mausoleum, Henry Bacon, 33, 34, Plates XXII-XXVI; House, Charles A. Platt, 167; House, C. F. Schweinfurth, 167; House, Watterson & Schneider, 131
Clifton, Mass.: House, Shepley, Rutan & Coolidge, 164
Cohasset, Mass.: House, Andrews, Jacques & Rantoul, 10
Conway, Mass. (Detail), Shepley, Rutan & Coolidge, Plate XXI
Cornish, N. H.: Garden Detail, Charles A. Platt, Plates XXIX, XXXIV
Cynwyd, Pa.: Country House, Mellor & Meigs, 82
Dallas, Tex.: House, Edward Overbeck and Geo. Willis, 83
Danbury, Conn.: Church, Howells & Stokes, 94
Dedham, Mass.: Garden Gateway, F. C. Brown, 10
Denver, Col.: U. S. Post-office and Court-house, Accepted Design, Tracy, Swartwout & Litchfield, 83; Competitive Designs, Arnold W. Brunner, 83; Competitive Design, H. Van Buren Magonigle, 83
East Boston, Mass.: Relief Station, Edward P. Dana, Plates XCI-XCIV
Englewood, N. J.: School, Davis, McGrath & Kiessling, 166
Far Rockaway, N. Y.: House, Edward I. Shire, 55
Germantown, Pa.: House, Thomas, Churchman & Molitor, 95; House, Wilson Eyre, 10

Glenridge, N. J.: House, Davis, McGrath & Kiessling, 154
Greenwich, Conn.: Club-house, Walker & Gillette, 95
Grosse Pointe, Mich.: House, Albert Kahn, 131
Hartford, Conn.: Office Building, Davis & Brooks, 166
Hollywood, Cal.: House, Myron Hunt & Elmer Grey, 143
Islip, L. I.: House, Grosvenor Atterbury, 143
Kenilworth, Ill.: House, Geo. W. Maher, 55
Kennebunkport, Me.: House, Green & Wicks, 40
La Crosse, Wis.: House, Handy & Cady, 40
Lake Forest, Ill.: House, Robert D. Kohn, 131; House, Richard E. Schmidt, Garden & Martin, 23, 24; House, Howard Van D. Shaw, 167; University Building, Howard Van D. Shaw, 54
Lansdowne, Pa.: House, Horace Trumbauer, 143
Lenox, Mass.: House (Detail), Hoppin, Koen & Huntington, 39
Los Angeles, Cal.: House, Maginnis & Walsh, 160, 161
Manchester, Mass.: House, Shepley, Rutan & Coolidge, 164
Manchester, Vt.: House, Shepley, Rutan & Coolidge, 164
McKeesport, N. Y.: Church, John T. Comes, 38
Maryland: Picturesque Country Buildings, 1-6
Merion, Pa.: Detail, House, Horace Trumbauer, 154
Milwaukee, Wis.: Civic Development Plan, Alfred W. Clas, 143; Houses, Brust & Philipp, 8, 132
Minneapolis, Minn.: Gateway Park, Edwin H. Hewitt, 10
Montclair, N. J.: House, Frank E. Wallis and J. Van Buren Magonigle, 83
Montgomery, Ala.: Church, Cram, Goodhue & Ferguson, 139, Plate LXXXVI
Montreal, Canada: Bank, McKim, Mead & White, 27, 120
Mt. Kisco, N. Y.: Stable, Albro & Lindeberg, 70
Mountain Station, N. J.: House, Squires & Wynkoop, 131
Mt. Vernon, N. Y.: House, Albro & Lindeberg and Thos. R. Johnson, 140
New Haven, Conn.: Bank, Gordon, Tracy & Swartwout, 27

New London, Conn.: Church, Edwin J. Lewis, Plate LXXVII; House, Charles A. Platt, 27
New Orleans, La.: Bank, Clinton & Russell and Emile Weil, 155; R. R. Station, D. H. Burnham & Co., 26
New York City: Apartment Building, Delano & Aldrich, 91, 92; Armory, (Accepted Design), C. C. Haight, 38; Banks, William Emerson, 11; McKim, Mead & White, 26, 54, 119; York & Sawyer, 103; Bathhouses, York & Sawyer, 106, 107; Bathroom, Walker & Gillette, 91; Chapel, Werner & Windolph, 11; City Hall (Governor's Room), Grosvenor Atterbury, 118; Club Building, Donn Barber, 39; Dining-room, H. Freedlander, 89; Gorham Building, McKim, Mead & White, 11; Hippodrome (Detail), Thompson & Dundy, 86, 87; Hospital, York & Sawyer, 101; Houses, Carrère & Hastings, 130; Cram, Goodhue & Ferguson, 75-79; Hale & Rogers, 55; Harry Allen Jacobs, 83; Charles A. Platt, 80, Plates XLVI-LI; York & Sawyer, 101; Lamp Standards, Bank, York & Sawyer, 102; Living-room, F. J. Sterner, 39; Office Buildings, Charles A. Platt, 19-22, Plates XIII, XIV, XVI, XX; Geo. B. Post & Sons, 118; Private Libraries, Charles A. Platt, 21, Plates XIX, XX; McKim, Mead & White, 26; School, Pell & Corbett, 38; Settlement House, York & Sawyer, 116; Studios, Charles A. Platt, 21, Plates XIII, XIV; Study for Court-house, Howells & Stokes, 38; Theaters (Detail), Herts & Tallant, 87; Mitchell & Fox, 39
Norfolk, Va.: High School, Neff & Thompson, Plates XCVII-C; Y. M. C. A., Wood, Donn & Deming and R. E. Mitchell, 55, Plates LXXXIII, LXXXIV
North Easton, Mass.: House, Shepley, Rutan & Coolidge, 167
Norton, Mass.: Dining-hall, Wheaton Seminary, Ripley & Russell, 17
Oak Park, Ill.: Temple, Frank Lloyd Wright, 10
Oceanic, N. J.: Country House, E. S. Hewitt, 87
Peapack, N. J.: Country House, E. S. Hewitt, 87
Philadelphia, Pa.: Baseball Pavilion, Wm. Steele & Sons Co., 94; Church, Thomas, Churchman & Molitor, 95; Island City Sketches, Louis H. Sullivan, 90

iv

THE ARCHITECTURAL REVIEW

Pittsburgh, Pa.: Altars for Church, John T. Comes, Plate xv; Bank, D. H. Burnham & Co., 131; Club Building, Janssen & Abbott, 38
Princeton, N. J.: Campus, Princeton University, R. A. Cram, Supervising Architect, 118; '79 Dormitory, B. W. Morris, 118; Stafford Little Hall, Cope & Stewardson, 118
Radnor, Pa.: Detail, House, Cope & Stewardson, 154
Richmond, Va.: House, Neff & Thompson, Plate LXXXV
Rochester, N. Y.: Bank, York & Sawyer, Plates LIII-LX, 98, 103; Church, Claude Bragdon, 11
Rockville, Conn.: House, Charles A. Platt, 162, Plates XCV, XCVI, CI, CII
Rondout, N. Y.: Mausoleum, York & Sawyer, 90, Plate LXII
Rosemont, Pa.: House, Cope & Stewardson, 95
San Francisco, Cal.: Office Building, Howells & Stokes, 155; Theater, Bliss & Faville, 70
Santa Monica, Cal.: House, 70
Scranton, Pa.: R. R. Station, Kenneth Murchison, 11
Sea Gate, N. Y.: House, Squires & Wynkoop, 131
Seattle, Wash.: Agricultural Building, Exposition Building, Howard & Galloway and Graham & Myers, 119; Alaska-Yukon Exposition Buildings, Howard & Galloway, 119; California Building, Exposition Building, Sellen & Heming, 119; Oriental Building, Exposition Building, Howard & Galloway and Bebb & Mendel, 119; Villa, Harlan Thomas, 94
Simsbury, Conn.: High School, E. F. Hapgood, 166
Somerville, Mass.: Church, Maginnis, Walsh & Sullivan, 94
South Manchester, Conn.: House, Charles A. Platt, 150
Springfield, Mass.: Accepted Design for Municipal Buildings, Pell & Corbett, 26
St. Augustine, Fla.: Courtyard, Carrère & Hastings, 95
St. Louis, Mo.: School, Wm. B. Ittner, 155
St. Paul, Minn.: House, James Alan MacLeod, 47; State Capitol, Cass Gilbert, 130
Summerville, Ga.: House, Kemp & Wendell, 83

University Heights, N. Y.: House, Squires & Wynkoop, 131
Vicksburg, Miss.: Monument, Jenney & Mundie, 127, Plates LXXIV-LXXVI
Washington, D. C.: Banks, York & Sawyer, 102, 108, 110, 112, 114, Plates LXIII-LXVIII; Club Building, B. Stanley Simmons, 70; Institution. Carrère & Hastings, Plates LXXXVII-XCI; Office Building, Wood. Donn & Deming, 54; Schools, Marsh & Peter, 167; York & Sawyer, 98, 104
Waterbury, Conn.: R. R. Station, McKim, Mead & White, 142
Westchester, Pa.: Bishop House, Charles Barton Keen, 167; Spring House, Charles Barton Keen, 167
West Point, N. Y.: Military Academy, Cram, Goodhue & Ferguson, 155
White Plains, N. Y.: Y. M. C. A., Albro & Lindeberg, Plates XLV, LII
Wilkes-Barre, Pa.: Court-house (Detail), McCormick & French, 154
Winnetka, Ill.: House, Perkins & Hamilton, 167

CANADA

Montreal, Canada: Banks, Frank Darling, 168; McKim, Mead & White, 27, 120; Club-house, McKim, Mead & White, 120
Toronto, Ontario: Houses, Eden Smith, 128

ENGLAND

Bassett: Church, Edward P. Warren (Modern English Churches), Plates XVII, XVIII
Blandford: Church, Edward P. Warren (Modern English Churches), Plate X
Bovingdon: Dormers, Walter E. Hewitt, 96
Berkshire: House, Ernest Newton (Modern English Country Houses), Plates IX-XII
Bishopthorpe, York: House, Walter H. Brierley, 168
Cardiff: County Hall, Harris & Moodie, 40
Chesterfield: Church. C. H. Reilly, 27
Dover: Garden, Thos. H. Mawson, Plate XXXVII
Durham: Church, J. W. F. Phillipson, 56
Dudley: Bank, Cossins, Peacock & Bewlay, 144

Elan Valley: House, Buckland & Farmer, 156
Gloucestershire: House, E. Guy Dawber, 84
Hampstead, N.: Gardens, Thos. H. Mawson, 41-45, Plates XXIX, XXX, XXXV; House, Geoffry Lucas, 84
Hampshire: House, Ernest Newton (Modern English Country Houses), Plate V
Kensington: Church, Late G. F. Bodley, R. A., 28
Kent: Church, Ernest Newton (Modern English Churches), Plates XV, XVI, House, T. P. Figgis, 96
Kingsway: Church, F. A. Walters, 168
Kingston Hill: House, A. J. Hardwick, 168
Limpsfield, Surrey: House, E. Turner Powell (Modern English Country Houses), Plates XIII, XIV
London: Bank, Prof. Beresford Pite, 120; Business Building, Wallace & Gibbs, 56; R. Frank Atkinson, 71; Club Buildings, Mèwes & Davis and E. K. Purchase, 71; Reginald Blomfield, 40; County Hall, A. Gilbert Scott, 84; Government Offices, Alfred Burr, 84, House, Edwin L. Lutyens, 144; Library, Henry T. Hare, 156; Museum, Sir Aston Webb, 120; National Gallery (Revised Design), H. Heathcote Statham, 12; Office Building, Late E. A. Gruning and Late E. W. Mountford, 168
Manchester: Pulpit, J. R. J. Swarbrick, 40
Middleton: Schools, Edgar Wood and J. H. Sellers, 28
North Cornwall: House, W. Curtis Green, 84
Northwood: House, Walter E. Hewitt (Modern English Country Houses), Plates VI, VII
Notting Hill Gate: Church, Ronald P. Jones, 55, 56
Rochester: House, Late A. H. Shipworth, 28
Roehampton: House, C. H. B. Quennell (Modern English Country Houses), 163, Plates XV, XVI
St. Giles: House, Forbes & Tate, 96
Somerset: Cottages, Sidrick & Reay, 96
Southport: Hospital, Adams & Holden, 168
Staffordshire: Church, Edward Goldie (Modern English Churches), Plate IX
Stratford, E.: Church, Edward P. Warren (Modern English Churches), Plates XI-XIV

Surrey: House, Buckland & Farmer, 144
Walmer Place: Gardens, Thos. H. Mawson, 40, 47, 52
Walsall: Bank, Cossins, Peacock & Bewlay, 144
Warwickshire: House, E. Guy Dawber, 156
Wiltshire: House, E. Guy Dawber (Modern English Country Houses), 7, Plates I-IV
Wimbledon: School, H. P. Burke Downing, 120
Windermere: Gardens, Thos. H. Mawson, 47, 48
Worcestershire: Church, Arthur Bartlett, 72; House, Cossins, Peacock & Bewlay, 132
Yorkshire: Church, Walter J. Tapper, 120

FRANCE

Paris: Building, M. Aumont, M. Ligny, 12; Church, M. Guilbert, 28; Gardens, Drawing by James F. Clapp, Plates XXXII, XXXIII; Hotels, M. Blanche, 144; M. Nenot, 121-126, Plates LXXI, LXXVIII; M. H. Valette, 40; School, M. G. Farcy, 132

GERMANY

Berlin: House, Alfred Messel, 42; Passage Kaufhaus, 29; School, Ludwig Hoffman, 142
Coblents: Villa, M. Willy Bock, 28
Dresden: Entrance, Exposition Building, Oswin Hempel, 89
Munich: Dance-hall, Franz Zell, 88; Entrance Arcade, Wilhelm Bertsch, 89; Restaurants, Emanuel Von Seidl, 89; Zell, Dietrich & Kurz, 88; Theater, Max Littmann, 80; Turin Exposition, Raim. d'Aronco, 88
Saxony: Half-Timber Buildings, 13-18

MISCELLANEOUS

Aberdeen, Scotland: Office Building, Paul Waterhouse, 84
Bologna, Italy: Church, E. Collamarini, 142
Calcutta, India: Memorial Hall, Wm. Emerson, 72
Edinburgh, Scotland: Church, P. MacGregor Chalmers, 28
Rome, Italy: School of Art, Lucian E. Smith, 96
Simla, India: Government Offices, James Ransome, 12

ACCORDING TO AUTHOR

Adams & Holden: Hospital, Southport, Eng., 168
Albro & Lindeberg: Stable, Mt. Kisco, N. Y., 70; Y. M. C. A. Building, White Plains, N. Y., Plates XLV, LII
Albro & Lindeberg and Thos. R. Johnson: Public School, Mt. Vernon, N. Y., 140
Allen & Collens and James W. O'Connor: Boston College Competition, 62, 65
Andrews, Jacques & Rantoul: House, Cohasset, Mass., 10
Aronco, d', Raim.: Turin Exposition, 88
Atkinson, R. Frank: Business Building, London, Eng., 72
Atterbury, Grosvenor: City Hall, New York City (Governor's Room), 118; House, Islip, L. I., 143
Aumont, M. and M. Ligny: Building, Paris, France, 12
Bacon, Henry: Mausoleum, Cleveland, O., 33, 34, Plates XXII-XXVI
Barber, Donn: Club Building, New York City, 39
Bartlett, Arthur: Church, Worcestershire, Eng., 72
Bebb & Mendel and Howard & Galloway: Building, Alaska-Yukon Exposition, Seattle, Wash., 119
Bertsch, Wilhelm: Exposition Building, 89
Blanche, M.: Hotel, Paris, France, 144
Bliss & Faville: Theater, San Francisco, Cal., 70
Blomfield, Reginald, A. R. A.: Club Building, London, Eng., 40

Bock, M. Willy: Villa, Coblentz, Germany, 28
Bodley, Late G. F., R. A.: Church, Kensington, Eng., 28
Bosworth & Holden: House, Oceanic, N. J., 70
Bradstreet, John S.: Theater (Detail), Minneapolis. Minn., 87
Bragdon, Claude: Church, Rochester, N. Y., 11
Brierley, Walter H.: House, Bishopthorpe, York, Eng., 168
Brite, Jasper: House, Brooklyn, N. Y., 66, 67, Plates XXXVII-XLI, XLIV
Brown, Frank Chouteau: Gateway, Dedham, Mass., 101; Plaster House, Brookline, Mass., 133, 138, Plates LXXX-LXXXII
Brunner, Arnold W.: Competition Design, U. S. Post-office and Court-house, Denver, Col., 83; Government Building, Cleveland, O., 39
Brust & Philipp: Houses, Milwaukee, Wis., 8, 152
Buckland & Farmer: House, Elan Valley, Eng., 156; House, Surrey, Eng., 144
Burnham, D. H. & Co.: Bank, Pittsburgh, Pa., 131; R. R. Station, New Orleans, La., 67
Burr, Alfred, F. R. I. B. A.: Government Building, London, Eng., 84
Carrère & Brunner: Civic Development Plan, Baltimore, Md., 143
Carrère & Hastings: Carnegie Institute, Washington, D. C., Plates LXXXVII-

XCI; Courtyard, St. Augustine, Fla. 95; House, New York City, 130
Chalmers, P. MacGregor: Church, Edinburgh, Scotland, 28
Clapp, James Ford: Gardens, Paris, France (Rotch Envoi Drawing), Plates XXXII, XXXIII
Clas, Alfred W.: Civic Development Plan, Milwaukee, Wis., 143
Clinton & Russell and Emilé Weil: Bank, New Orleans, La., 155
Codman & Despradelle: Competition for Peter Bent Brigham Hospital, Boston, Mass. (Winning Design), Plates 1, 11, V-IX
Collamarini, Edoardo: Church, Bologna, Italy, 142
Comes, John T.: Altars for Church, Pittsburgh, Pa., Plate xv; Church, Butler, Pa., Plates LXXII, LXXIII; Church, McKeesport, Pa., 38
Coolidge & Carlson: Competition for Boston College, Boston, Mass., 64, 65; House, North Easton, Mass., 155
Cope & Stewardson: House (Detail), Radnor, Pa., 154; House, Rosemont, Pa., 95; Stafford Little Hall, Princeton University, 118
Cossins, Peacock & Bewlay: Bank, Dudley, Eng., 144; Bank, Walsall, Eng., 144; House, Worcestershire, Eng., 132
Cram, Goodhue & Ferguson: Church, Buerne, W. Tex., 139, Plate LXXIX; Church, Montgomery, Ala., 139, Plate

LXXXVI; House of Mr. Goodhue, New York City, 75-79; Military Academy, West Point, N. Y., 155
Crunelle, Mr.: Fountain, Chicago, Ill., 57; Rustic Figure, Chicago, Ill., 58
Dana, Edward Percy: Relief Station, East Boston, Mass., Plates XCII-XCIV
Darling, Frank: Bank, Montreal, Canada, 168
Dawber, E. Guy: Houses, Gloucestershire, Eng., 84; Warwickshire, Eng., 156; Wiltshire, Eng. (Modern English Country Houses), 7, Plates I-IV
Davis & Brooks: Office Building, Hartford, Conn., 166
Davis, McGrath & Kiessling: House, Glenridge, N. J., 154; School, Englewood, N. J., 166
Delano & Aldrich: Apartment Building, New York City, 91; House, Bronxville, N. Y., 159
Downing, H. P. Burke: School, Wimbledon, Eng., 120
Dyer, J. Milton: Bank. Cleveland, O., 130
Emerson, William: Bank, New York City, 11
Emerson, Sir William: Queen Victoria Memorial Hall, Calcutta, India, 72
Eyre, Wilson: House, Germantown, Pa., 10
Figgis, T. P.: House, Kent, Eng., 96
Forbes & Tate: House, St. Giles, Eng., 96
Freedlander, J. H.: Dining-room, House, New York City, 89
Gilbert, Cass: Capitol, St. Paul, Minn., 130; Competition for Peter Bent Brig-

ham Hospital, Boston, Mass., Plates I, II, IV, V
Goldie, Edward: Church, Staffordshire, Eng. (Modern English Churches), Plate IX
Gordon, Tracy & Swartwout: Bank, New Haven, Conn., 27
Farcy, M. G.: Fencing-School, Paris, France, 132
Gibbons, J. & Sons: Addition to Church, England, 15b
Graham & Myers and Howard & Galloway: Building, Alaska-Yukon Exposition, Seattle, Wash., 119
Graham, E. T. P.: Boston College Competition (2d Prize Design), 61, 63
Green, W. Curtis: House, North Cornwall, Eng., 84
Green & Wicks: House, Kennebunkport. Me., 40
Gruning & Mountford: Office Building, London, Eng., 168
Guillaume, M. Henri: Pavilion for W. K. Vanderbilt, 156
Guilbert, M.: Church, Paris, France, 28
Haight, C. C.: Armory, New York City (Accepted Design), 38
Hale & Rogers: House, New York City, 55
Handy & Cady: House, La Crosse, Wis., 40
Hapgood, E. F.: School, Simsbury, Conn., 106
Hardwick, A. J.: House, Kingston Hill. Eng., 168
Hare, Henry T.: Fulham Library, London, Eng., 156
Harris & Moodie: County Hall. Cardiff, 40
Hempel, Oswin: Entrance, Exposition Building, 89
Hering, Oswald C.: House, Ardsley, N. Y., 155
Herts & Tallant: Theater (Detail), New York City, 87
Hewitt, Edward S.: House, Peapack, N. J., 82
Hewitt, Edwin H.: Gateway Park, Minneapolis, Minn., 10
Hewitt, Walter E.: Houses, Bovingdon, Eng., 96; Northwood, Eng. (Modern English Country Houses), Plates VI, VII; Surrey, Eng. (Modern English Country Houses), Plate VIII
Hill & Woltersdorf: Laboratory Building, Chicago, Ill., 166
Hoffman, Ludwig: School Building, Berlin, Germany, 142
Hoppin, Koen & Huntington: House, Lenox, Mass., 39
Howard & Galloway: Building, Alaska-Yukon Exposition, Seattle, Wash., 119
Howard & Galloway and Bebb & Mendel: Building, Alaska-Yukon Exposition, Seattle, Wash., 119
Howard & Galloway and Graham & Myers: Building, Alaska-Yukon Exposition, Seattle, Wash., 119
Howells & Stokes: Church, Danbury, Conn., 94; Office Building, San Francisco, Cal., 155; Study for Court-house, New York City, 38
Hunt, Myron, and Elmer Grey: House, Hollywood, Cal., 143
Itner, Wm. B.: School, St. Louis, Mo., 155
Jacobs, Harry Allen: House, New York City, 83
Janssen & Abbott: Club Building, Pittsburgh, Pa., 38
Jenney & Mundie: Monument, Vicksburg, Miss., 127, Plates LXXIV-LXXVI
Jones, Ronald P.: Church, Notting Hill Gate, Eng., 55, 56
Kahn, Albert: House, Grosse Pointe, Mich., 132
Keen, Charles Barton: Houses, Chestnut Hill, Pa., 95; Westchester, Pa., 167
Kellogg, Joseph M.: A Night Shelter, 26

Kemp & Wendell: House, Summerville, Ga., 83
Kohn, Robt. D.: House, Lake Forest, Ill., 131
Lehman & Schmitt: Club-house, Cleveland, O., 83
Lewis, Edwin J.: Church, New London, Conn., Plate LXXVII
Little, J. Lovell, Jr.: Houses, Almont, Mass., 151; Brookline, Mass., 151; Chestnut Hill, Mass., 151
Littmann, Max: Theater, Munich, Germany, 89
Lord & Hewlett: Masonic Temple, Brooklyn, N. Y., 70
Lowell, Guy: Competition for Peter Bent Brigham Hospital, Boston, Plates III, XI, XII
Lucas, Geoffry: House Group, Hampstead, N., Eng., 84
Lutyens, Edwin L.: House, London, Eng., 142; Temple Dinsley, Herts, 144
MacLeod, James Alan: House, St. Paul, Minn., 27
McCormick & French: Court-house (Detail), Wilkes-Barre, Pa., 154
McKim, Mead & White: Bank, Montreal, Canada, 27, 120; Bank, New York City, 26, 54, 119; Club, Montreal, Canada, 120; Gorham Building, New York City, 11; J. P. Morgan Library, New York City, 26; Railway Station, Waterbury, Conn., 142
Maginnis & Walsh: Boston College Competition (1st and 3d Prize, Designs), 60, 65; House, Los Angeles, Cal., 160, 161
Maginnis, Walsh & Sullivan: Church, Somerville, Mass., 94
Magonigle, H. Van Buren: Competition Design, U. S. Post-office and Court-house, Denver, Col., 83; House, Auburn, N. Y., 35, 36, Plate XXVII; House, Briarcliff Manor, N. Y., 68, Plates XLII, XLIII; McKinley Memorial, Canton, O., 82; Music Room, New York City, 82
Magonigle, H. Van B. and Wilkinson & Magonigle: Court-house, Brooklyn, N. Y., 82
Maher, Geo. W.: House, Kenilworth, Ill., 55
Marsh & Peter: School, Washington, D. C., 167
Marshall & Fox: House, Barrington, Ill., 40; Theater, New York City, 39
Marye, P. Thornton: Terminal Station, Birmingham, Ala., 142
Mawson, Hon. Thos. H., A. R. I. B. A.: Gardens, Eng., 41-52, Plates XXIX, XXX, XXXV, XXXVI
Mellor & Meigs: House, Cynwyd, Pa., 82
Messel, Alfred: Dwelling-house, Berlin, Germany, 142
Mêwès, Chas. F.: Château, France, 84
Mêwès & Davis and E. K. Purchase: Royal Automobile Club, London, Eng., 71
Mitchell, Rossel Edward and Wood, Donn & Deming: Y. M. C. A. Building, Norfolk, Va., 55, Plates LXXVII, LXXXIV
Morris, Benj. W.: '79 Dormitory, Princeton University, 118
Mowbray & Uffinger: Bank, Brooklyn, N. Y., 38
Murchison, Kenneth: Railroad Station, Scranton, Pa., 11
Neff & Thompson: House, Richmond, Va., Plate LXXXV; School, Norfolk, Va., Plates XCVII-C
Nenot, M.: Hotel Meurice, Paris, 121-126, Plates LXXI, LXXVII
Newton, Ernest: Church, Kent, Eng. (Modern English Churches), Plates XV, XVI; House, Berkshire, Eng. (Modern English Country Houses), Plates IX-XII; House, Hampshire, Eng. (Modern English Country Houses), Plate V

O'Connor, James and Allen & Collens: Boston College Competition, 62, 65
Overbeck, Edward and George Willis: House, Dallas, Tex., 83
Palmer & Hornbostel: Subway Entrance, Queensboro Bridge, 71
Parker, Thomas & Rice: Competition for Peter Bent Brigham Hospital, Boston, Mass., Plates I, II, X
Peabody & Stearns: Competition for Boston College, Boston, Mass., 63; Competition for Peter Bent Brigham Hospital, Boston, Mass., Plates III, XI, XII
Pell & Corbett: Accepted Design for Springfield Municipal Buildings, 26; School, New York City, 38
Perkins, Dwight H.: Schools, Chicago, Ill., 166
Phillipson, J. W. F.: Church, Durham, Eng., 56
Pite, Beresford: Bank, London, Eng., 120
Platt, Chas. A.: Garden, Cornish, N. H., Plates XXXI, XXXII; Houses, Cleveland, O., 167; New London, Conn., 27; New York City, 82, Plates XLVI-LI; Rockville, Conn., 102, Plates XCV, XCVI, CI, CII; So. Manchester, Conn., 150; Office Buildings, New York City (Exterior and Interior), 19-22, Plates XIII, XIV, XVI-XX; Private Libraries, 22, Plates XX, XX.
Perkins & Hamilton: House, Winnetka, Ill., 167
Pond & Pond: Woman's Baptist Home Mission Society, Chicago, Ill., 71
Post, Geo. B., & Sons: Office Building, New York City, 158
Powell, E. Turner: House, Limpsfield, Surrey, Eng. (Modern English Country Houses), Plates XIII, XIV
Quennell, C. H. B.: House, Roehampton, Eng. (Modern English Country Houses), 163, Plates XV & XVI
Ransome, James: Government Offices, Simla, India, 12
Reilly, C. H.: House, Chesterfield, Eng., 27
Ripley & Russell: Dining-hall, Wheaton Seminary, Norton, Mass., 71
Rogers, Wm. J. and Frank E. Wallis: Country House, Montclair, N. J., 131
Schmidt, Richard E., and Garden & Martin: House, Lake Forest, Ill., 39, 24
Schweinfurth, C. F.: House, Cleveland, O., 167
Scott, A. Gilbert: Design for Glamorgan County Hall, 84
Sellen & Heming: Building, Alaska-Yukon Exposition, Seattle, Wash., 119
Shaw, Howard Van Doren: Dining-hall, Lake Forest University, Lake Forest, Ill., 54; House, Chicago, Ill., 83; House, Lake Forest, Ill., 67
Shepley, Rutan & Coolidge: Administration Building, Harvard Medical School, Boston, Mass., Plate XXVIII; Competition for Peter Bent Brigham Hospital, Boston, Mass., Plates I, XI, XII; Houses, Clifton, Mass., 164; Manchester, Mass., 164; Manchester, Vt., 164; Library (Detail), Conway, Mass., Plate XXI
Shipworth, Late A. H.: House, Rochester, Eng., 28
Shire, Edw. I.: House, Far Rockaway, N. Y., 55
Silcock & Reay: Houses, Somerset, Eng., 96
Simmons, B. Stanley: Elks Club, Washington, D. C., 70
Smith, Eden: Houses, Toronto, Ontario, 128
Smith, Lucian E.: School of Art, Rome, Italy, 96
Squires & Wynkoop: Houses, Bronxville, N. Y., 26; Mountain Station, N. J., 131; Sea Gate, N. Y., 131; University Heights, N. Y., 131
Statham, H. Heathcote: National Gallery, London, Eng., 12

Steele, Wm., & Sons Co.: Baseball Pavilion, Denver, Col., 94
Sterner, F. J.: Living-room, New York City, 39
Stores, M.: Chapel, Normandy, 156
Sullivan, Louis H.: Sketches Island City, Philadelphia, Pa., 90
Swarbrick, J. & J.: Pulpit, Manchester, Eng., 40
Tapper, Walter J.: Church, Yorkshire, Eng., 128
Thomas, Harlan: Villa, Seattle, Wash., 94
Thomas, Churchman & Molitor: Church, Philadelphia, Pa., 142; House, Germantown, Pa., 95
Thompson & Dundy: Detail of Hippodrome, New York City, 86
Tracy, Swartwout & Litchfield: Accepted Design U. S. Post-office and Court-house, Denver, Col., 83
Trumbauer, Horace: House, Lansdowne, Pa., 143; House (Detail), Merion, Pa., 154
Valette, M. H.: Hotel, Paris, France, 40
Von Seidl, Emanuel: Restaurant, Munich Exposition, 89
Walker, Harry Leslie: Building, Atlanta, Ga., 118
Walker, Nellie V.: Sculpture, "Afterward," Chicago, Ill., 95
Walker & Gillette: Bathroom, Leow House, New York City, 95; Club-house, Greenwich, Conn., 95
Wallace, W., and James S. Gibson: Business Building, London, Eng., 56
Wallis, Frank E., and Wm. J. Rogers: Country House, Montclair, N. J., 131
Walters, F. A.: Church, Kedgeway, Eng., 168
Warren, Edw. P.: Church, Bassett, Eng. (Modern English Churches), Plates XVII, XVIII; Church, Stratford, E., Eng. (Modern English Churches), Plates XI-XIV
Warren & Welton: Dining-hall Polytechnic Institute, Auburn, Ala., 166; House, Birmingham, Ala., 95
Waterhouse, Paul: Office Building, Aberdeen, Scotland, 84
Webb, Sir Aston: Museum, London, Eng., 120
Werner & Windolph: Chapel, New York City, 94
Westgate, W. L.: A Night Shelter 26
Wheelwright & Haven: Opera House, Boston, Mass., 166
Wood, Donn & Deming: Union Trust Co. Building, Washington, D. C., 54
Wood, Donn & Deming and Rossel Edward Mitchell: Y. M. C. A. Building, Norfolk, Va., 55, Plates LXXXIII, LXXXIV
Wood, Edgar, and J. Henry Sellers: Schools, Middleton, Eng., 28
Wright, Frank Lloyd: Temple, Oak Park, Ill., 10
York & Sawyer: Banks: Albany, N. Y., 100, 113, 115, Plates LXI, LXX; Babylon, L. I., 99; Baltimore, Md., 97; Rochester, N. Y., 98, Plates LIII, LX; Washington, D. C., 108, 110, 112, 114, Plates LXIII-LXVIII; Bank Doorways, 105; Study for Banks, 97, 100; Bathhouses, 101; House, New York City, 101; Lamp Standards for Banks, 102; Mausoleum, Rondout, N. Y., 99, Plate LXII; Office Building, Buffalo, N. Y., 99, 101; Schools, Dobbs Ferry, N. Y., 105; Washington, D. C. 98, 104; Settlement House, New York City, 116
York & Sawyer and Joseph Evans Sperry: Bank, Baltimore, Md., 111, 114, Plate LXIX
Zell, Franz: Dance-hall, Munich, Germany, 88
Zell, Dietrich & Kurz: Restaurant, Munich Exposition, 88

The Architectural Review

Volume XVI   January, 1909   Number 1

Picturesque Country Buildings of Maryland

By Julian A. Buckly

THE layman seldom sees any beauty in a building unless it is large in extent and represents the expenditure of thousands of dollars. To the architect, or to any one interested in the picturesque, it is quite the contrary, for they are ever ready to admire any building possessing architectural merit. The small buildings of our own country are frequently overlooked, and few realize we have many well worth a considerable journey to see. Even the smallest types of domestic buildings are often very picturesque and possess a vast amount of architectural interest. Generally old buildings of this class are more valuable than ones that are new, for a century ago the designers and builders seemed to have a better idea of what made a structure beautiful than most men who design small buildings at the present day. It is true that generally owners of small buildings do not think that they are of enough importance to be carefully considered by the architect; and in our time the customary method of contracting buildings makes it impossible for the workman to be left by himself and expected to make anything look well. Then, again, we do not find in our Labor organizations the same intelligence and pride among the workmen that characterized all labor a century ago.

In some sections of the country the old buildings possess a unique architectural value, due almost solely to the use of the natural material at hand and the local methods of building. In the South a country residence required many more small buildings about the estate than was thought necessary in the North. In Baltimore County, Maryland, there are many of these little buildings still in use just as they were a century ago. The bakehouses, ice houses and — especially — dairies, were necessary on every country estate.

The bakehouses were quite near the main dwelling and were generally of one large room, with a paved floor and a brick oven at one end; the chimney was usually on the outside. The dairy houses were built close by a swift running brook; the water, entering at one side through a gate, was carried around through a trench just inside the wall, about fourteen inches deep and twenty inches wide, and passed out at the lower end. Crocks of milk and cream were placed in the water, — the height necessary to cover the contents and yet not overflow the jar's edge being regulated at the outer gate. The trenches and floor were paved with brick or stone. The floor space was used for cold storage for the butter. The churning was generally done on the square of paving placed just outside the door.

On the estate now owned by Mr. Douglas Gordon, just north of Baltimore, there remain two very charming little buildings, — a bakehouse and a dairy. These buildings are of a stone of good color and very well laid. They were built in the simplest method of that age, and time has done much toward beautifying them. The front wall of the dairy is covered with stucco and the side walls are left rough. The bakehouse is all of stone, with exceptionally well-pro-

Entrance Gate, Estate of the Late Thomas Cradock, Trentham, Md.

Entrance Gate, "Ulm," Owings Mills, Md.

Copyright, 1909, by Bates & Guild Company

Bakehouse, Mr. Douglas Gordon's Estate, Baltimore County, Md.

Ice-house, Oakland Farm, Md.

Dairy, Mr. Douglas Gordon's Estate, Baltimore County, Md.

portioned wall-surfaces.

In some of the old buildings the picturesque side may not have been very much considered by the builder, their beauty being due to the material at hand and the method of building. Combined with good workmanship to meet utilitarian requirements, with good lines, good color and texture, they could not be otherwise than picturesque.

This was not the case at Oakland Farm, for here the small buildings were carefully designed, though, unfortunately, only one of the old buildings now stands, and that one is the dairy. Oakland Farm had originally a great many of these small buildings, built by General Robert Goodloe Harper in about 1805. The dwelling was burned many years ago and, judging from the other buildings, must have been of quite a little architectural pretense. The ice-house, which was on

Bath-house, Estate of the Late Thomas Cradock, Trentham, Md.

Ice-house, Estate of the Late Thomas Cradock, Trentham, Md.

the side of a hill in the grove, was built of stone and brick covered with stucco. The three Gothic-shaped panels in the front wall gave it a very dignified appearance. The color of the stucco was a warm brownish gray. The roof, which was as mellow as one could wish, and covered here and there with moss, fell in during the winter of 1905, and the side wall fell down during the following year. All that remains is the front wall, which faces a little winding road through the woods. The dairy, which is still in use, is of stone covered with stucco, and is quite white in color. The front, which is not far from the highway, is adorned with a portico worthy of a much more important structure; it has four well-shaped columns with Ionic capitals carved in wood (not *papier-mâché*). They support a pediment with a rich and very well wrought cor-

Dairy, Estate of the Late Thomas Cradock, Trentham, Md.

nice; the architrave being ornamented with a wave ornament cut in the wood.

The little buildings at "Ulm" were built by Samuel Owings, 2d, a few years after his marriage, which took place in 1765. They are of brick, painted white, and are located quite near the mill-race. The bakehouse remains much as it was originally, but the dairy has a few modern improvements, such as pumps and granolithic paving. "Ulm" is an old-time Maryland county estate some fifteen miles north of Baltimore, and, like most Maryland estates, is set back about a half-mile from the highway. There are many larger buildings about the estate, which make quite a little village by themselves.

The most interesting group of small buildings is at "Trentham," at Garrison Forest, in the western part of the Green Spring Valley. They are the oldest and best preserved, and their surroundings have been better cared for than the others mentioned.

The ice-house, placed at some distance from the others, is built of a rough field stone, while the dairy and bath-house are of quarry stone, roughly cut. The bath-house, octagonal in plan, is located on the lower terrace opposite the entrance to the mansion. These buildings were built by the Rev. Thomas Cradock, the first rector of St. Thomas (Church), located about one and a half miles away. Mr. Cradock came to Maryland from England in 1744, and on January 14, 1745, he was appointed minister in St. Thomas' Parish by His Excellency, Thomas Bladen, Esq., Governor of the Provinces of Maryland. The following year he was married to Catharine, daughter of John Risteau, Esq., a Huguenot, who had fled to Maryland from France. He presented his daughter with a farm, then a part of his estate, and the buildings were built soon thereafter. The mansion was remodeled about 1835, but the little buildings are as they were first built. Mr. Cradock called the place "Trentham," doubtless from his fond recollections of the school at Straffordshire.

Dairy, Oakland Farm, Md.

Gate and Green, Estate of the Late Thomas Cradock, Trentham, Md.   Rear Garden Gate, Estate of the Late Thomas Cradock, Trentham, Md.

Dairy and Bakehouse, "Ulm," Owings Mills, Md.

Dairy, "Ulm," Owings Mills, Md.

MODERN ENGLISH COUNTRY HOUSES

SOUTH ENTRANCE AND TERRACE GARDEN, CONKWELL GRANGE, WILTSHIRE, ENGLAND.
E. GUY DAWBER, ARCHITECT.

PLATE I.

MODERN ENGLISH COUNTRY HOUSES

DETAIL, GARDEN TERRACE AND ENTRANCE, CONKWELL GRANGE, WILTSHIRE, ENGLAND.
E. GUY DAWBER, ARCHITECT.

PLATE II.

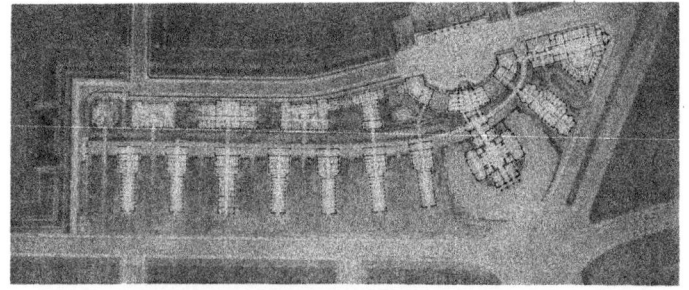

GROUP PLAN, WINNING DESIGN, CODMAN & DESPRADELLE, ARCHITECTS.

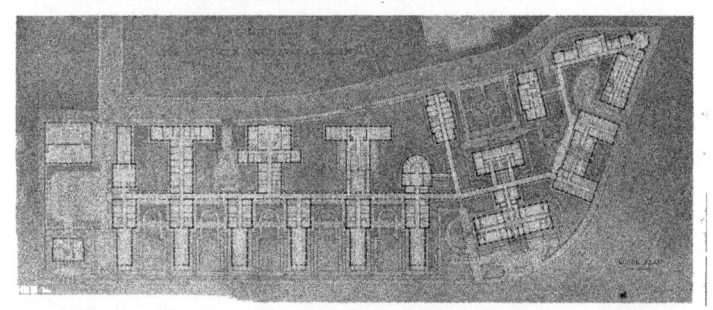

GROUP PLAN, CASS GILBERT, ARCHITECT.

GROUP PLAN, PARKER, THOMAS & RICE, ARCHITECTS.
GROUP PLANS, COMPETITION FOR THE PETER BENT BRIGHAM HOSPITAL, BOSTON, MASS.

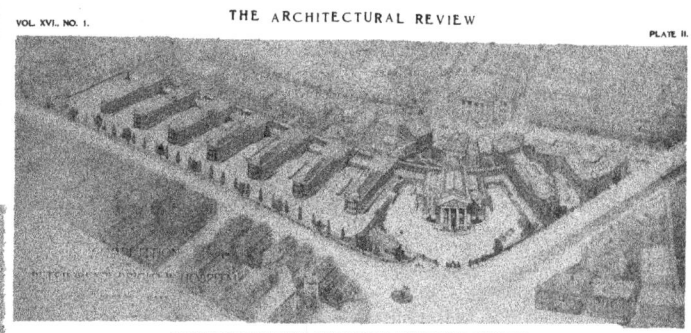

GROUP PERSPECTIVE, WINNING DESIGN, CODMAN & DESPRADELLE, ARCHITECTS.

GROUP PERSPECTIVE, CASS GILBERT, ARCHITECT.

GROUP PERSPECTIVE, PARKER, THOMAS & RICE, ARCHITECTS.

GROUP PERSPECTIVES, COMPETITION FOR THE PETER BENT BRIGHAM HOSPITAL, BOSTON, MASS.

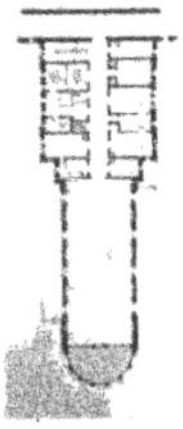

WARD PLAN.  ADMINISTRATION BUILDING, GUY LOWELL, ARCHITECT.  WARD PLAN.

ELEVATIONS, WARD PAVILION, GUY LOWELL, ARCHITECT.

ELEVATION ON SQUARE, PEABODY & STEARNS, ARCHITECTS.

ELEVATION ON VAN DYKE STREET, PEABODY & STEARNS, ARCHITECTS.
COMPETITION FOR THE PETER BENT BRIGHAM HOSPITAL, BOSTON, MASS.

ADMINISTRATION BUILDING.

DISPENSARY.

NURSES' HOME.

COMPETITION FOR THE PETER BENT BRIGHAM HOSPITAL, BOSTON, MASS. CASS GILBERT, ARCHITECT.

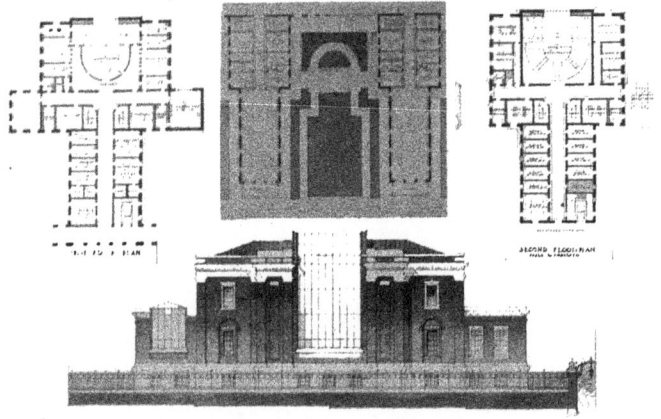

OPERATING AND WARD BUILDINGS, CASS GILBERT, ARCHITECT.

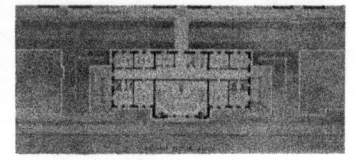

OPERATING BUILDING

OPERATING BUILDING, WINNING DESIGN, CODMAN & DESPRADELLE, ARCHITECTS.
COMPETITION FOR THE PETER BENT BRIGHAM HOSPITAL, BOSTON, MASS.

PATHOLOGICAL BUILDING

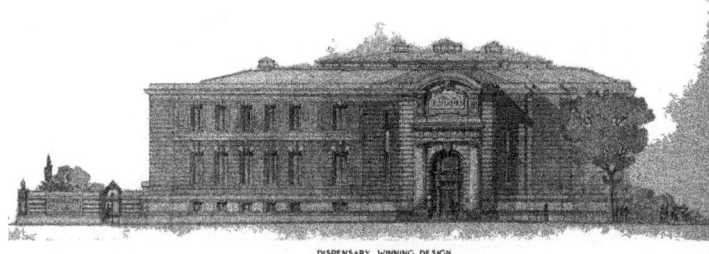

DISPENSARY, WINNING DESIGN.

TYPICAL WARD WINNING DESIGN. COMPETITION FOR THE PETER BENT BRIGHAM

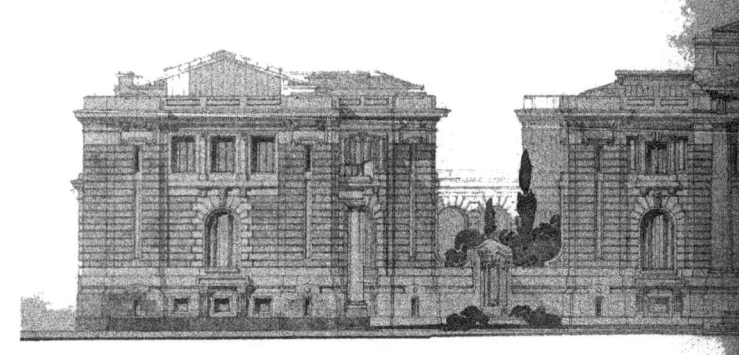

REVIEW

PLATES VI, VII.

MEDICAL CLINIC BUILDING

NURSES' HOME, WINNING DESIGN.

TYPICAL WARD, WINNING DESIGN.

CODMAN & DESPRADELLE, ARCHITECTS.

ADMINISTRATION BUILDING, WINNING DESIGN.

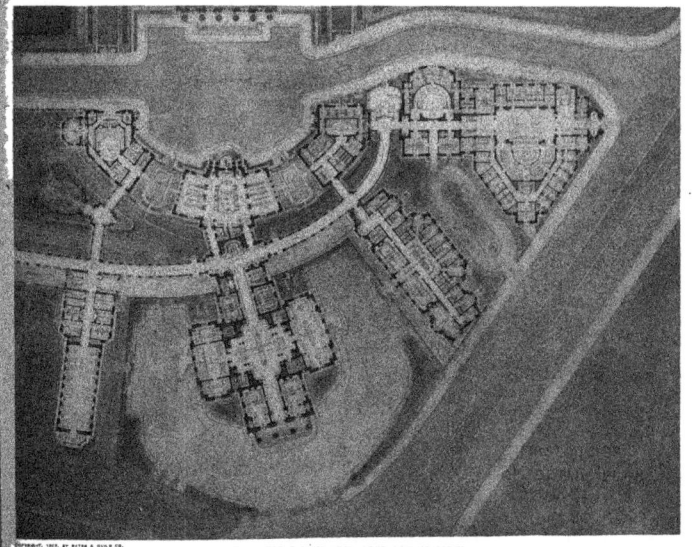

DETAIL GROUP PLAN, FIRST FLOOR, WINNING DESIGN.
COMPETITION FOR THE PETER BENT BRIGHAM HOSPITAL, BOSTON, MASS. CODMAN & DESPRADELLE, ARCHITECTS.

SIDE ELEVATION, DISPENSARY, WINNING DESIGN.

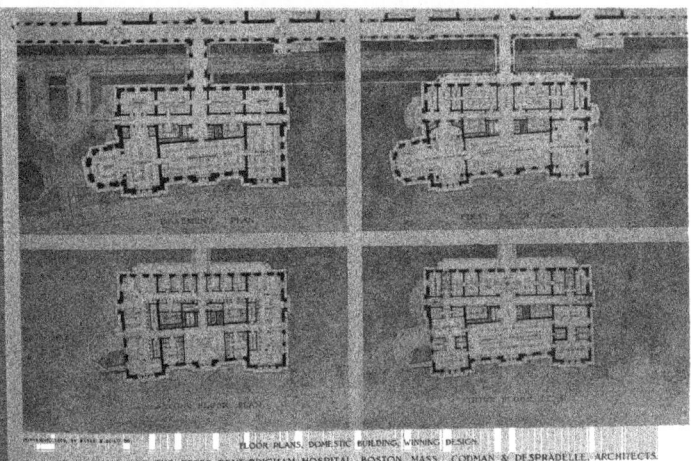

END ELEVATION, NURSES' HOME, WINNING DESIGN.

FLOOR PLANS, DOMESTIC BUILDING, WINNING DESIGN.
COMPETITION FOR THE PETER BENT BRIGHAM HOSPITAL, BOSTON, MASS. CODMAN & DESPRADELLE, ARCHITECTS.

WARD PLAN. ADMINISTRATION BUILDING, PARKER, THOMAS & RICE, ARCHITECTS. WARD PLAN.

DISPENSARY, PARKER, THOMAS & RICE, ARCHITECTS.

WARD PLAN. ADMINISTRATION BUILDING, SHEPLEY, RUTAN & COOLIDGE, ARCHITECTS. WARD PLAN.

APOTHECARY BUILDING, SHEPLEY, RUTAN & COOLIDGE, ARCHITECTS.   NURSES' HOME, SHEPLEY, RUTAN & COOLIDGE, ARCHITECTS.

COMPETITION FOR THE PETER BENT BRIGHAM HOSPITAL, BOSTON, MASS.

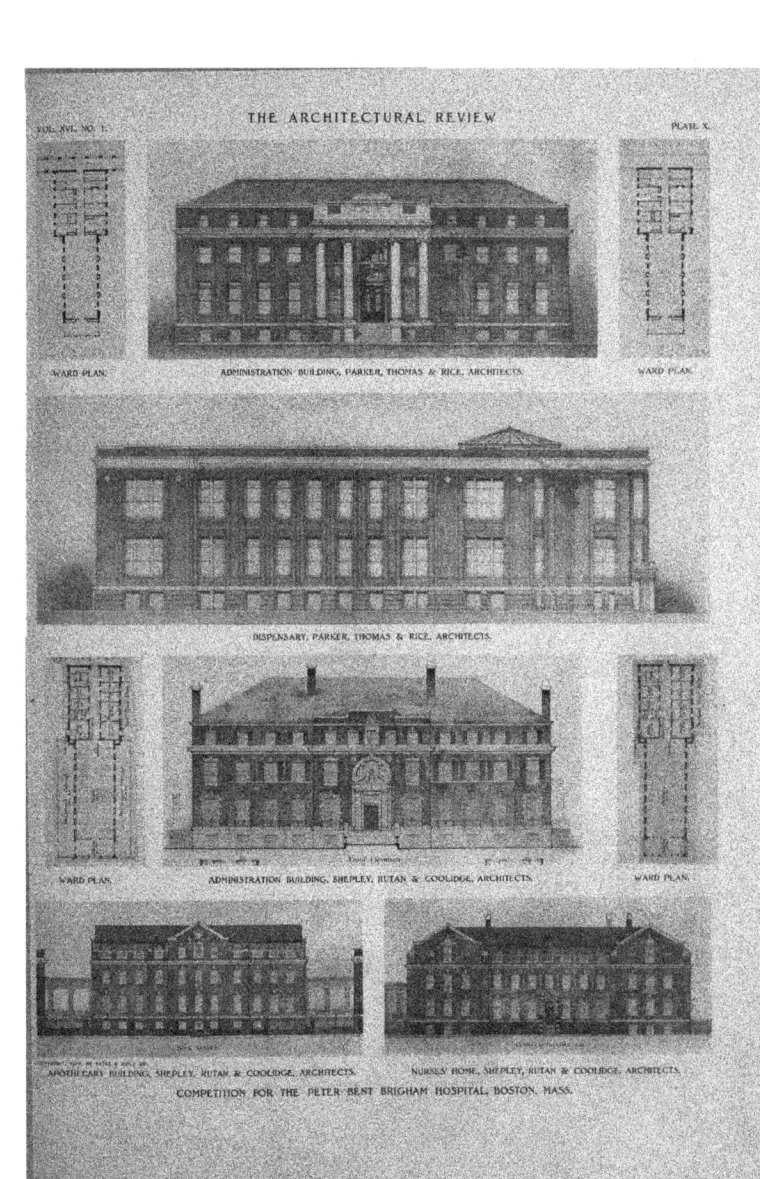

GROUP PERSPECTIVE, GUY LOWELL, ARCHITECT.

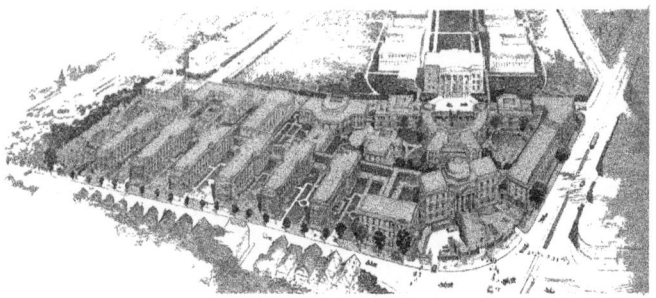

GROUP PERSPECTIVE, PEABODY & STEARNS, ARCHITECTS.

GROUP PERSPECTIVE, SHEPLEY, RUTAN & COOLIDGE, ARCHITECTS.
GROUP PERSPECTIVES, COMPETITION FOR THE PETER BENT BRIGHAM HOSPITAL, BOSTON, MASS.

GROUP PLAN, GUY LOWELL, ARCHITECT.

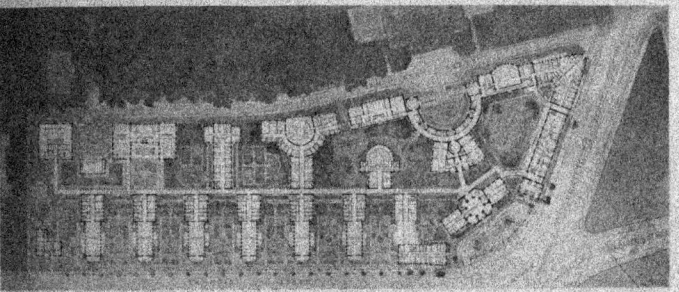

GROUP PLAN, PEABODY & STEARNS, ARCHITECTS.

GROUP PLAN, SHEPLEY, RUTAN & COOLIDGE, ARCHITECTS.

GROUP PLANS, COMPETITION FOR THE PETER BENT BRIGHAM HOSPITAL, BOSTON, MASS.

MODERN ENGLISH COUNTRY HOUSES

KITCHEN COURTYARD AND SIDE ENTRANCE, CONKWELL GRANGE, WILTSHIRE, ENGLAND.
E. GUY DAWBER, ARCHITECT.

PLATE III.

MODERN ENGLISH COUNTRY HOUSES

HALL, SHOWING FIREPLACE.

THE HALL, CONKWELL GRANGE, WILTSHIRE, ENGLAND.
E. GUY DAWBER, ARCHITECT.

PLATE IV.

MODERN ENGLISH COUNTRY HOUSES
CONKWELL GRANGE, WILTSHIRE, ENGLAND
By E. Guy Dawber, Architect

MR. DAWBER'S design for Conkwell Grange, near the city of Bath, Wiltshire, England, shown in the photographs on this page and in the four plates bound into this number, has been selected as the first of the dwellings to be reproduced in the series of "Modern English Country Houses," that we recently announced. It is as distinctive and typical an example of English Country House architecture of to-day as could be found to initiate this series. The selection of an appropriate local stone — taken mostly from old walls about the estate; the exceptionally suitable roofing — old stone slate — also obtained in the vicinity; and the utilization — fused into the one design — of motives easily separated under the heads of "Classic" and "Gothic", are all representative of the modern type of residence design in England.

While it is not desirable that, in America, we should slavishly imitate these mannerisms, or adopt, without reason, these forms or these details, yet the lessons to be learned from modern English work of this type might with benefit be inculcated into the domestic architecture of America to-day. And these lessons are not solely in æsthetics! — although the word "Home" is nowhere better defined than in the moderate priced English dwelling. It is, in England, the rule — rather than the exception — to build enduringly,— of fire-proof, non-burning materials and construction; to use only the best and hardest woods for finish; to use good plasterwork, frankly as such; or else to carve wood — where such carving is in assured taste — instead of imitating that carving in papier-mâché.

It is also the custom to suit the plan first to the location and needs of its inhabitants, and then allow the arrangement and surroundings largely to determine and dominate the exterior character of the dwelling.

Entrance Door and Vestibule.

Dining-room, Conkwell Grange, Wiltshire, England. E. Guy Dawber, Architect.

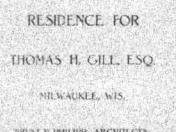

RESIDENCE FOR
THOMAS H. GILL, ESQ.
MILWAUKEE, WIS.
BRUST & PHILIPP, ARCHITECTS

The Architectural Review
VOLUME XVI. NUMBER 1
JANUARY, 1909

BATES & GUILD COMPANY, Publishers
42 Chauncy Street, Boston
NEW YORK OFFICE, PARK ROW BUILDING

Published monthly. Price, mailed flat to any address in the United States or Canada, five dollars per annum, in advance; to any foreign address, six dollars per annum, in advance. Subscriptions begin with the issue following their receipt. Single copies, fifty cents. Special number, two dollars. Entered as second-class mail-matter at the Post-office, Boston, Massachusetts, November 27, 1891.

PLATES

PLATES I., II.— BRIGHAM HOSPITAL COMPETITION, BOSTON, MASS. (GROUP PLANS AND PERSPECTIVES.) — CODMAN & DESPRADELLE; PARKER, THOMAS & RICE; CASS GILBERT; ARCHITECTS.
PLATE III.— BRIGHAM HOSPITAL COMPETITION, BOSTON, MASS. (PLANS AND ELEVATIONS.) — GUY LOWELL, ARCHITECT.
PLATE III.— BRIGHAM HOSPITAL COMPETITION, BOSTON, MASS. (PLANS AND ELEVATIONS.) — PEABODY & STEARNS, ARCHITECTS.
PLATES IV., V.— BRIGHAM HOSPITAL COMPETITION, BOSTON, MASS. (PLANS AND ELEVATIONS.) — CASS GILBERT, ARCHITECT.
PLATES V.-IX.— BRIGHAM HOSPITAL COMPETITION, BOSTON, MASS. WINNING DESIGN. (PLANS AND ELEVATIONS.) — CODMAN & DESPRADELLE, ARCHITECTS.
PLATE X.— BRIGHAM HOSPITAL COMPETITION, BOSTON, MASS. (PLANS AND ELEVATIONS.) — PARKER, THOMAS & RICE, ARCHITECTS.
PLATE X.— BRIGHAM HOSPITAL COMPETITION, BOSTON, MASS. (PLANS AND ELEVATIONS.) — SHEPLEY, RUTAN & COOLIDGE, ARCHITECTS.
PLATES XI., XII.— BRIGHAM HOSPITAL COMPETITION, BOSTON, MASS. (GROUP PLANS AND PERSPECTIVES.) — GUY LOWELL; PEABODY & STEARNS; SHEPLEY, RUTAN & COOLIDGE; ARCHITECTS.

THE trade magazines published in the interests of the Portland Cement manufacturers teem with contributions, editorial and otherwise, berating the architects for their slowness in taking up and using the various new methods of construction in which cement plays the part of a prominent structural element. An amusing side-light on the situation is found in some correspondence we have recently seen, that passed between two important cement associations, namely A and B, and an inquiring architect, who had written to both A and B for information. From the replies we have borrowed the following quotations, taken from letters dated but one day apart. Cement man A writes to the architect: "We would refer you to the ——" (cement men B) "for securing data of concrete houses. We have tried to do so several times, but have been unable to obtain any." Now to quote from the letter received from cement men B (the very people to whom the above writer had "referred" his questioner!): "We regret to advise you of our inability to furnish you with *any*" (pardon these italics; they are ours!) "information concerning methods of construction and application of plaster or stucco on concrete. We are at the present time preparing a book in which this subject will be considered." (Consistency, thou' art a jewel!) "We would suggest that you communicate with ——" (naming cement man A, the very writer of the other letter!) "for this information."

The Gilbertian satire of the situation rests in the fact that the very publications used for propaganda by the two concerns from whom these letters had been received are those cement journals that keep insinuating most persistently that the *architect* is the one who does not give to the subject of building in cement the consideration they claim it deserves; and yet here, in an attempt to obtain material upon this very subject, the principal association of cement manufacturers confess themselves as being unable to furnish "any information concerning methods of construction . . . or stucco on concrete," while they complain in their publication, issued the very same month, of the lack of interest of the architect who "seems to be rather passive and unsympathetic on the subject of concrete houses!" Pray, who is "passive" — even, one might say, "negative" — "and unsympathetic" in *this* instance!

AND *this* sort of advertising, containing several misrepresentations of fact, continues to be advocated by even the most important cement interests, and accepted, without hesitation, by *reputable* publications. The accompanying clipping is taken from a recent number of *The Saturday Evening Post*.

SOME publications have now been commenting for years on the reckless fire losses incurred by the American people, until the public at last appears to be taking some interest in the matter — and even the popular magazines are beginning to do their part toward spreading information as to the enormous amount of money actually consumed year after year by fire in the United States. Anything that can make this matter more effective will undoubtedly tend toward the earlier arrival of a day when we would build durably and permanently. Might not the arrival of that much-to-be-desired time be hastened if the newspapers would print, regularly each day, at the head of a certain column upon their front page, a brief succession of paragraphs giving the fire losses sustained throughout the country on the day preceding; and summarizing the entire total by a head-line stating the money value of the property burned! The Sunday papers could give the "Fire Record" totals for the preceding week.

We believe that such a campaign would soon become effective, as we doubt if even the most reckless and happy-go-lucky American could long withstand the subtile psychology of head-lines reiterating, over and over again, a series of fire losses aggregating almost three-quarter million of dollars each day!

IN the matter of the appointment of a Governmental Commission on the Fine Arts it is more than probable that President Roosevelt's hand was forced by Speaker Cannon's scheme for a three-and-a-half-million-dollar memorial to Lincoln to be erected on the Plaza in front of the Union Station at Washington. Otherwise it is doubtful if the President would have followed his recommendation for the appointment of a Committee on Art by publishing so soon the list of members selected upon the advice of the officers of the Institute of Architects. It is to be regretted that there should have appeared to be a conflict between Senator Newlands, who had introduced a bill providing the machinery to make such a commission effective, and the President, in appointing the list as he did, before the legislation that would make the approval of this commission obligatory for works of art was passed by Congress.

Nevertheless, this action, precipitate as it may have appeared, is certainly not to be regretted by those having the interests of this movement at heart. Probably in no other way could the actual need for this commission have been so well visualized before the country as a whole. The mass of the people undoubtedly now realize the necessity as they would never otherwise have done. The instant response from all over the States made to the appeal of the Institute was also a revelation, to that body as well as to Congress; as both can now realize how well prepared and awake the country is to protest an action of this sort when the proper authoritative bodies make an appeal to them for assistance. The flood of protest that poured in upon Congress from all over the country when the facts in regard to Speaker Cannon's bill for locating a Lincoln Memorial in "Graft Square" became known was a surprise to every one concerned, and proved — when backed up by the dominating personality of the President — to be immediately effective.

Current Periodicals

A Review of the Recent American And Foreign Architectural Publications

Terrace, House at Cohasset, Mass.
Andrews, Jacques & Rantoul, Architects.
(From "The Island Architect.")

Perspective, Gateway Park, Minneapolis, Minn.
Edwin H. Hewitt, Architect.
(From "The Western Architect.")

Garden Gateway, Dedham, Mass.
Frank Chouteau Brown, Architect.
(From "Architecture.")

WE are glad to be able, for once, to give first place in this review to *The Western Architect*, which has issued a number of particular interest among the December architectural magazines. It is always a question, in the conduct of any technical journal, whether or not it is merely to "hold a mirror up to nature," by illustrating desultorily from number to number that work that has been done within the realm it purposes to reflect; or whether it is to take a position in advance of the movement for progress, and perform its allotted function in the direction of the energies of its subscribers toward the attainment of the best and highest ideals. In arriving at a decision, it may or may not be definitely settled that the paper is to follow the latter — and more difficult — course. Yet, in the editorial conduct of any publication, this question must either be solved — or avoided. If the problem is *not* once stated and thoroughly faced it is inevitable that the magazine become merely a hanger-on at the heels of what actual progression — or retrogression — there may occur in the field that it is its province to cover. Certainly, this course is much easier than assuming the hardships and misunderstandings of assaulting the obstacles and encountering the prejudices that must be the lot of the paper whose conception of its reason for existence is of the bolder type. It undoubtedly takes courage, and a somewhat egotistic belief in one's ability, judgment, or intuition, to assume the rôle of prophet and leader in an untried and little-known field. Yet, as almost the sole means of education for the profession, especially those members established at remote distances from the centers of progress, or in those little known backwaters where the direction of the current may not so strongly evidence itself, is from the pages of the architectural journal, whatever that journal may happen to be, it is most important that it provide him with the proper incentives for betterment.

Undoubtedly one of the big fields for the future practice of architecture is going to lie in the domain of City Building, and *The Western Architect*, by deviating for once from its accustomed habit of reproducing illustrations of mediocre works selected from an arbitrarily restricted field, has undoubtedly done something toward influencing its subscribers to give thought and consideration to a problem the analysis and discussion of which cannot help but benefit them. While the number that has suggested these improvements is incomplete, and its illustrations fragmentary in many

House of William Jay Turner, Esq., Germantown, Pa.
Wilson Eyre, Architect.
(From "The American Architect.")

Unity Temple and Unity House, Oak Park, Ill.
Frank Lloyd Wright, Architect.
(From "The Inland Architect.")

Detail, House of William J. Turner, Esq.
Wilson Eyre, Architect.
(From "The American Architect.")

Interior view, Unity Temple, Oak Park, Ill.
Frank Lloyd Wright, Architect.
(From "The Inland Architect.")

ways, yet it remains largely given to the consideration of "Civic Planning in America" — than which no better nor more important text could have been chosen.

The plates include several suggestions for developing the entrance plaza in Minneapolis, a city where the diverging lines of two main avenues of traffic, uniting at the bridge across the Mississippi immediately above the Falls of St. Anthony, already contain the basis of a stately and dignified city entrance. This natural asset is rendered rarely effective from the fact that one of the largest railroad stations is located immediately at this point of intersection — instead of in some remote slum district; as is the case in every other American city of which we have any knowledge. It remains merely to combine the many other railroad interests converging at and entering the place — and a slight expenditure of money in this square will enable the stranger to enter this Western metropolis under those conditions most calculated to produce a favorable impression upon him.

The Western Architect having thus pointed the way, it remains only for the citizens of Minneapolis to appropriate the idea and make it a reality. We reprint on this page one of the best of the schemes suggested. Other illustrations include Mr. Maher's now well-known Rubens House at Glencoe, Ill., and exteriors and interiors of houses by Mr. Whitney, in Minneapolis, and by Mr. Clarence Johnson, of St. Paul, along with a number of attractive pictures of garden architecture, all generally picturesque.

The Inland Architect follows a close second, particularly by its illustrations of Mr. Frank Lloyd Wright's completed church (or "Temple," as it is here called) at Oak Park, Ill., one of the most interesting designs that he has done. It is also rather a surprise to find a house at Cohasset by Andrews, Jacques & Rantoul first shown in this Western publication. The remainder of the number reproduces a considerable amount of detail from the Boston School report, a Post-office in Michigan, and a page of sketches of projected buildings at West Point, covering, all in all, rather more of a range than is often attempted by our Western architectural journals.

The Brickbuilder contains an article on "The Denominational Church," by C. Howard Walker, illustrated by rather a wide variety, in point of location and in design, of American churches. Distinctly among the most interesting views reproduced is Mr. Howard Shaw's interior for a Presbyterian church at Chicago, that is more than a little suggestive of some of the Austrian architecture to which we elsewhere refer. This magazine also recognizes, at last, one modern branch of the practice of architecture to-day, in an article dealing with "The Development and *Financing* of Apartment-Houses!" The plate illustrations include a church at Rochester by Claude Bragdon, a general view of which we reproduce; A. W. Longfellow's town hall at Lancaster, and a country house by Wilson Eyre that — particularly in the way brick is utilized for porch columns and balustrades — is of considerable value to the house designer. The utilitarian buildings by Winslow & Bigelow are not among the least interesting examples of brick work shown in this month's issue.

The American Architect for December 2 reproduces a plaster house by Wilson Eyre and a number of illustrations of picturesque Colonial architecture. The issue of the same magazine for December 9 is devoted to Cope & Stewardson's new building for the College of Physicians at Philadelphia, and to a description of the proceedings of the Eighth International Congress of Architects last May at Vienna, accompanied by a number of plate illustrations of Viennese architecture — Art Nouveau and otherwise. The drawings for the College of Physicians and Surgeons show a building based upon conservative Georgian precedent that is something of a contrast to the more original works from Austria — especially those by Otto Wagner. The beautiful view along the Ringstrasse is shown in a photograph in this same issue, and is perhaps as comprehensive and effective a plea for the proper layout of our large cities as could be found. We have already reproduced in these columns a view of this same section of Vienna, and therefore do nothing more than call attention to the matter here. This article is continued in the issue for December 16, the plates of which reproduce a number of "Neo-Grec" banks and improved tenements by Mr. William Emerson.

December 23 begins a report of the 42d Convention of the American Institute of Architects at Washington. The plates illustrate several schools in the vicinity of Philadelphia by David Knickerbacker Boyd, and a school at Porto Rico by Clarke, Howe, and Homer. We reproduce a building by Werner & Windolph for a "Sunshine Chapel" that, though more nearly resembling a bank, possesses considerable architectural interest.

The last issue of the month, for December 30, contains further reports brought in at the Convention of the American Institute, along with some notes from Europe; and the plates illustrate Kenneth Murchison's new station at Scranton for the Delaware, Lackawanna and Western Railway, of which we give a general view of the exterior.

The December *Architectural Record* illustrates the Chicago and Northwestern Terminal in the city of Chicago (that has already just been illustrated in *The American Architect*) and the new German Theater in New York City, especially the decorations by Alphons Mucha. One article describes some of the bridges and new railroad stations, the latter by Cass Gilbert, along the ' Harlem River branch;" along with a number of interesting illustrations of chimneys and factory buildings, car-barns, etc., that quite accord with the architectural repute in which these buildings are generally held. An article descriptive of the vicinity around Los Angeles abounds in illustrations of residence architecture of a type that is rather consistently disappointing throughout; while an article of somewhat general interest is that on the Châteaux of the Loire. All in all, a number of rather more general and popular than of architectural value.

Architecture prints a New York apartment-house ("the largest in the world"), along with three pages of Palmer & Hornbostel's drawings for the State Educational buildings at Albany, doubtless interesting enough in the originals, but so reduced and obscured in these miniature reproductions that it is impossible quite to tell what they are all about. This appears to be an apartment-house number. Certainly it contains a number of unusual apartment types, generally from New York; perhaps the worst we have ever seen being "The Gainsboro Studios." The Verona, while distinctly of better style, is not notable for any great originality; and the building for the Hendrik Hudson apartment has the effect of attempting to reproduce the sky-line of lower New York in a single block along the Hudson at 110th Street. The Stoneholm apartment in Brookline is the single building outside the city of New York; while the only representation of residence architecture in this issue is the restoration of an old house at Derlham. As the editor possessed sufficient courage to give an entire plate to a most picturesque photograph of a garden gateway, we have chosen to reproduce it rather than the more conventional and architectural view of this building.

The November *New York Architect*, just received, is given to McKim, Mead & White's buildings for the Gorham Manufacturing Company and Colony Club, New York City, and the Girard Trust Company, Philadelphia. We believe we have already remarked on the entire preceding number having been given to the Importers' and Traders' National Bank, and one again wonders at those determining factors that caused an editor to devote an entire number to a building of *that* type, and reduces the illustration of the Gorham Building — one of the two most important modern architectural monuments in New York City — to a bare half-dozen of plates!

Christian Art for December deals with the Church of Brou, Chipping-Campden and its Craftsmanship, and Canterbury Cathedral, all three articles of considerable architectural value. The carvings of I. Kirchmayer are also thoroughly illustrated.

The English *Architectural Review* illustrates some of the familiar buildings "Around and about Paris;" completes the review of the work of Sir Gilbert Scott; describes and illustrates several historic and architectural monuments recently destroyed or on their way towards destruction; and, for current work, Mr. Reginald Blomfield's additions to the Goldsmith College and the Manchester Royal Infirmary, both already illustrated in these columns.

Of the other foreign magazines, *The Builder's Journal* devotes its plates mostly to photographs and drawings of old English work, save for a recent County Hall competition at Cardiff, shown in the issue for December 23. *The Architect* for the month of December, however, has not given us architecture of any importance. In *The Builder* we note the single important architectural design for the month — in the extension of the front block of the National Gallery, Trafalgar Square, that we reprint. Extended comment hardly seems necessary, inasmuch as the design itself speaks far more eloquently than dull type! Another plate from the same publication is the Government Offices at Simla that certainly does *not* belong to the scenes of which Kipling has written so many times and oft.

La Construction Moderne presents the usual number and kinds of "Hotels" and "Projets"— but, in the last issue of the year, it publishes a plate that for pure hideousness surpasses anything previously seen, and therefore irresistibly demands republication!

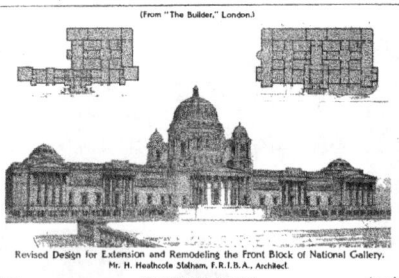

Revised Design for Extension and Remodeling the Front Block of National Gallery.
Mr. H. Heathcote Statham, F.R.I.B.A., Architect.
(From "The Builder," London.)

Government Offices, Simla.
James Ransome, Architect.
(From "The Builder," London.)

Gare D'Epinay.
M. Aumont, Engineer. M. Ligny, Architect.
(From "La Construction Moderne.")

The Architectural Review

Volume XVI   February, 1909   Number 2

Half-Timber Buildings of Saxony

By C. A. Whittemore

THE origin of half-timbered work in Germany is lost far back in the mist of the ages. A number of individuals have written on this subject, but their deductions are, in a measure, mere conjecture, as they frequently cannot be substantiated by accepted facts. Undoubtedly the most valuable and definitive contribution to the history of German half-timber work, although it deals mostly with buildings in the province of Saxony, resulted from a survey undertaken by a governmental commission, headed by Dr. O. Doering, the "provincial conservator," that is summarized in the following text and illustrations.

While there are still in existence plenty of examples to illustrate the characteristics of the different epochs, yet so many links are missing that it is impossible to establish a continuous chain of development. Neither can the influence exercised by German half-timber work on the architecture of other countries be estimated with any degree of certainty. There is little doubt but that it extended wherever this type of construction has been adopted. France, Scandinavia, England, all received their inspiration from this source; and thence the movement spread throughout the continent, to finally appear — centuries later — in America; — there blossoming forth as an applied surface treatment that preserved its decorative qualities while losing its former utilitarian, historical, and political significance.

Doubtless this style primarily arose from exigencies of structural conditions. The oldest examples extant are probably of the same general character as its earliest progenitor; i.e., a skeleton construction in wood, with filled-in panels of other materials.

Fig. 1. House near St. Martin's Church, Stolberg, 1500.

Fig. 2. House near St. Sylvester's Church, Wernigerode, 16th Century.

Copyright, 1909, by Bates & Guild Company.

In the days of Pliny and Tacitus the German village houses were noted for their good domestic character and harmonious coloring. With the gradual transition from town to city the scope of development was greatly increased; and in its later form, the city house, early influence is still predominant, despite the various periods through which it has passed. Used even in castles and churches, half-timber work has adhered, with a wonderful steadfastness and veracity, to its individual character as originally derived from the peasant builders. Only after a long, hard, and constant struggle did it yield to the influences of the more pretentious forms of building.

Whether half-timber work first arose in Northern or Southern Germany is an indeterminate question. Doubtless it developed almost simultaneously from a common source in those regions which abounded in oak, beech, and other woods. Its growth and extension, constantly influenced by local conditions, is not so remarkable when we consider the nomadic character of the artisans of the time. This may also account for the fact that a group of houses may be found in one locality which resembles more strongly the character of the work in a distant town than it does its own companions. Thus also we see different characteristics in different localities — in some, rich forms; in others, severe, dignified lines; here, artistic and refined handiwork; there, crude attempts at carving.

On account of the great antiquity of this style, the oldest of the existing half-timbered houses is relatively young. The Rathskeller in Halberstadt (Fig. 5), built in 1461, is the earliest building in this

Fig. 3. 338 Rittergasse, Stolberg. Street Front. 14th-15th Century.

Fig. 4. 338 Rittergasse, Stolberg. Garden Side.

section of which there is any authentic record. Some buildings, such as the house in Quedlinburg (Fig. 6), seem to bespeak a greater age than this; but the date of erection cannot be definitely established. Stolberg had up to recent years a house which was conceded as a relic of the thirteenth century (Figs. 3 and 4), but it is now entirely destroyed.

The following division of the development of the timber-work in Germany into periods has been accepted by many good authorities, — Early (thirteenth century to fifteenth century); Late Gothic (fifteenth century to sixteenth century); Transitional — Gothic to Renaissance (1520-1580); Renaissance (1580-1620); Baroque (seventeenth to eighteenth century).

The earliest form of construction is shown in the houses at Quedlinburg and Stolberg (Figs. 3, 4, and 6, and in Figs. 7, 9, and 12). This form is also the simplest, and consists of laying a heavy sill on a masonry wall or foundation; erecting upon this the studs, unbroken to the roof, braced, and tied by cross-bars. Into these cross-bars and studs the floor-timbers were mortised; and these cross-bars mark, on the exterior of the building, its separation into stories. At Quedlinburg we can see where the floor-timbers are cut clear through the studs and pinned on the outside with wooden pins. It is interesting to note that the Stolberg house had a painted decoration in the spaces between the studs in the upper story, and also a painted frieze. The colors were, as far as can now be conjectured, principally red and brown.

Fig. 5. Rathskeller, Halberstadt, 1461.

Fig. 6. 3 Wordgasse, Quedlinburg, 15th Century.

We have numerous evidences that the old method of tenoning was not forgotten in later years. In several instances these tenons, where they extended beyond the face of the wall, were protected from the rain by small projecting boards or caps. Three framing-drawings (Figs 7, 9, and 12), of a house at Marburg, dating from 1320, will help explain these customs.

A most noticeable feature is the overhanging of the upper stories, marking an epoch in the history of wood construction, and adopted in all work from this period up to the decline of the movement. The oldest known house, in Halberstadt, previously mentioned, is a brilliant link in the chain binding the new era with the old prototypes. The construction of the overhanging portion is practically the same as is done to-day. The floor-timbers which were the same width as the studs, projected beyond the street faces. Either above or on the ends of these floor-timbers was placed a sill similar to that on the ground; and then on this the studs, etc., were built up as below. The support for the projecting timbers was furnished by a three-cornered brace which was mortised into both the stud and the cross-timber. Between these timbers filling-in blocks were sometimes placed, in order to strengthen the frame and incidentally to soften the outline of the overhang. The reason for this overhang was probably a practical requirement, inasmuch as it certainly was not a constructive necessity. It may have been a protection for the lower part against the rain, or it may have been to increase the space in the upper floors.

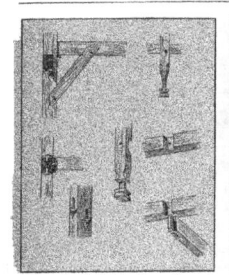

Fig. 7. Detail of Timber Frame, House at Marburg, 1320.

Fig. 8. 2 Moritzplan, Halberstadt, 15th Century.

Fig. 9. Skeleton Framework, House at Marburg, 1320.

Fig. 10. The "Alte Klopstock," Quedlinburg, 16th Century.

Fig. 11. 9 Neukirchenstrasse, Osterwieck, 16th Century.

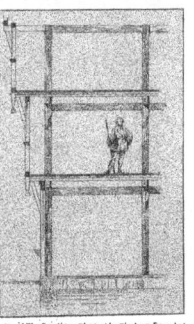

Fig. 12. Section Through Timber Framing House at Marburg, 1320.

Fig. 13. 5 Hagenstrasse, Neuhaldensleben, End of 16th Century.

or, again, it may have originated for defensive purposes in time of war.

The height of the upper projecting stories was varied solely by practical demands, but the ground floor was almost invariably very massive and high. Sometimes parts of this story would, for domestic reasons, be lower than others; and, where full height was not required, a lower or mezzanine floor was added. This mezzanine was never projected beyond the lower part; nor were the timbers cut through the studs, as was the case with the main floor-timbers.

When the house was on a corner of two streets, or stood alone, the overhang was frequently carried along the side, or even — on occasion — entirely around the building. In Northern Germany the corner studs, instead of continuing the regular spacing, were at first made much wider than the others. As a result of this increased width, three brackets were at first used at the corners to make a better finish. One was placed on the diagonal and was frequently increased in length over the other two (Fig. 5), in order to soften the line of the corner when seen in perspective.

In many cases the sills and studs were of considerable size — partly for the sake of greater stability, partly because of labor. Gradually, under the changing influences, these sizes were diminished until all the principal members became approximately of the same dimensions. There were, however, in the upper stories (and, in some examples, in the lower also), cross-braces put in at the sill to brace the studs. These were held in place by wood pins. Many times the crossing-points were covered with a rosette

Fig. 14. Detail of 5 Sandstrasse, Gardelegen.

Fig. 15. Detail of Castle, Flechtingen, End of 15th Century.

(Fig. 16), or another piece of ornament. The arrangement of these braces became a distinguishing mark of the different periods. The St. Andrew's cross, three-part, and four-part divisions were most frequently adopted in the early epochs. In the Baroque period this form of decoration assumed its highest development, and a radical departure from simple early treatments and use of straight lines may be seen. The work of this period (Fig. 32) is generally rather noticeably elaborate.

The spaces between the sills, studs, cross-bars, etc., were filled in with various materials. In the earlier buildings they were frequently closed with latticework, smeared with lime; later, tiles of different size and color were used. In this medium (Fig. 27), the builders displayed considerable ingenuity in working out patterns and designs. In almost every epoch there may be found examples which show that the use of a lime putty or mortar was handed down from generation to generation. There are also places where brick was employed — sometimes, in rather exceptional instances, covered with a coating of plaster. Another interesting material which was adopted in a few cases, as in Fig. 25, was the wooden block.

In the case of the house at Liebschütz, the lower part of the dwelling was filled in with wood block and the upper part with mortar. The blocks were set back from the face of the studs, and were bound together by the braces and cross-pieces. The joints between the horizontal layers of blocks were filled with mortar, much the same as in brickwork. The inside of the new block wall was usually lined with plank.

The treatment of the roof was also an important feature of half-timber work. Frequently the roof and rafters projected beyond the face of the wall far enough to protect the lower part of the house from the weather. The gables were usually plain and undecorated, but some examples are to be found showing the employment of decoration in low relief. The roof was covered with straw, shingles, and reeds in the olden times; but in the later periods slate and tile were adopted as being less combustible.

A further advance along ornamental lines took place in the treatment of the sills. In the Gothic period a system of square recesses was adopted as a decoration of this plain surface. Sometimes these surfaces were left unornamented, and sometimes they were enriched by carved leaf or plant forms. A later development cut off the corners of the timbers, making a deep

Fig. 16. House at Wernigerode, Courtyard Front, 16th Century.

Fig. 17. 309 Dammstrasse, Homburg, 1672.

Fig. 18. Old School, Schleusingen, 1681.

Fig. 19. Die Rose (Breitestrasse), Original Condition, Quedlinburg, 1612.

Fig. 20. House in the Hohestrasse, Quedlinburg, 1548.

Fig. 21. Upper Part of 1 Mittelstrasse, Osterwieck, 1549, Restored, 17th Century.

Fig. 22. Halle, 13 Rannische Strasse, 16th Century.

Fig. 23. 14 Lichtengraben, Halberstadt, 16th Century.

Fig. 24. Ratswage, Wernigerode, End of 15th Century.

Fig. 25. Farmhouse in Block Framing, Liebschütz, 18th Century.

Fig. 26. Reichartswerben, Province of Weissenfals, 17th Century.

Fig. 27. 24 Neuperverstrasse Salzwedel, 16th Century.

sinkage with rounded edges (Fig. 14). This form, variously developed, continued in use up to a late period, and was similar to the stone treatment used so frequently by the Romans. In its highest type, the rounded edge of the sill was ornamented with a bead motive, the background of the sinkage being decorated with carvings.

In the earlier periods the sills and even the trim around the entrance-doors were often ornamented with inscriptions (Fig. 14). These related the name of the builder and his wife, the date of the construction, the circumstances incident with its erection — and were carved in verse or prose, sometimes in German, sometimes in Latin, and sometimes even in Greek script!

The consoles, or brackets, which served both a constructive and an æsthetic purpose, were also subjected to a decorative development. In the Gothic period they were mostly square or octagonal in section. The outer face was hollowed and filled with carved figures, usually of saints or Old Testament characters. In the Renaissance the figure-work was gradually replaced by molded and carved forms continued throughout the console, while the sides were occasionally decorated with rosettes. In later times, as the projection of the upper stories was reduced, these consoles, with their accompanying ornament, gradually disappeared.

The diagonal braces also assumed new forms in the later periods. At first they were used only in the spaces beneath windows, at the foot of the studs. Gradually this paneling extended over the building's surface. These members, instead of being straight, were curved and modeled in various ways. In the province of Saxony there rose, about 1540, the rosette motive which we find so often decorating the crossing of these members. As it developed it assumed new forms, sometimes appearing as rays streaming from a central point, sometimes as a cross, sometimes fan-shaped (Fig. 28). These ornaments gradually increased in number, even overlapping (Fig. 21).

Fig. 28. House at Stolberg. 16th Century.

Fig. 29. House on the Breitenstrasse, Wernigerode. 1674.

Fig. 30. 34 Wasserstrasse, Homburg. 1563.

The development and growth of the various types of timber ornament passed from the early figure-carving to the more conventional leaf and plant forms; which are similar to much of the work now prevalent in modern Germany.

Door and window trims were also influenced by the decoration of other parts of the construction. Rich molded and carved architraves, ornamented doors, and decorative motives around the openings were all but a part of the general elaboration given to the whole exterior.

About the beginning of the eighteenth century appeared the first evidences of decline. Ornament vanished, the projection of upper stories disappeared, and the whole wall-surface was plastered over. From this time the study of German half-timber loses its fascination, and there ended a type of constructive decoration which, in its highest development, was so architecturally and æsthetically individual that its influence still survives,—although present-day half-timber work is hardly to be recognized as a lineal descendant of an ancestor so illustrious!

Fig. 31. 405 Rittergasse, Stolberg. 15th Century.

Fig. 32. Town Hall, Heinrichs. 17th Century.

Fig. 33. Town Hall, Stolberg. 1482. Restored, 1600.

Fig. 34. House in the New City, Stolberg. 16th Century.

Fig. 35. Farmhouse, Hainichen. 17th Century.

Fig. 36. Farmhouse near Geismar. 1769.

131 AND 133 E. 66TH ST., NEW YORK CITY.
CHARLES A. PLATT, ARCHITECT.

ENTRANCE DETAIL, 131 E. 66TH ST., NEW YORK CITY.
CHARLES A. PRATT, ARCHITECT.

I

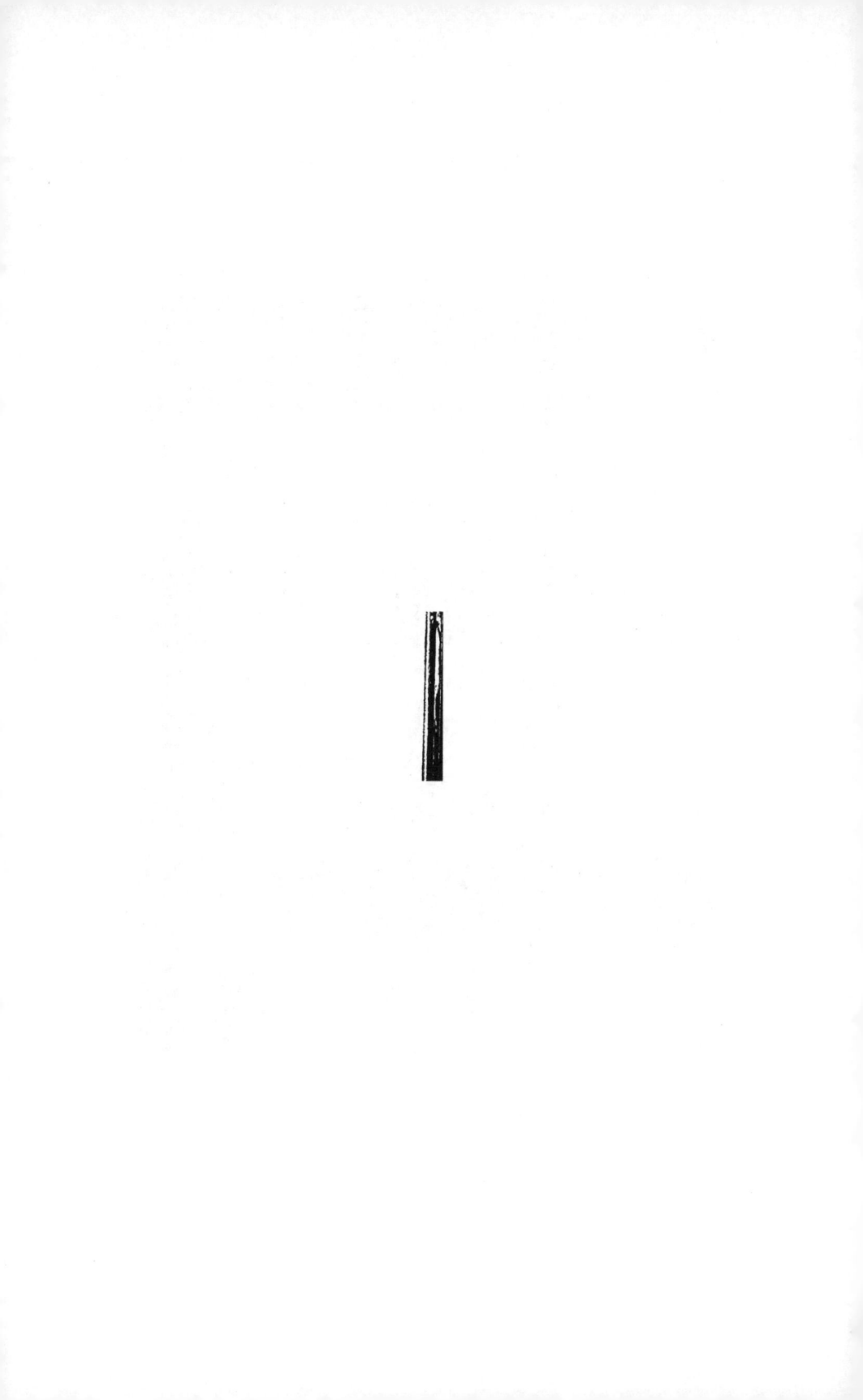

THE REREDOS, HAWKESYARD PRIORY, STAFFORDSHIRE, ENGLAND.
EDWARD GOLDIE, ARCHITECT.

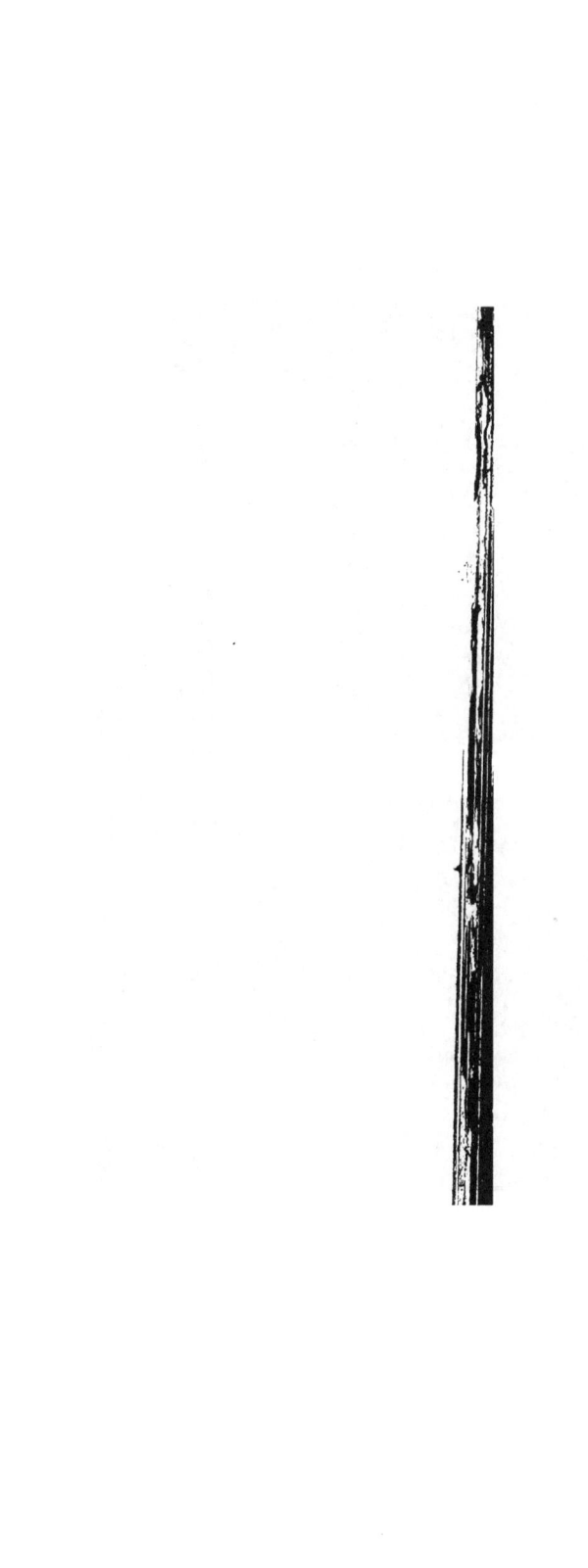

MANTEL, STUDIO OF MR. HOWARD HART, 131 E. 66TH ST., NEW YORK CITY.
CHARLES A. PLATT, ARCHITECT.

INTERIOR, STUDIO OF MR. HOWARD HART, 131 E. 66TH ST., NEW YORK CITY.
CHARLES A. PLATT, ARCHITECT.

II

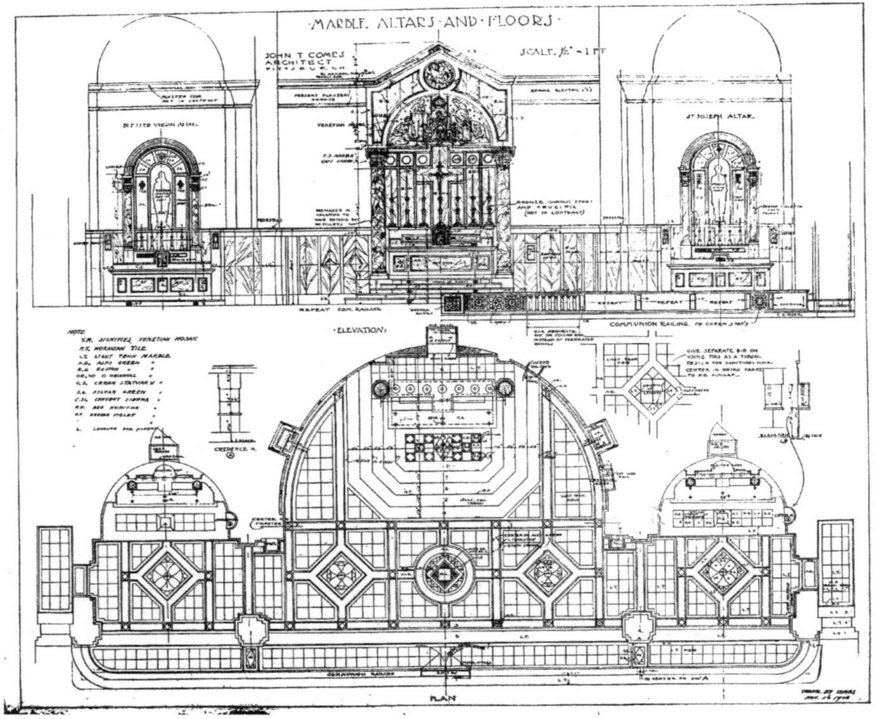
·MARBLE·ALTARS·AND·FLOORS·
JOHN T COMES
ARCHITECT
SCALE ½" = 1 FT
BLESSED VIRGIN ALTAR
ST JOSEPH ALTAR
·ELEVATION·
COMMUNION RAILING
REPEAT
REPEAT COM. RAILING
BRONZE CANDLESTICKS AND CRUCIFIX (NOT IN CONTRACT)
NOTE
V.M. SIGNIFIES VENETIAN MOSAIC
M.T. MORAVIAN TILE
L.T. LIGHT TENN. MARBLE
GIVE SEPARATE BID ON USING THIS AS A TYPICAL DESIGN FOR SANCTUARY FLOOR
CREDENCE
ELEVATION
PLAN
COMMUNION RAILING

PLANS, AND DETAIL OF ENTRANCE AT 131.
BUILDING AT 131 AND 135 E. 66TH ST., NEW YORK CITY.
CHARLES A. PLATT, ARCHITECT.

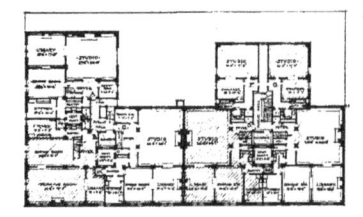

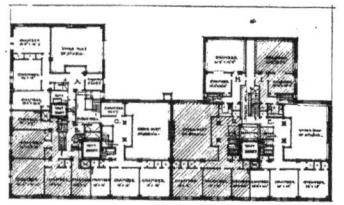

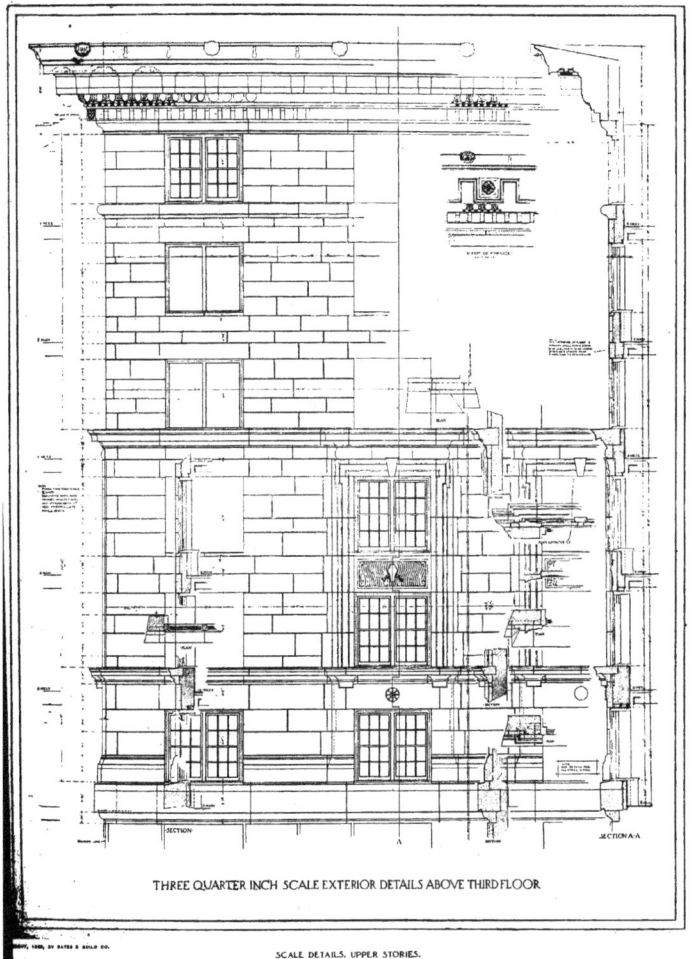

THREE QUARTER INCH SCALE EXTERIOR DETAILS ABOVE THIRD FLOOR

SCALE DETAILS, UPPER STORIES.
BUILDING AT 131 AND 135 E. 66TH ST., NEW YORK CITY.
CHARLES A. PLATT, ARCHITECT.

LEXINGTON AVENUE ELEVATION. WEST HALF OF ELEVATION ON 66TH ST.
BUILDING AT 131 AND 135 E. 66TH ST., NEW YORK CITY.
CHARLES A. PLATT, ARCHITECT.

INTERIOR, LIBRARY OF CHARLES A. PLATT, 135 E. 66TH ST., NEW YORK CITY.
CHARLES A. PLATT, ARCHITECT.

MANTEL IN LIBRARY OF CHARLES A. PLATT, 135 E. 66TH ST., NEW YORK CITY.
CHARLES A. PLATT, ARCHITECT.

MODERN ENGLISH CHURCHES

NORTH SIDE VIEW, BRYANSTON CHURCH, BLANDFORD, DORSET, ENGLAND.
EDWARD P. WARREN, ARCHITECT.

PLATE X.

INTERIOR, MR. HOWARD HART'S STUDIO, 131 E. 66TH ST., NEW YORK CITY.
CHARLES A. PLATT, ARCHITECT.

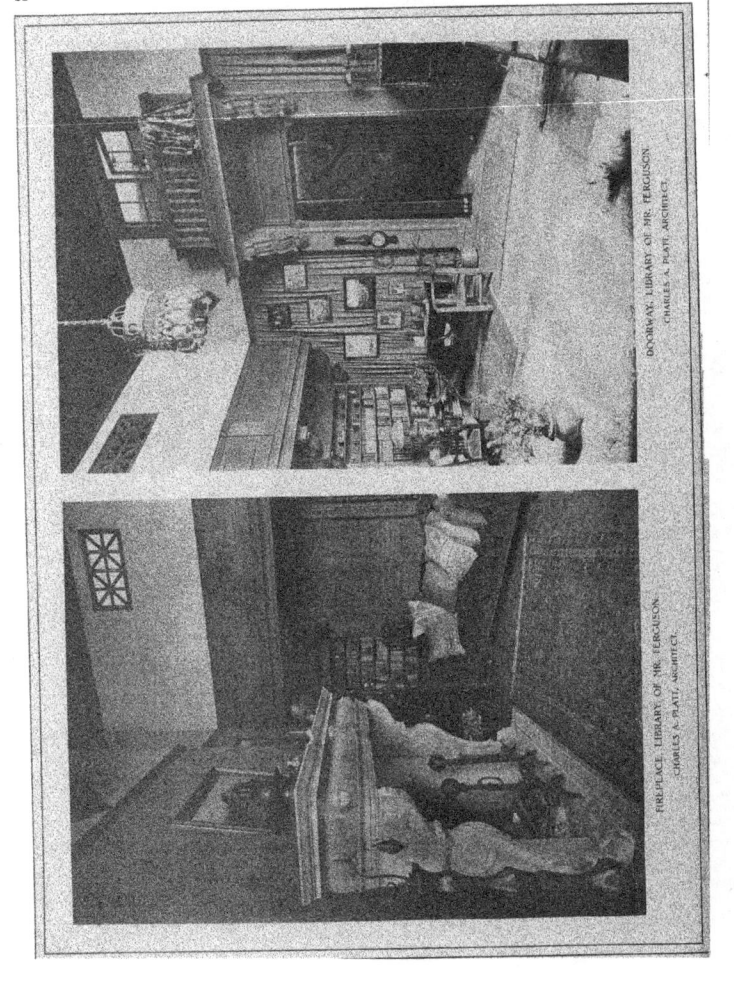

DOORWAY, LIBRARY OF MR. FERGUSON.
CHARLES A. PLATT, ARCHITECT.

FIREPLACE, LIBRARY OF MR. FERGUSON.
CHARLES A. PLATT, ARCHITECT.

ENTRANCE HALL

LIVING-ROOM
A HOUSE AT LAKE FOREST, ILL.
RICHARD E. SCHMIDT, GARDEN & MARTIN, ARCHITECTS

GENERAL VIEW.

DETAIL OF PORCH.
A HOUSE AT LAKE FOREST, ILL.
RICHARD E. SCHMIDT, GARDEN & MARTIN, ARCHITECTS.

The Architectural Review

VOLUME XVI. NUMBER 2

FEBRUARY, 1909

BATES & GUILD COMPANY, Publishers
42 Chauncy Street, Boston

NEW YORK OFFICE, PARK ROW BUILDING

Published monthly. Price, mailed flat to any address in the United States or Canada, five dollars per annum, in advance; to any foreign address, six dollars per annum, in advance. Subscriptions begin with the issue following their receipt. Single copies, fifty cents. Special number, two dollars. Entered as second-class mail-matter at the Post-office, Boston, Massachusetts, November 27, 1891.

PLATES

PLATES XIII.-XIV.— INTERIORS, STUDIO OF MR. HOWARD HART, 131 E. 66TH ST., NEW YORK CITY (PHOTOGRAPHIC VIEWS) — CHARLES A. PLATT, ARCHITECT.

PLATE XV. — MARBLE ALTARS, CHURCH AT PITTSBURGH, PA. — JOHN T. COMES, ARCHITECT.

PLATES XVI.-XVIII.— BUILDING AT 131 AND 135 E. 66TH ST., NEW YORK CITY (PLANS, ELEVATIONS, AND DETAILS) — CHARLES A. PLATT, ARCHITECT.

PLATES XIX., XX. — INTERIORS, LIBRARY OF CHARLES A. PLATT, 135 E. 66TH ST., NEW YORK CITY (PHOTOGRAPHIC VIEWS) — CHARLES A. PLATT, ARCHITECT.

A SHORT year ago we delivered ourselves, in these columns, of a definition of the artistic temperament that we believed at the time to be as clear an analysis of that somewhat baffling quantity as it was possible to give. In the light of a recent event we can realize this analysis may have been possibly overoptimistic, as the profession has since been treated to an exhibition showing the obverse of the shield; indicating how a spirit of egotism will feed on self-esteem until it has malformed all channels of outlook upon the world, and of communion with one's fellowmen. We still opine this not to be the case with a *great* artist. Such an one can never forget his gift is God-given. It dowers him within sight without his conscious volition, and — as the momentary possessor of a priceless gift — he is properly humble and thankful for being selected as a medium for the benefit and inspiration of his less-favored fellows. He never requires the plaudits of the crowd so long as his art meets with his own approbation; though his outlook is too broad for him ever to make the initial error of looking down upon his associates, or of regarding himself as better than they.

The *little* master is an artist of more human mold! His feet, at least, are clay. He murmurs and repines at restrictions that his master welcomes as the final inspiration that will add a higher individualism to even his most personal ideas. He is always inventing excuses to palliate his defects; or demanding his artproduct be seen — as did Richard Wagner! — only under impossible conditions or among physically unobtainable surroundings. The true master of his art is also the master of its limitations. His genius suffices to surpass all. His works make for great results; and these results he obtains by first accepting those conventions that are held by the greater part of humanity, and then — by these same very means — he so surpasses their limitation of vision — while still keeping in touch with their imagination — that they are bound to realize some part of the ideals he establishes for them.

THERE can be no doubt whatsoever that we are doomed to go through in this country a certain period of experiment in the attempt to utilize architectural forms and motives that will be borrowed from the so-called "Art Nouveau" schools of Europe. Since the beginning of architectural history in America we have always been influenced — a few years after — by the passing "styles" in design fashionably current across the water; and there is little likelihood, in this instance, of history failing to repeat itself. Already the first evidences are indeed beginning to appear amongst us in a few stray examples that have crept into the margins of our city streets. It is to be regretted that this invasion threatens at a time when we are experimenting throughout the country in the use of fluid concrete as a building-material, inasmuch as many of these perpetrations will inevitably take form in this easily modeled, yet time-resisting, material, so earning a lien upon perpetuity that would not have been otherwise granted them.

It seems impossible to prevent by any mere argument this threatened inundation, — rather, as heretofore, we will probably have to "grin and bear it," — and we may be certain that there will be examples sure to arouse our levity. It is a foregone conclusion that at least ninety-five one-hundredths of the work that will be produced under this influence will be bad, and an equal proportion of that amount irredeemably so; for it will appeal from its very appearance of facility to many designers whose training and education have not permitted them successfully to cope with the more easily comprehended styles that have been reduced to rules and formulæ by long years of use. How much the less able will they be to apprehend the subtler refinements and unconventional treatments of a style that raises the merit of simplicity to the Nth degree and that is based upon the most subtile refinements of Greek and Gothic architectural precedent!

So, too, from long accustomed disuse, we are little able to appreciate architectural treatments that do not deal with the conventional A B C's of architectural forms and moldings that our draughtsmen unthinkingly perpetuate day after day over the office drawing-board. Sweep out of their hands these cut-and-dried conventional forms, and how many architectural designers are there with sufficient facility in their fingers and inventiveness and inspiration in their minds to conceive and bring into being substitutes such as will merit execution in such enduring materials as stone and concrete?

"RUINED and stricken Reggio is to rebuild itself," was the announcement recently published in the American press. This head-line conveys a different idea to the initiate than many will gather from its simple statement of fact. Reggio *will* rebuild — and it will be her endeavor and her pride to have the reconstructed city based as closely as possible upon the picturesque architectural lines of the old city that was lost!

The Campanile of St. Mark that fell is rising again upon the identical lines and of, indeed, the identical materials in which it was previously constructed. Possibly the Campanile will be better built — at least that will be the intention of its builders — and probably the buildings of the new Reggio will be more convenient and sanitary than of yore; but that an endeavor will be made to retain their original beauty and picturesqueness, no person understanding the Italian temperament can doubt. Indeed, the "foreigner," with a canny eye for profit that the self-satisfied American business man doth lack, realizes the money value of architectural beauty, and does not scorn to make appeal to the eye in a way that the more practical and up-to-date (?) civilizations continue to overlook. Many cities of Europe, Chester-within-the-Gates as an example — even in "commercial" Germany! — include regulations in their building laws requiring new buildings to be built upon the architectural lines of the old, that are as stringent as any portion dealing with construction; with sanitation; or with the prevention of fire! One conjures in his mind's eye a vision of future tourists visiting America and peering round amongst an artistically desert city of tablets and of stones inscribed with sentences, evermore beginning, "Here once stood this — or that — memorial of American liberty and history," and "This square contained a structure emblematic of American architecture; torn down in the year 190- to make place for this brewery — or this office building." Truly, an interesting tourist pilgrimage! Let us imagine him — returned to his homeland — descanting daily on the wonders of American architecture, so that succeeding generations of friends and neighbors will be moved to yearly travel and study in this same marvelous and beautiful (?) land!

Current Periodicals
A Review of the Recent American And Foreign Architectural Publications

(From "The American Architect.")

Entrance Loggia, J. Pierpont Morgan Library.
McKim, Mead & White, Architects.

(From "The American Architect.")

Union Station, New Orleans, La.
D. H. Burnham & Co., Architects.

(From "The American Architect.")

Mantel, East Room, J. Pierpont Morgan Library.
McKim, Mead & White, Architects.

(From "Architecture.")

Accepted Design for Springfield Municipal Buildings.
Pell & Corbett, Architects.

(From "Architecture.")

House at Lawrence Park, Bronxville, N. Y.
Squires & Wynkoop, Architects.

(From "Architecture.")

National City Bank, New York.
McKim, Mead & White, Architects.

(From "The American Architect.")

A Night Shelter.
Joseph M. Kellogg, Student, Society of Beaux-Arts Architects.

(From "The American Architect.")

A Night Shelter.
W. L. Westgate, Student, Society of Beaux-Arts Architects.

THE *American Architect* starts the year 1909 with the announcement that in its issue for January 6 "is merged *The Inland Architect*." So far as appears in this month's numbers, *The Inland Architect* has been entirely *submerged*. This same issue gives very inadequate reproductions of interior views of Mr. McKim's private library building on East 36th St., New York, for Mr. Morgan, probably the most beautiful and refined bit of classic architecture in that city. A bare and disappointing brick church at Andover is illustrated in the same number. In this pagan age we would suggest it is more necessary for the Church to call to its aid what attraction may exist in beauty of form, color, light, music, and art; rather than revert to the Puritan spirit and repudiate such aid as these influences can lend! From the issue of January 13 we reprint D. H. Burnham's new Union Station at New Orleans, one of the best and most virile expressions of the problem that we ever remember to have seen.

The issues of January 20 and 27 — entirely given to reproduction of the working drawings for the new Union Theological Seminary, New York City — but confirm an opinion we have long since held, that drawings showing *pseudo*-Gothic architecture of rock-face stone (*sic*) and thoroughly conventional repetition of detail — which is never, by any chance, to be found in work containing the true Gothic spirit — are of no practical value to the profession. As we have occasionally carped at the printing of Beaux-Arts student drawings, we take pains to note that the last issue of the month contains two remarkably interesting solutions of a Beaux-Arts Society problem for a "night shelter." These designs are reasonable, practicable, and modern, both in plan and elevation, and would be effective in the material suggested for their construction.

The text-pages of all the numbers for the month contain various portions of the proceedings of the American Institute at its last convention, along with some of the reports there made.

The Western Architect — to which both the western and northwestern fields have now been abandoned — starts the new year with laudable — if poorly realized — intentions, whereby the magazine evidently desires to enlarge its field and increase its interest for its subscribers by giving a number of plates to Eastern work. It is therefore doubly to be regretted that the editors unfortunately chose, for the first effort, four already well-published views of Mr. Murchison's station at Scranton *and* Mr. Freedlander's mongrel design for the Importers' and Traders' National Bank! The remainder of the issue reproduces houses at La Crosse, Duluth, and Detroit, the

House at New London, Conn.
Charles A. Platt, Architect.
(From "The Brickbuilder.")

House at St. Paul, Minn.
James Alan MacLeod, Architect.
(From "The Brickbuilder.")

Bank of Montreal, Montreal, Can.
McKim, Mead & White, Architects.
(From "The New York Architect.")

Connecticut Savings Bank, New Haven, Conn.
Gordon, Tracy & Swartwout, Architects.
(From "The Architectural Review," London.)

Belmont, Chesterfield, Garden Side.
C. H. Reilly, Architect.

later, by an Eastern architect, of which the first named is considerably the more interesting and picturesque, despite various minor defects in detail.

Architecture for January contains an interesting department entitled "Architectural Criticism," in which the designers of the Home Club, the Pittsburg Synagogue, and the Palisades Trust Company all criticise their own designs. The result is so amusing and instructive that we hope this feature will be continued in future issues. We reprint Pell & Corbett's successful design for the Municipal buildings at Springfield, and a sketch by Birch Burdett Long of the alteration of the Old Custom-house into the National City Bank, of which we spoke in a recent number. The remainder of the issue contains several banks, governmental buildings, and "studio apartments," and, among the dwellings, the extremely attractive country house by Squires & Wynkoop that we reprint. This is one of those rare exceptions where a design executed in shingles is yet sufficiently original and forceful to even surpass what it might have been in plaster. We believe, in this instance, the effect is largely obtained by the peculiarly appropriate use made of the material.

In the January *Brickbuilder* the second article on "The Denominational Church" continues to show illustrations quite as interesting as the first installment, upon which we have already remarked. They include a number of churches quite above the average, and valuable plans. The same issue gives further information as to "The Financing of Apartment-houses," and the actions of the Institute at the convention are briefly described. The plates publish a number of Western houses, as well as some drawings of Palmer & Hornbostel's Western University buildings. Of the houses, certainly the most picturesque is Mr. McLeod's house for himself at St. Paul; Mr. Platt's house at New London being a dwelling of more dignified type. We also note a reserved Georgian dwelling in Philadelphia by Messrs. Newman & Harris, and a somewhat overpowering and futile arch motive in brick, dwarfing the remainder of a railroad-station at Chattanooga, Tenn.

We notice, rather regretfully, that both *The Brickbuilder* and *The American Architect* start the new year with frontispieces of somewhat dubious architectural interest. *The Brickbuilder* announces a series of Piranesi's engravings, of which much of the charm cannot fail but be lost in their line-plate engraving and printing, in cold black-and-white, on modern coated paper. *The American Architect*, "the newspaper of the profession," shows a tendency to publish old European buildings, whereas we believe that this publication would better serve the public by restricting itself — so far as plate illustrations, at least, are concerned — to recent, and *not* to historic architecture.

The January *Architectural Record* is entitled "A Bank Number," and reproduces, as might be expected, a number of buildings with which architects would be fairly familiar through earlier printings. We do not recall, however, that McKim, Mead & White's alterations for the Bank of Montreal have before appeared in an American magazine. Certainly the front, which retains intact the old and familiar portico, is an extremely successful bit of reconstruction, while the new rear façade is equally dignified, if simpler; and the interior far more impressive than one would realize from the illustrations. A number of buildings, such as the Girard Trust Company in Philadelphia, the Suffolk Bank in Boston, the Farmers' National Bank at Owatonna, the Union Trust and Savings and the National Metropolitan Banks in Washington, are already familiar to the subscribers of the architectural magazines. Mr. Freedlander's omnipresent Importers' and Traders' Bank (for its *fifth* recent publication!) again "bobs up serenely" in this company. Among a great number, one especially notices the New England Trust Build-

(From "The Builder," London.) *(From "The Builder," London.)* *(From "The Architect.")*

House at Shorne, near Rochester.
The Late A. H. Shipworth, Architect.
(From "The Builder," London.)

The Armenian Church, Paris.
M. Guilbert, Architect.

Triptych, Kensington Church.
The Late G. F. Bodley, R.A., Architect.

St. Luke's Church, Edinburgh.
P. MacGregor Chalmers, Architect.

ing in Boston as a structure of less blatant advertising and pretension than the majority of those others illustrated. We also commend the buildings of the Second National Bank in New York and the Savings Bank of Baltimore for their successful and simple treatments. On the whole, one rather wonders that the artistic average of these banks is not higher, until a closer scrutiny discloses the fact that there are included a great number of such uninteresting buildings as those for the Dime Savings and Trust Company of Peoria, Ill., and the Cleveland Trust Company, which much reduce the average.

The New York Architect for December inaugurates an announced policy of reproducing in each issue a number of plates of contemporaneous foreign — which in this case means "French"— architecture. The Palace Hotel in the Champs-Elysées starts the series in quite the sort of conventional pastry-shop rococo that we rather expect of modern French architecture. The remainder of the number is given to the work of Gordon, Tracy & Swartwout, including their very excellent Home Club, several Bank buildings, and other somewhat less interesting and older works. The Connecticut Savings Bank at New Haven, which we reprint, illustrates how undesirable it is to attempt to reproduce "Erechtheums" and "Parthenons" in modern America. When commercial business backgrounds are substituted for the magnificent locations and beautiful natural sites so lovingly selected by the Greek builders, no matter how carefully proportion and detail may be studied, the effect of these buildings can never be anything else but disappointing.

The English *Architectural Review*

has been somewhat lacking in interest now for several months, probably from the saving up of material for the number on "Country Houses." "Architecture in the United States" still deals with commercial buildings, though now containing some more modern examples, such as the Frick Building at Pittsburg and the Mutual Life at Newark. We reprint an attractive plaster-house alteration at Chesterfield; the interiors being evidently based on American Colonial forms, or their immediate English precedents. We cannot refrain from harping on an old text and reprinting a modern English idea of "Business Premises"! The name of the architect we carefully suppress. Certainly everything that ought *not* to be done in city architecture is — in this design — most painstakingly expressed.

The Architect contains a number of street façades and one or two attractive houses; as well as a very severe and dignified Norman church at Edinburgh by P. MacGregor Chalmers.

The Builder publishes, January 2, M. Guilbert's new Armenian church in Paris, located on the same street as his well-known Commemorative Chapel; also the rather atavistic design for schools at Middleton and, for contrast in period and style, an Art Nouveau house. January 23 is printed a Triptych for Kensington Church, by the late Mr. Bodley. Our readers should be glad to know it is proposed to erect this reredos as a memorial to the designer.

The Builder's Journal publishes nothing we feel called upon to reprint; and *La Construction Moderne* provides us only with an appealing though flamboyant design by that versatile artist, Mr. Willy Bock.

(From "The Architectural Review," London.)

Royal Insurance Bldgs.,
St. James St. Elevation.

(From "The Builder," London.)

Borough of Middleton Elementary Schools.
Edgar Wood & J. Henry Sellers, Architects.

(From "La Construction Moderne.")

Villa a Coblentz.
M. Willy Bock, Architect.

The Architectural Review

Volume XVI   March, 1909   Number 3

The Passage Kaufhaus, Berlin

By Julius Grundmann

THERE has recently been completed in the German capital a building that, from the standpoint of the architect, the shopper, or the business man, is unlike anything else, either at home or abroad. This structure, known as the *Passage Kaufhaus*, was originally intended as an ordinary business arcade, connecting two principal streets, and providing space for a large restaurant, cafés, offices, and shops. Through the influence of a clever and clear-headed Berlin manufacturer this plan was finally abandoned and a new kind of store was built, which has met with so much success as to suggest it may mark the beginning of a new era of retail business coöperation. To be brief, the *Passage* as carried out is not a department-store and not a special retail-shop, but an exhibition and sales building for an organization of about sixty retail merchants, placed under one roof, taking advantage of all the best features of a department-store, and yet being entirely independent as regards selling goods and making profits!

A central office, maintained at the expense of all the retailers occupying space in the building, undertakes the delivery of merchandise, cashing and collecting money, advertising generally and for special events, providing floor-space for special sales and exhibitions, and also takes charge of the heating, lighting, insurance, cleaning, etc. It is clear that, by undertaking these portions of the business on a scale such as this, considerable savings would be made, and each individual shopkeeper has to contribute only one sixtieth of the total cost of conducting these departments, which is much less than it would cost him to do all the above services himself. In addition, he obtains the best imaginable service, as each different line of business is conducted by a trained staff of experts. The public also derives an equal profit and advantage, for it can buy every conceivable article in this single building, enjoy all the advantages of a big store, and have the use of parlors, restaurants, reading-room, and other conveniences. At first sight this scheme may not appear to possess any advantages over the ordinary department-store; but a second thought will make it apparent that each establishment, maintaining its own individuality as it does, is more likely to attain a higher level of excellence.

The location is one of the best in Berlin, a few minutes only from the principal railway-station; the two ends of the arcade, and the building fronts, facing along crowded and much traveled streets. These two streets for a long distance had no connection, and the arcade contained in the *Passage Kaufhaus* will shorten the way for many a person. This, of course, at the same time draws buyers to the store. The structure itself covers about 93,548 square feet, seven city houses having to be pulled down to obtain the necessary area; requiring an outlay of eight million marks (about $2,340,000), while the building itself cost another eight and one-half millions.

This new and unusual business scheme has resulted in a design almost as novel and bold for this immense building. In the structure itself reinforced concrete has been used wherever practicable. This material is noted for its durability and fire-proof qualities,— both essentials of European construction,— and made it possible to complete this immense building within a rather short period. Foundations, pillars, ceilings and roofs, including the immense cu-

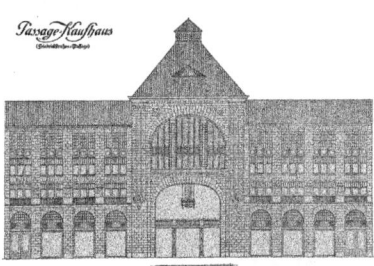

Main Front on the Friedrich Strasse.

Copyright, 1909, by Bates & Guild Company

Detail of Carving, Circular Court.

pola, which has a diameter of 98 feet and a height of 148 feet, are made of reinforced concrete. The concrete ceilings were an interesting experiment. The building department, being in doubt respecting plaster ceilings on concrete, required a guaranty that the plastering should not fall off. In this building all the ceilings are therefore left without any plaster covering, being treated directly by the painter with a certain preparation, and afterwards painted over with a coating that is not affected by vibrations, moisture, and heat — the whole treatment also resulting in a considerable saving of time.

Inside, as well as out, some entirely novel methods have been followed. New methods of design required new architectural forms. The mechanical production of details by stamping or casting in moulds rather restricts the use of projecting members or overhanging cornices. It might seem as if the elimination of projecting moldings and ornaments might limit the inventive power of an architect. On the contrary, the difficulties inherent in the material offer in themselves a considerable attraction for the artist. When dealing with this form of construction, so massive and yet so plastic, one soon finds that many and effective means of handling it are at his disposal; — the technical resources of the stone-cutter, the painter, the bronze and mosaic workers, are all appropriate and available for its architectural treatment.

A great deal could be written about the many interesting details of this store, but a brief description will show in what ways it is different from the usual types. Along the Friedrich Strasse, which is probably the most important business street in Berlin, this store has a frontage of

Entrance Feature on the Oranienburger Strasse.

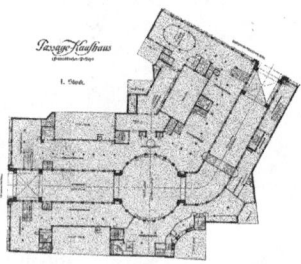

Plan of the Passage Kaufhaus.

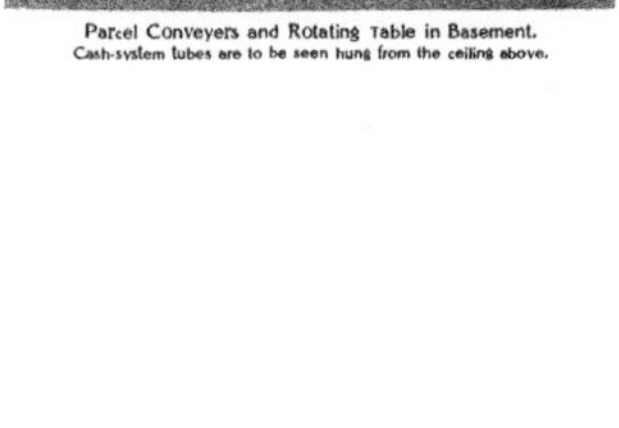

Parcel Conveyers and Rotating Table in Basement.
Cash-system tubes are to be seen hung from the ceiling above.

Detail of Carving, Circular Court.

187 feet; the other front, on the Oranienburger Strasse, being 285 feet long. These two streets are connected through the middle of the store by the arcade, a glass-covered walk 43 feet wide and nearly 492 feet long. Both entrances are immense portals, two stories high. The arcade is not straight, but forms an angle near the center, and it is here surmounted by a tremendous cupola. The whole building is constructed of only the best and most durable materials, limestone and marble being chiefly used. The majolica works belonging to the Emperor furnished a considerable part of the decoration of the building; and statues and ornaments of stone and bronze, designed by well-known German artists, are to be found everywhere.

An unique feature, which does not exist in any other city of Europe, is the railway-station contained within the store. In the city of Berlin there is being built an underground line from North to South, cutting through the central portion of the city; and, upon request, a station — already completed, though not yet in use — was provided underneath this store. We therefore find in the cellar a waiting-room, with ticket-office, toilets, etc., and elevators going directly down to this platform; so that a customer can go in town by train, shop, lunch, and return directly home again, all without leaving cover — a system that will be welcomed by everybody, especially during wet weather!

The arcade, or passageway, itself, is lined with about sixty show-windows, to one of which each retail concern is entitled. These show-cases are all made of glass and bronze. Several doors open from the arcade to those salesrooms on the ground floor; while several monumental stair-

Detail of Restaurant.

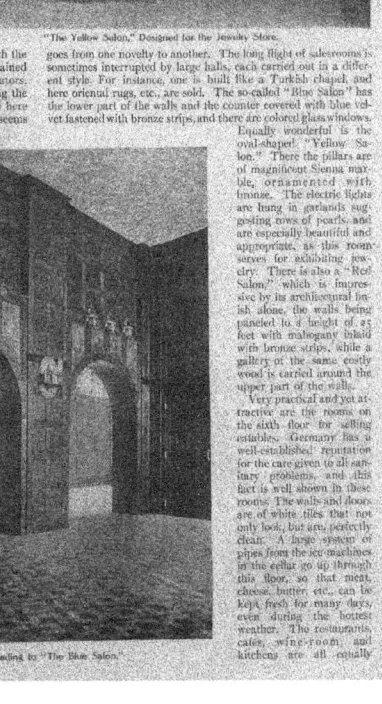

"The Yellow Salon," Designed for the Jewelry Store.

Portals Leading to "The Blue Salon."

ways, conveniently located, lead to the second story. To reach the shops on other floors one can use the numerous stairways contained within the store itself — or any one of the twenty-three elevators. At certain places the arcade is spanned by bridges connecting the different levels, some of them as high as the fifth floor, and here the band plays every afternoon, furnishing a concert which seems to come from the sky.

The stairways are made of artificial stone, richly ornamented, with railings of heavy forged iron, inlaid with porcelain. The stairways inside the enclosure and in the salesrooms are of steel and polished marble, and the treads are of tallowwood and oak or marble. There are ten principal staircases in the building, going through all the stories, and nine more inside the salesrooms. In addition, eleven elevators help to carry the public up and down, while ten special lifts, varying in size, are provided for freight; and six spiral chutes care for all smaller articles. The largest elevator occupies a floor-space of 3,453 square feet and can lift 5,500 pounds. It will be used for pianos, safes, motor-cars, etc. The doors separating the elevator-shafts from the floors are constructed after the latest fire regulations, being absolutely fire-proof and, contrary to American practice, having no openings. From the outside, those for passengers are masterpieces of art, showing a rich inlay in colors, glass and bronze.

When a customer walks through the big building he goes from one novelty to another. The long flight of salesrooms is sometimes interrupted by large halls, each carried out in a different style. For instance, one is built like a Turkish chapel, and here oriental rugs, etc., are sold. The so-called "Blue Salon" has the lower part of the walls and the counter covered with blue velvet fastened with bronze strips, and there are colored glass windows.

Equally wonderful is the oval-shaped "Yellow Salon." There the pillars are of magnificent Sienna marble, ornamented with bronze. The electric lights are hung in garlands suggesting rows of pearls, and are especially beautiful and appropriate, as this room serves for exhibiting jewelry. There is also a "Red Salon," which is impressive by its architectural finish alone, the walls being paneled to a height of 25 feet with mahogany inlaid with bronze strips, while a gallery of the same costly wood is carried around the upper part of the walls.

Very practical and yet attractive are the rooms on the sixth floor for selling eatables. Germany has a well-established reputation for the care given to all sanitary problems, and this fact is well shown in these rooms. The walls and doors are of white tiles that not only look, but are, perfectly clean. A large system of pipes from the ice-machines in the cellar go up through this floor, so that meat, cheese, butter, etc., can be kept fresh for many days, even during the hottest weather. The restaurants, cafés, wine-room, and kitchens are all equally well-arranged, modern, sanitary, and up-to-date.

In the cellar all the most modern machines have been installed: such as a vacuum apparatus for cleaning the whole building; several exhaustors for the pneumatic cash system, which contains 150 cash stations; an ice-machine, as mentioned before; and last, but not least, a conveying arrangement for parcels, which, so far as is known, cannot be found in any other store in the world. When a customer has made a purchase the parcel is placed on spiral chutes which have openings conveniently located on each floor. It slides down through these tubes and falls out upon a continuously moving endless belt in the cellar, which carries it to the central room beneath the cupola. Here the parcel drops upon a rotating table, around which several men are sitting, which carries it at last in front of the man having in charge the certain delivery district of Berlin to which the parcel is addressed, and he distributes the packages among the wagons, which make deliveries four times a day, within his district. If the articles are destined for customers outside of Berlin, the delivery is made direct to the railway-stations.

Of the whole area acquired, only seven-tenths were allowed to be built upon, and it was a special favor of the Berlin police that caused the arcade and rotunda beneath the cupola to be regarded as "unoccupied space." The remaining three-tenths are formed by these areas and the nine courtyards that furnish light and air to the various upper offices. The construction of the building itself was extraordinarily difficult, especially in such a crowded neighborhood; and no less than 3,500 team-loads of waste material from the old houses pulled down had to be carted away. The adjoining very old buildings had also to be carefully timbered and braced. Yet this building, a master product of German architecture, engineering, and business sense, has been completed and opened to the public within a year and a quarter of the time when the work of demolition was begun!

View within the Outside Corridors, Showing Stairways and Elevator Enclosures.

Looking from the Arcade into the Court under the Central Cupola.

One of the Double-storied "Venetian" Bridges across the Passageway.

Hanna Mausoleum, Lake View Cemetery, Cleveland, Ohio.
Henry Bacon, Architect.

Model End of Sarcophagus. 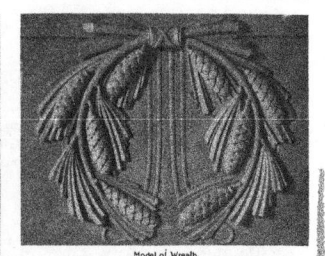 Model of Wreath. 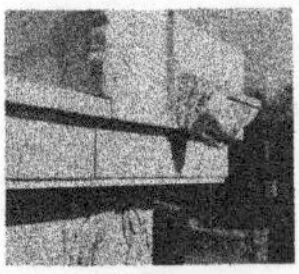 Detail of Cornice.  Detail of Frieze.

Interior.
Hanna Mausoleum, Lake View Cemetery, Cleveland, Ohio.
Henry Bacon, Architect.

II

MODERN ENGLISH CHURCHES

VIEW OF WEST END, CHURCH OF ST. COLUMBA, WANSTEAD SLIP, STRATFORD, E., ENGLAND

PLATE XI.

DETAIL OF ENTRANCE, FIELD MEMORIAL LIBRARY, CONWAY, MASS.
SHEPLEY, RUTAN & COOLIDGE, ARCHITECTS.

SOUTH ELEVATION, HANNA MAUSOLEUM, LAKE VIEW CEMETERY, CLEVELAND, OHIO.
HENRY BACON, ARCHITECT.

LONGITUDINAL SECTION, HANNA MAUSOLEUM, LAKE VIEW CEMETERY, CLEVELAND, OHIO.
HENRY BACON, ARCHITECT.

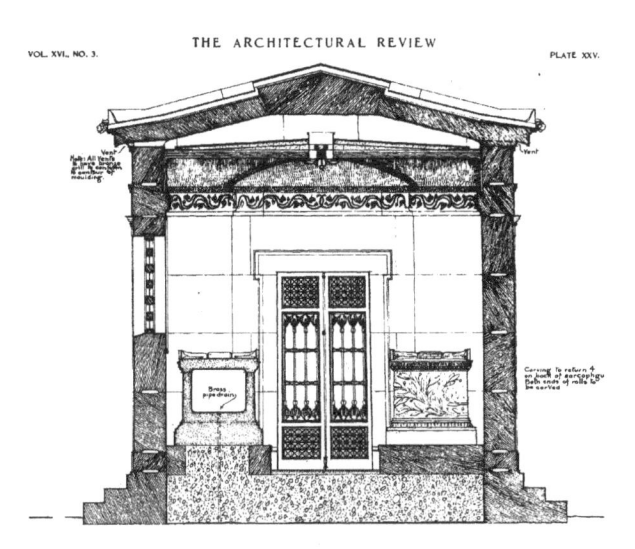

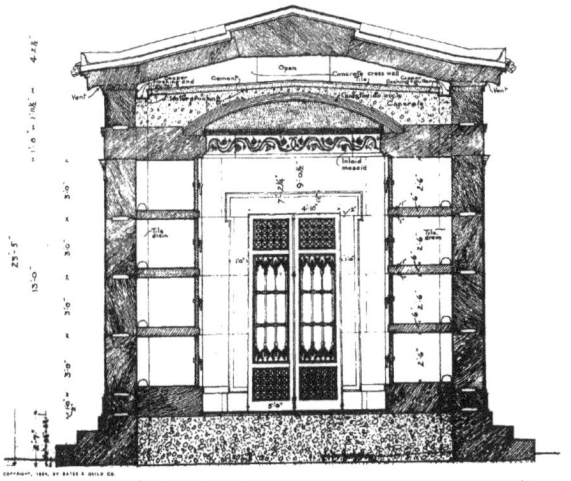

SECTIONS THROUGH CATACOMBS, HANNA MAUSOLEUM, LAKE VIEW CEMETERY, CLEVELAND, OHIO.
HENRY BACON, ARCHITECT.

DETAILS OF SARCOPHAGUS.

CEILING OF MAUSOLEUM.

PLAN, HANNA MAUSOLEUM, LAKE VIEW CEMETERY, CLEVELAND, OHIO.
HENRY BACON, ARCHITECT.

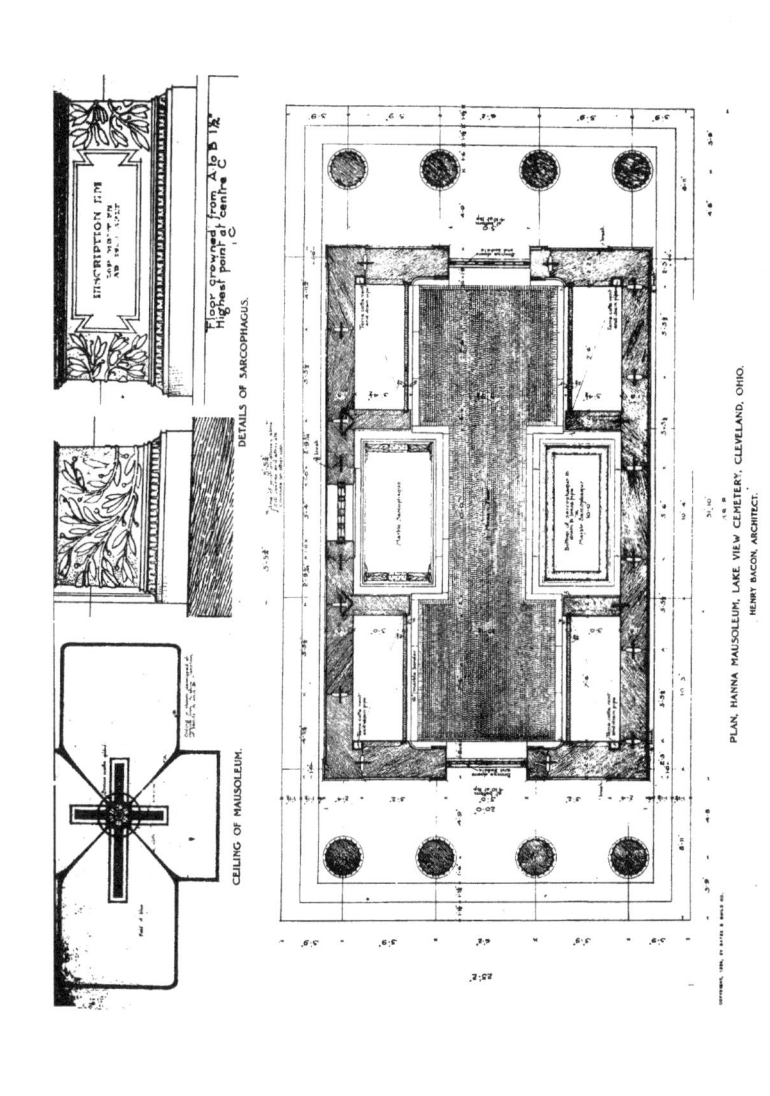

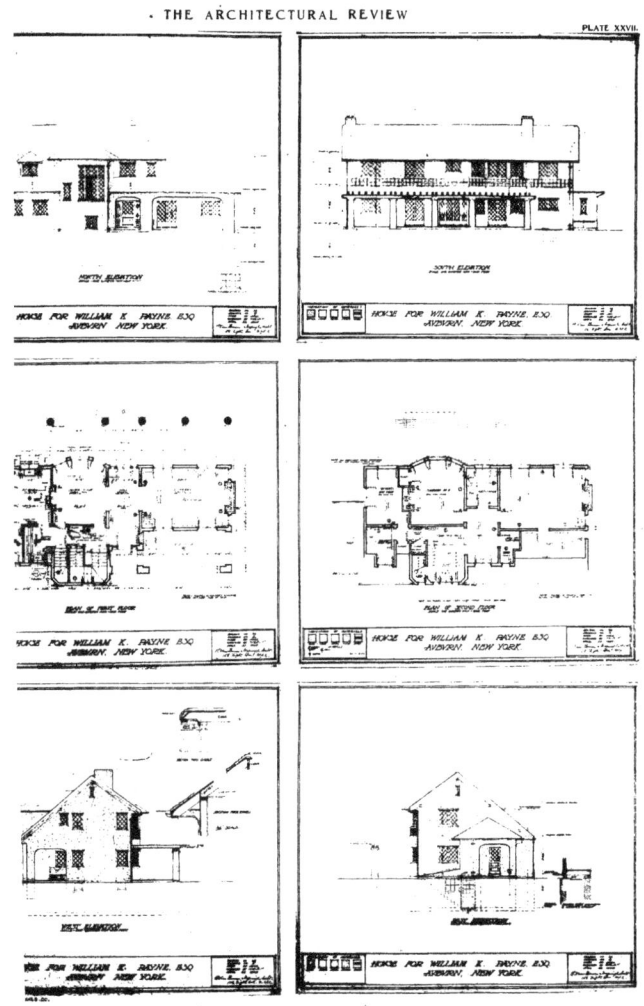

PLANS AND ELEVATIONS, HOUSE FOR WM. K. PAYNE, ESQ., AUBURN, N. Y.
H. VAN BUREN MAGONIGLE, ARCHITECT.

ADMINISTRATION BUILDING, HARVARD MEDICAL SCHOOL, BOSTON, MASS.
SHEPLEY, RUTAN & COOLIDGE, ARCHITECTS.

MORNING CHAPEL, CHURCH OF ST. COLUMBA, WANSTEAD SLIP, STRATFORD, E., ENGLAND.
EDWARD P. WARREN, ARCHITECT.

House for William K. Payne, Esq., Auburn, N. Y.
H. Van Buren Magonigle, Architect.

House for William K. Payne, Esq., Auburn, N. Y.
H. Van Buren Magonigle, Architect.

The Architectural Review

VOLUME XVI.   NUMBER 3

MARCH, 1909

BATES & GUILD COMPANY, Publishers
42 Chauncy Street, Boston

NEW YORK OFFICE, PARK ROW BUILDING

Published monthly. Price, mailed flat to any address in the United States or Canada, five dollars per annum, in advance; to any foreign address, six dollars per annum, in advance. Subscriptions begin with the issue following their receipt. Single copies, fifty cents. Special number, two dollars. Entered as second-class mail-matter at the Post-office, Boston, Massachusetts, November 27, 1891.

PLATES

PLATE XXI.—DETAIL OF ENTRANCE, FIELD MEMORIAL LIBRARY, CONWAY, MASS. (PHOTOGRAPHIC VIEW)—SHEPLEY, RUTAN & COOLIDGE, ARCHITECTS.

PLATES XXII-XXVI.—THE HANNA MAUSOLEUM, LAKE VIEW CEMETERY, CLEVELAND, OHIO (PLANS, ELEVATIONS, AND SECTIONS)— HENRY BACON, ARCHITECT.

PLATE XXVII.—RESIDENCE AT AUBURN, N. Y. (PLANS AND ELEVATIONS)—H. VAN BUREN MAGONIGLE, ARCHITECT.

PLATE XXVIII.—ADMINISTRATION BUILDING, HARVARD MEDICAL SCHOOL, BOSTON, MASS. (PHOTOGRAPHIC VIEW)—SHEPLEY, RUTAN & COOLIDGE, ARCHITECTS.

CERTAINLY the times have become ripe for systematizing — in some way — the conduct of competitions. Some competitions recently held have been decided in such ways as to leave both architects and public excessively dissatisfied with the results, while one or two have achieved to a newspaper notoriety much to be regretted. In the conduct of the competition for the New York State Prison, for instance, it would appear that the Commission did not consider itself in any way held by the requirements set down in that law by which alone they were in existence! In another recent instance, it happened that the personal leaning of a judge for one type of solution threw out, in a preliminary competition, all those arrangements differing from his preconception of the problem. This resulted much to the detriment of their authors, as appeared when the final competition was settled, when it was found that the design awarded first place (submitted by one of the new competitors) had the same *parti* as those systematically discarded in the first competition!

Authorities do not even agree among themselves! Despite any amount of talk upon the subject, architects have not yet formulated any set of rules to which they would subscribe when competing — or acting as judges for competitions. Two individuals much in demand as expert judges were recently overheard in a lively discussion as to whether a competition was held for the purpose of selecting a *plan* or an *architect* and whether, in a scheme necessitating some minutiæ of detail, it would be most expedient for the winning design to express a thorough grasp and comprehension of these complex individual parts, or merely to show "a large conception" of the general layout and handling of the problem; believing that the person with this grand concept would be able afterward to incorporate those technical details most requisite for the business conduct of the institution for which the competition was being held!

It even frequently happens that an architect submitting a design obeying stringent regulations laid down in the program may be a successful competitor in preference to others who have kept these requirements strictly in mind. Of course, in the matter of amount of expense, this is common; — a disregard, by the way, easily traceable to the program, which customarily demands less than can possibly be obtained within the amount stipulated. Further, however, when limitations are set by the program as to number of drawings, size or style of rendering, or of the arrangement of plans and drawings, it is to be supposed that there may exist some reason for these stipulations being made; and yet it frequently happens that an architect taking the risk of disregarding these demands is awarded the prize; — often perhaps largely because by this very disregard he has been able to prepare his drawings in a more effective or taking manner! Surely, when doctors disagree — even in *this* profession — it is to be expected that those with less understanding of the complications of the situation should fail in the acceptance of a common point of view.

Possibly it will help the cause for us to once again formulate the ideals that we believe would make for the best presentation of a competitive program. First, that no great amount of intricate details of arrangement be required of the competitors. Provided the general scheme they submit is acceptable, they will be able, without much trouble, afterwards to inculcate these desired peculiarities of arrangement into their general design. Second, that the matter not be complicated by too minute specifications of the *way* in which drawings shall be presented. As a rule, these details might be much better left to a general agreement among the architects competing. Third, that the program entail the least possible amount of work and expense upon the contestants. It is obvious that the best members of the profession are prevented from going into competitions because of the great detailed labor and study required of them — that, they only too well know, is likely to be largely if not entirely thrown away.

Aside from the improvements necessary in the preparation of the program, the most important essential would seem to be the systematizing of those points upon which a program is to be judged. While it is evident that these might vary somewhat with different types of competitions, it should yet be possible to formulate a general and a specific set of conditions upon which the judges should be required to base their awards, in strict accordance with the completeness with which these stipulations were met by the competitors. A set of stringent general conditions could probably be made to apply to nearly all competitions, while a few specific requirements should be made mandatory and binding upon both competitor and judge.

It does not seem to us that the double competition should be encouraged as an improvement upon the old form. It is cumbersome and slow in employment, and generally gives cause for dissatisfaction by its preventing certain of the competitors from being considered in the final award. Provided only that the competition be made simple enough, it would seem to be much more valuable to occasionally substitute, in cases of extreme doubt or difficulty, a secondary set of studies, in which those architects who had first produced the most interesting or suggestive plans might be given opportunity to further elaborate or work out their ideas.

IN an editorial note accompanying Volume II. of "American Competitions," we find the editors to have arrived independently at conclusions much the same as we have stated above. Their suggestion for nullifying personal leanings on the part of an expert is to require *three* such judges or experts. They also advise the publication by the judges of their reasons for making the awards, believing this would enhance the educational value of the competition for those entering it for that purpose, as well as add increased interest to their decisions, and, incidentally, result in the drawing of better considered programs and the making of more careful awards. They also suggest that the judges state distinctly in the program which conditions are obligatory and which optional; and that the awards be required to be made *strictly* in accord with the more stringent set of conditions!

It seems to us that if the competition — undignified, disadvantageous, and economically unproductive of desired results as it is! — is to be longer officially countenanced by the Institute and reputable architects of these United States, it is time to stop argument and theoretical discussion and "get down to bases;" to determine once and for all such general conditions as are to govern the competitor (and govern the expert judge in deciding among such competitors!), so that a competition, instead of being a matter of good luck and chance — as is now confessed largely to be the case — would become a matter of absolute mathematics, determined strictly on merit and craftsmanship.

Current Periodicals
A Review of the Recent American And Foreign Architectural Publications

WE are glad to find the February number of *Architecture* continues its interesting columns on "Architectural Criticism;" this month with screeds by Messrs. Murchison, Newman, Morris, and Hill, dealing respectively with the same architects' Hoboken Terminal, Hoyt House at Stamford, Hartford State Bank, and German-American Insurance buildings. A Babylonian design for a New York Court-house, expressing on a city block the "pyramidic" type of construction that has been recently much advocated in the public press, is probably the most interesting single plate in the issue; Warren & Wetmore's Court-house at Hudson, N. Y., the most disappointing; principally, we would say, from the quite impossible central feature — exactly the sort of splash one might expect from a classically untrained designer, but not from so erudite an office as this. The School of Applied Design for Women strikes one as a drastically modern use of Greek forms that might be more pleasing were it not for the entablature broken over the columns, with what would appear to be — from this view-point — aggravating obstreperosity! Mowbray & Uffinger's Dime Savings Bank, Brooklyn, carries an effective colonnade, and provides a good interior; while Janssen & Abbott's Pittsburg Athletic Association is another of those *Italianate* designs that are, apparently, to be the architectural "fashion" for the coming season! Other plates show two essays in Gothic, the last preceding *mode* — one by Edward Pearce Casey for a house in New York City, the other by C. C. Haight for the Second Battery Armory, the latter conforming rather better than the former to the Mediæval limitations of the style.

We note with regret that the publishers of *Architecture* persist in their undignified policy of perverting their magazine into a building trades journal by incorporating advertising among the plate-titles in more and more of grant undisguise,— some of the plates in the February issue carrying three and four announcements of advertising materials used in the illustrated buildings.

The Western Architect publishes several buildings in Detroit, including Donaldson & Mcier Y. M. C. A.; a new school; and a rather florid terra-cotta office building for the Detroit Gas Company that is nevertheless one more experiment in the expression of the "steel frame type" of modern skyscraper. Other plates show some Chicago park refectories and bath-houses, a picturesque house at La Crosse, and a thoroughly charming and attractive house and stable at Barrington, Ill., by Marshall & Fox, the architects of the Maxine Elliott Theater. We reprint a general view, in detail, of as simple and attractive an American dwelling as we have seen in the architectural magazines for six months.

The February *Brickbuilder's* leading article is on "Gymnasiums," while a travel article by Mr. Reed contains some attractive illustrations of architecture in Western France. We reproduce a view of Mr. Comes' Roman Catholic Church at McKeesport, Pa., illustrated in this issue, and of two attractive houses — at Old bridge by Richard Arnold Fisher and in Rochester by Claude Bragdon — and an estate at Kennebunkport, Me., by Green & Wicks, from which we reproduce the Gardener's Cottage The interesting brickwork of Donn Barber's Lotus Club, so attractive in its details; and a house at Lenox, by Hoppin, Koen and Huntington, is rather more dignified than their two or

St. Mary's R. C. Church, McKeesport, Pa.
John T. Comes, Architect.
(From "The Brickbuilder.")

Study for Court-house on a Single Block, New York City.
Howells & Stokes, Architects.
(From "Architecture.")

Accepted Competitive Design, 2d Battery Armory, N. Y. City.
C. C. Haight, Architect.
(From "Architecture.")

Dime Savings Bank of Brooklyn, N. Y.
Mowbray & Uffinger, Architects.
(From "Architecture.")

Proposed Building, Pittsburg Athletic Association, Pittsburg, Pa.
Janssen & Abbott, Architects.

School of Applied Design for Women
New York City. Pell & Corbett, Architect
(From "Architecture.")

(From "The American Architect.")   (From "The Brickbuilder.")   (From "The American Architect.")

...room, House on West 75th St., New York City.
J. H. Freedlander, Architect.

Living-room, House in East 19th St., New York City.
P. J. Sterner, Architect.

...nown houses at Newport.
New York Architect for January appeared ...e for review last month — with more illus... ...s of the Palace Hotel in the Champs- ...s; which include, this month, the exterior — ...y wonderful and horrible design that would ...not have been divulged at all! Mr. Brun- ...conservative classic Federal Building at ...nd is shown in this issue, al- ..., we rather doubt the titling on ...ates showing the sculptures — ...Mr. Brunner still alone receives ...dit! The same designer's School ...nes at Columbia, and Mount ...Hospital Buildings, along with in- ...s of the Lewisohn house in New ..., complete the issue.

...February *Architectural Record* ...article on "Sicilian Gardens," ...ted by sketches and snap-shot ...graphs; another dealing with ...te" construction in the Forum; ...third, illustrating the Château de ...or, that is hardly as *châ- ...que* as Mr. Charles C. Boldt's ...ng home in the Thousand Is- ...The rest of the number, except ...ry at Cleveland by R. D. Kohn ...distinctively interesting and ...away piece of brickwork — ...re or less given to short and flip- ...*feuilletons*.

...*American Architect* passes this ... — undisputed — to the foot of

the class by publishing little work of architectural value. On February 3, a gross city dwelling jostles shoulders with Maxine Elliott's delicately refined new playhouse. This *bijou* little theater (it becomes absolutely necessary, in describing its architecture, to revert to its native language!), despite its somewhat modest location, is noticeable — in New York — largely because of the "prettiness" and charm of its dainty detail and somewhat effeminate elegance. Inside it impresses one rather as an enlarged drawing-room than a theater; and outside it might be, as well, a fashionable ballroom or restaurant entrance. We do not know whether it be necessary to go as far afield as Chicago to find architects capable of designing in this sort of taste, but certainly no other theater in New York exteriorly possesses any claims to good breeding; and — with the possible exception of the Hudson — the same is equally, if not even more noticeably, true of their interiors.

We believe we have — in recent numbers — devoted perhaps overmuch of this space to calling attention to what we believe to be a regrettable tendency toward the mongrelizing of modern French architectural forms now in process of accomplishment in the city of New York, until we hesitate to make further reference to examples testifying the fact. Otherwise we would have to

New Lotus Club, New York City.
Donn Barber, Architect.
(From "The Brickbuilder.")

Entrance, House at Lenox, Mass.
Hoppin, Koen & Huntington, Architects.

(From "The American Architect.")   (From "The New York Architect.")

Maxine Elliott's Theatre, West 39th St., New York City.
Marshall & Fox, Architects.

U. S. Post-office, Custom-house, and Court-house, Cleveland, O.
Arnold W. Brunner, Architect.

THE ARCHITECTURAL REVIEW

(From "The Western Architect.") 
Residence, La Crosse, Wis.
Hancly & Cady, Architects.

(From "The Brickbuilder.") 
Gardener's Cottage, House at Kennebunkport, Me.
Green & Wicks, Architects.
(From "The Western Architect.")

(From "The Western Architect.")
Detail, Residence, Barrington
Marshall & Fox, Architects

North Front, Residence, Barrington, Ill.
Marshall & Fox, Architects.
(From "The Architect.")

CENTRAL AVENUE ELEVATION

DRILLYARD ELEVATION
First Premiated Design for Glamorgan County Hall, Cardiff.
E. Vincent Harris & T. A. Moodie, Architects.
(From "The Architectural Review," London.)

United University Club, Pall Mall East.
Reginald Blomfield, A.R.A., Architect.
(From "The Builder.")

Eadie Memorial Pulpit, Manchester.
J. and J. Swarbrick, Architects.

Hotel Particulier à Paris.
H. H. Valette, Architect.
(From "La Construction Moderne.")

revert to the same adjectives for even a guarded and reserved expression of our feelings when this same style is applied to a private residence! Failing in language, we are content to depend upon a reproduction of contrasting expressions of quite different ideals of "homeliness," believing that the sane common sense of Americans can be depended upon to choose properly between them.

For February 10 the plates are Warren & Wetmore's Fort Gary Terminal; while Howells & Stokes' house for Mark Twain, and the New York Architectural League exhibition, are described and illustrated in the text.

The issue of February 17 contains a number of plates of houses by Messrs. Green & Wicks, of which two most attract our attention. February 24 is printed the first article on "Old English Mansions," with illustrations in part taken from Mr. Batsford's new book on "The Tudor Period." One of the most individual city houses we have seen in some time is Mr. Sterner's house at 139 East 19th Street, the interiors being thoroughly delightful and livable, yet simple.

The English *Architectural Review* shows a church at West Ealing and two private se the first following a publi second a more residential We reproduce the memorial pit in the Congregational at Manchester, by J. & J. brick, as a distinctively use of architectural motive suggest somewhat the Ar veau period in Austria. tecture in the United Sta its fourth part is still deali commercial buildings, but so far as Warren & Wet store for Mrs. Osborne, Flagg's Scribner's Book Louis Sullivan's Gage and anty buildings, and Mead & White's Tiff Gorham stores.

The Builders' Journal chitectural Engineer for Fe 24 shows the Blackpool L competitive designs. *The A tect* for February 5 illustra sketches for small country by Messrs. Ernest, Geo Peto; and, on February 20, the Glamorgan Count drawings. We reprint two premiated elevations as better type of English building than usual. In *struction Moderne* for Fe 13 we find a commendable sian dwelling by M. H. V

The Architectural Review

April, 1909

Garden Design in England

By Thomas H. Mawson, Hon. A. R. I. B. A.

IN every branch of art and in all matters of taste feuds are unending. It is impossible to settle peacefully and limit the respective claims of the Idealists and the Realists. The former maintain that it is the first duty of the artist, in representing scenes or objects, to purify them from all non-essential ugliness or anything that militates against the predominant characteristic or expression, and that the result must always be conventional and decorative. The latter insist that a transcript be rendered, as all attempts at classification and idealization are perversions of the truth.

Personally I am convinced that all art is conventionalism, either wittingly or unwittingly, because no man can either portray pictorially, or tell descriptively the real truth, the whole truth, and nothing but the truth. The infinity and rapidity of change in nature is beyond man's subtlest skill, or the deftness of the most rapid impressionist. Truth in art is constantly being preached, but we are as far from achieving it as we ever were. Realism precludes symbolism, whereas the first principle that a designer truly learns and the idealist believes is that visible things, by their outward form, shape, and semblance, have all both a meaning and have affinities which are to be combined or contrasted with similar or differing forms or presentments, and need behind their outward representations a mind to interpret them to the multitude, between whom and the forms of nature the designer occupies the intermediary place of priest; that is, if he rightly understands his calling. In one way the designer professionally serves the public, and takes the tone from it; but on the other hand he has, or ought, to educate the public. He ought not to stand on a high, exalted pedestal far above their ken, and yet, on the other hand, he ought not to pander to every passing whim and fashion.

Has it not occurred to every one whose soul is in any way responsive to deep emotions, perhaps in some art such as music supposing for the moment we are unlearned therein), that we are instinctively conscious that the composer is behind the notes and tones leading us to indefinable, and to us inexpressible, themes — to "heights unsearched and depths unfathomed"— which give us both surprise and joy? Ruskin somewhere applies a similar test to a poet where he says, ' Rhythm and rhymes are thoroughly injurious where there is no mystery; when there is not some under-meaning, some repressed feeling. In five-sixths of Scott's poetry, as it is called, the meter is an absolute excrescence, the rhythm degenerates into a childish jingle, and the rhyme into unseemly fetters to yoke the convicted verses together. To put plain text into rhyme and meter is easy; but not so to write a passage which every time it is remembered shall suggest a new train of thought. This is the mystic secret of beauty, which is the secrecy of the highest art, which opens itself only to close observation and long study."

It is claimed that this, the indefinable and inexpressible quality in the highest forms of art, may appear in even a constructive and practical art, which has mostly to incorporate and express practical needs, such as architecture. And if it can be secured for architecture, which is accorded the place of leader in the constructive arts, I think it can be justly accorded to civic design and to landscape architecture. Most people in England, until recently, looked down upon the latter two arts as consisting merely of a few subterfuges for rounding off the architects' erections; but now there is evidence, thanks to the lead set by the American universities, that many are waking up to see that they have more to do with influencing the landscape than architecture, and that to adapt the far-reaching spurs of a city, or the outlying wings of a demesne, to the freer natural features and to the surface of the landscape contour is not to be relegated to clumsy novices and allowed to go haphazard, as it has so often in the past.

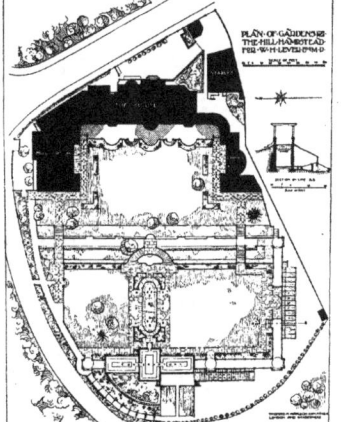

Plan of the Gardens. "The Hill." Hampstead, for W. H. Lever, Esq.

In all arts, whether constructive or not, there must be the objective and the subjective sides, and in the constructive arts the practical usually gains readier recognition than the imaginative or objective view. It is not intended to set the ethical side at enmity with the practical in designing and constructing a garden, nor is the latter to be despised; both parts are needed for success. It is more a question of which should take the lead.

About this there should be no doubt! The ethical is that which

Copyright, 1909, by Bates & Guild Company

Garden for W. H. Lever, Esq. Upper Terrace Near the "China-room."

Garden for W. H. Lever, Esq. Fountain and Pool.

breathes in the region of romance and should always be in advance. The objective lives in the ideal atmosphere, and yearns for the garden which belongs to the realm of picture and imagination: the cloistered place of uninterrupted meditation and reflection, wherein — comparatively speaking — we are weaned from all outside; where, in a kind of rapture undisturbed, we may rest deep hidden in avenues and glades of solitude which lead through imaginary gates to the pleasure-house designed, shaped, and beautified according to the inner consciousness. Only occasionally it is given us to view in execution our most cherished combination of forms, features, and images.

In contrast, the practical is the needful department which must be up and doing to keep pace with nature's calls for pruning and trimming; all the forces arrayed against it bristle with life. An overlay or a little abstraction may cost the practical man dearly, and result in an increased strain of disaster. Even in winter, the time when the forces which demand his energies are in comparative rest, like a capable general he has to be amassing forces and stores to cope with the forthcoming multitudinous outburst of living energy on all hands and sides. For him there is no time for rest and reflection; it is "touch-and-go" almost the whole year round; if not, he wakes up some morning to find all scattered, mystified, and mixed. This is what I may call the subjective and practical side of gardenage, and it should always be subordinate to the objective.

One of the most foolish things about garden literature is that these two sides are always being arrayed antagonistically; whereas, each in its place is as harmonious as the first and second fiddle — perhaps the most appropriate simile would be as conductor and first fiddle! Some people suggest merging the one into the other. That you cannot do. You must have both. You may get a measure of both combined in one man, but my judgment is that each half is sufficient for any one individual. Certainly the latter, with its perennial call to activity, leaves no time for the former

Garden for W. H. Lever, Esq.   The Arbor at the End of the Greenhouse.

The practical may be susceptible to the romantic side, and the romantic may appreciate and, to a limited extent, understand the practical; but the two are no one man's work. Each, as I said before, plays a different part, yet there is no discord—at any rate, there need not be. There exist, however, many short-sighted people who delight to set them in opposition, antagonizing those who wish to study the principles of a delightful art profitably in quiet, and bringing even the helpful literature dealing with it, and which seeks charitably to advance the art, into disrepute.

In all art, whether pictorial, descriptive, or constructive, the true artist knows how to reach his ideal expression by the shortest and most direct methods, and not by haphazard. He must have a logical and coherent system of plan; his proportion, groupings, and balance must bear the stamp of the ease of a master, and his detail must be well considered and telling in its rhythm. If the art is not exactly a constructive one, there is that which in all arts must know how to resolve the component

Garden for W. H. Lever, Esq.   A Corner of the Pergola.

parts, apportioning to each its own desirable counterpart by so much or by so little that each may find its own resemblance or contrast, consonant with the expression to be reached.

There are men of cleverness, possessed of ample natural powers and keenly observant, who are adept in all the constructive knowledge and skill which is one part of the making of an artist; who gain an entrance into the temple of fame and would almost persuade you that they have the secret and mystic faculties of soul that alone reach to the high level of an artistic success, which is so difficult to describe. The two qualities, namely the inward and indefinable and the outward and manifest, are to the most indistinguishable the one from the other; and by the multitude the latter is higher esteemed than the former, because it manifests more of that which is patent and palpable. The majority, however, are capable of response to the "fire elemental and essential" when tempered by rigidly directed advances.

It has of late come to be recognized that certain gardens

Garden for W. H. Lever, Esq.   Steps from Upper to Lower Level.

have the power to stir the emotions, and that others, which have all the well-kept qualities to commend them, fail so to do,— they lack that indescribable something which is only to be imparted by the soul of the designer.

In every site, no matter how unpromising, there are some suggestions or hints to be gleaned as a basis for a design; and oftentimes the more chaotic the better. What I find to be fatal is to bring preconceived notions to a site — for every site suggests its own solution. "Considerable imagination and a dash of artistic feeling not unmixed with poetry are absolutely essential for the success of a garden that is the least out of the common." I remember, in a certain office, a form of diversion in great favor amongst the pupils was to take the surplus colors left over on the palettes and dash them in vigorously on to spare pieces of drawing-paper, and then to pick and limn out, by the aid of the memory and the imagination, the elements of a picture to be finished later if deemed worthy. There was one most promising fellow who was ever full of fresh ideas, the fruit of an observant and imaginative mind, who could, with the aid of his lead-pencil and colors, always fashion into form the suggestions of architecture, foliage, and what-not, with an atmospheric softness betimes, and a wealth of suggestiveness that often eludes the painstaking worker who seeks to make a transcript from nature. Many were the pictured gems carried away and stored as reminders of that young, brilliant mind. These playful exercises were only an index to his abilities in his profession; but alas for the pitfalls that beset the young, and more particularly the brilliant, who are too easily led. This career never ripened according to the bud of promise, or perhaps the writer would have had to say, as Turner, the artist, said of Girtin, "If Tom Girtin had lived I would have starved." From such acorns great oaks grow.

A designer can never be possessed of too much knowledge in every specific branch of his art,— but knowledge will never design. To design a garden without a knowledge of the growth and acclimatization of trees and plants, or lacking the essentials of architecture and a knowledge of structural efficiency, and so forth, is but to court failure; but these adjuncts, although they may surround your house creditably, will never design. True design is indefinable. It is easy to criticize and to find fault with parts that might have been done better, and it is the present-day fashion to try and dissect the soul of the artist; but the soul-reaching quality always eludes. It is the birthright of genius, and, like the wind, the effort of it can be seen and experienced, but none can tell whence it comes or whither it goes.

Photographs of a garden seldom render the designer's intention, those representing an old garden, or even a ruined garden, making the strongest appeal to the imagination when there are plenty of lichens, when the raw edge of newness has been lost and the trees have grown branch and branch into one another and are gnarled and rugged; but age is no guaranty that the personal qualities of the designer are there. The Japanese have a ready method of at once securing the appearance of age within the garden by buying or transporting their ancient and gnarled trees which they weave into each and every design.

It is always better, from an educational standpoint, to show gardenage by plans, clear views, and a description of one, rather than insert detached views of many gardens; and a plan — of itself — is an indeterminate way of showing a designer's intentions. I have therefore included, as an object-lesson, a plan and views of the gardens at Hampstead Heath for Mr. W. H. Lever. This garden may be classified as a typical suburban garden, being purchased, remodeled, and equipped for residence during the parliamentary sessions. It comprises about three acres, and is situated near the famous Golders Hill, now devoted to the purposes of a public park.

The middle part of the residence existed at the time of purchase, but the curved corridors and side pavilions were erected for the ac-

Garden for W. H. Lever, Esq. View Across Lower Level, with House in Background.

Garden for W. H. Lever, Esq. Terrace, Showing Pergola and Greenhouses.

Rock Terrace and Fountain, Walmer Lodge.

commodation of a superb collection of china and works of art, the architect being the late E. A. Ould, of Liverpool. Later, the center portion will assume a more regular and architectural guise by the addition of a classical stone loggia or veranda, covering in the entire house terrace. From the terrace opens out a magnificent view across the Weald of Harrow, terminating in Harrow-on-the-Hill Church and its shapely spire. The retention of this view, and the necessity of a screen from the public on the adjoining common, partly accounts for the several deep terraces and the pergola and conservatories on the outer fringe of the gardens. Essentials settled, the problem was to give a peaceful place of seclusion and a garden of shade interspersed with the gaiety of flowers and noble architectural adjuncts, and meanwhile to sustain the classical note throughout. Whatever of breadth was in the lawns, that could be counted upon to give the idea of expanse, was retained; and the floral effects were kept low and grouped in their several separate colorings, as is to-day usual in formal schemes of garden-design with those who are strict purists in the matter of formalism, in contrast with the present-day overpopular and more heterogeneous herbaceous borders.

By way of contrast, two views of an exposed seaside garden at Walmer Place, Kent, are inserted. In a seaside garden it is always a more or less difficult problem to secure the necessary protection, until by plantations or architectural screens the forces of the wind are broken. Walmer Place is where the late Lady Curzon was removed from the adjoining Walmer Castle during her last illness.

Another series of views represent a house built and a garden laid out to my designs, in accord with lakeland traditions, for my brother, Mr. Robert Mawson, at Windermere. The tinted rough-cast, which is a local speciality and has been the delight of Wordsworth and Ruskin and all the lakeland poets, is almost as enduring as the rugged stone to which it forms so admirable a contrast. In this district, owing to the variety of views, it is not often necessary to do more than to give the immediate presence of the house a suitable aspect of seclusion and an interesting surrounding and to plant sparingly and effectively. Lavish nature herself supplies all else needed to influence the imagination.

Sun-dial, Walmer Lodge, for Albert Ochs, Esq.

A Walk in the Garden, Walmer Place, England.

The Rustic Pergola, Robert Mawson's House at Windermere, England.
Thomas H. Mawson, Landscape Architect.

Rustic Steps, Terrace, and Pergola.

Rock Terraces and Garden-house, Robert Mawson's House at Windermere, England.
Thomas H. Mawson, Landscape Architect.

I

MODERN ENGLISH COUNTRY HOUSES

GARDEN FRONT. "FOURACRE," WINCHFIELD, HAMPSHIRE, ENGLAND.

PLATE V.

THE ARCHITECTURAL REVIEW

VIEW ACROSS LOWER TERRACE, "THE HILL," HAMPSTEAD, ENGLAND, FOR W. H. LEVER, ESQ.
THOMAS H. MAWSON, LANDSCAPE ARCHITECT

UPPER TERRACE AND MUSIC-ROOM, "THE HILL," HAMPSTEAD, ENGLAND, FOR W. H. LEVER, ESQ.

TERRACE, RESIDENCE OF MR. PLATT, AT CORNISH, N. H.

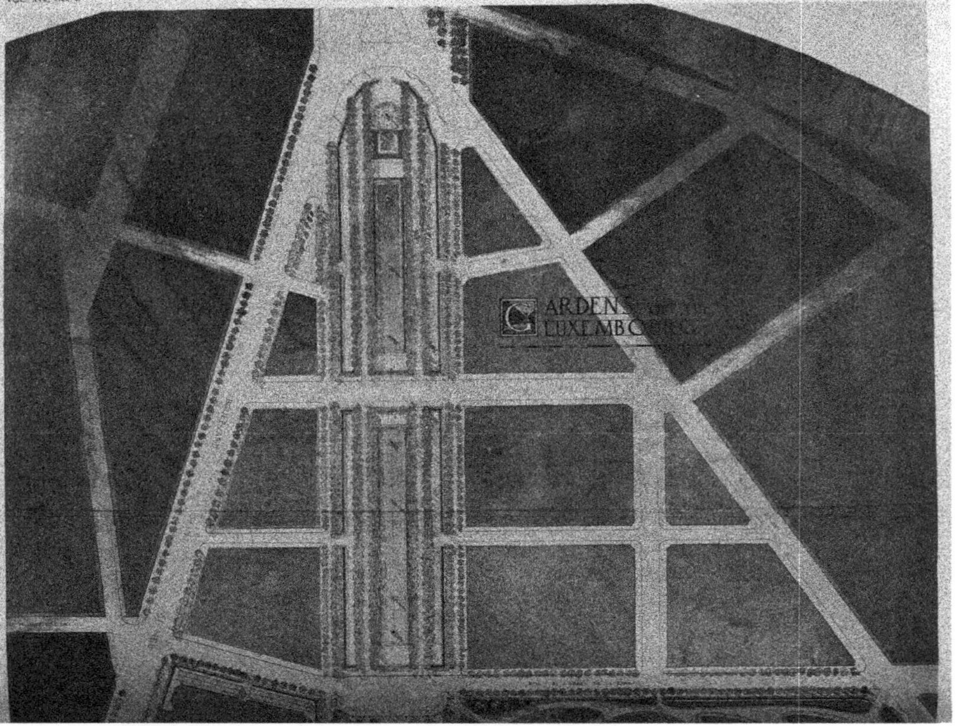

THE GARDENS OF THE LUXEMBOURG, PARIS, FRANCE.
SKETCH FROM DRAWING BY JACKS FORD CLUNE.

VISTA FROM STUDIO OF MR. PLATT AT CORNISH, N. H.
CHARLES A. PLATT, ARCHITECT.

LILY POOL, "THE HILL," HAMPSTEAD, ENGLAND, FOR W. H. LEVER, ESQ.
E. A. OULD, ARCHITECT. THOMAS H. MAWSON, LANDSCAPE ARCHITECT

VIEW FROM TERRACE, KEARSNEY COURT, NEAR DOVER, ENGLAND.
THOMAS H. MAWSON, LANDSCAPE ARCHITECT.

FRONT VIEW, "FRITHCOTE," NORTHWOOD, ENGLAND.
WALTER F. HEWITT, ARCHITECT.

VIEW ACROSS GRASS TERRACE TOWARD CHINA-ROOM, "THE HILL," HAMPSTEAD, ENGLAND.
THOMAS H. MAWSON, LANDSCAPE ARCHITECT.

VIEW ACROSS WATER-POOL TOWARD GARDEN-HOUSE, "THE HILL," HAMPSTEAD, ENGLAND.
THOMAS H. MAWSON, LANDSCAPE ARCHITECT.

DETAIL, INSIDE PERGOLA, "THE HILL," HAMPSTEAD, ENGLAND
THOMAS H. MAWSON, LANDSCAPE ARCHITECT

GAZEBO AND TERRACE, WALMER PLACE, ENGLAND
THOMAS H. MAWSON, LANDSCAPE ARCHITECT

The Architectural Review

VOLUME XVI. NUMBER 4

APRIL, 1909

BATES & GUILD COMPANY, Publishers
42 Chauncy Street, Boston

NEW YORK OFFICE, PARK ROW BUILDING

Published monthly. Price, mailed flat to any address in the United States or Canada, five dollars per annum, in advance; to any foreign address, six dollars per annum, in advance. Subscriptions begin with the issue following their receipt. Single copies fifty cents. Special numbers, one dollar. Entered as second-class mail matter at the Post-Office, Boston, Massachusetts, November 20, 1891.

PLATES

PLATES XXIX., XXX.— GARDEN AT "THE HILL," HAMPSTEAD, ENGLAND, FOR W. H. LEVER, ESQ. (PHOTOGRAPHIC VIEWS)— THOMAS H. MAWSON, ARCHITECT.

PLATE XXXI.— TERRACE, HOUSE FOR MR. PLATT AT CORNISH, N. H. (PHOTOGRAPHIC VIEW)— CHARLES A. PLATT, ARCHITECT.

PLATES XXXII., XXXIII.— THE GARDENS OF THE LUXEMBOURG, PARIS (PLAN)— ROTCH ENVOI DRAWING BY JAMES FORD CLAPP.

PLATE XXXIV.— VISTA FROM STUDIO, HOUSE FOR MR. PLATT AT CORNISH, N. H. (PHOTOGRAPHIC VIEW)— CHARLES A. PLATT, ARCHITECT.

PLATE XXXV.— LILY POOL, "THE HILL," HAMPSTEAD, ENGLAND, FOR W. H. LEVER, ESQ. (PHOTOGRAPHIC VIEW)— THOMAS H. MAWSON, ARCHITECT.

PLATE XXXVI.— VIEW FROM TERRACE, KEARSNEY COURT, ENGLAND (PHOTOGRAPHIC VIEW)— THOMAS H. MAWSON, ARCHITECT.

WE recently spoke of the general disregard among architects, even those of the best standing, of taking into account the buildings that surround the sites upon which they are to build important structures, so making our city architecture a jumble of warring and conflicting styles and scales. This disregard is not confined to any one branch of the profession. It crops out in all directions, and — if anything — the architect having to do with smaller dwellings is more likely to adjust his designs to meet the conditions set by the natural environment in which they are to be placed, than is the designer of more important and expensive structures.

On the occasion of a "Garden Number" it is perhaps especially pertinent to again point out how our architecture lacks in distinction and individuality, largely because of the tendency on the part of the architect, in viewing a lot of uneven grades and difficult of treatment, to solve the problem merely by "leveling it off," which is undoubtedly the treatment easiest for him — if most expensive for his client — and most unfortunately monotonous in its final results. If only he could be persuaded to accept the natural outlines, the natural growths with which the site is already garbed by nature, as a part of the problem set to him, these limitations would of themselves help to point the way in which the most successful solution was to be found; and we would, as a result, have architecture of individuality, architecture of picturesqueness, and architecture suitable to the larger aspects of the landscape in which it is placed, and not architecture obtrusive, uninteresting, and monotonous in its more intimate details, while a jarring and conflicting element to all the rest of the landscape other than the small plot of land upon which it happens to be forced!

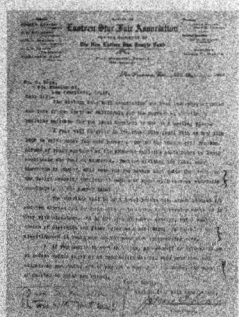

A "SKYSCRAPER SCHOOLHOUSE" was, perhaps, some day to be expected, but yet it can at once be seen how conservatives — especially with a few recent disasters vividly before them — should hesitate at what appears, at first sight, to be a somewhat startling proposition. There have been, afloat now, for some time, various and persistent rumors that in Chicago, "the home of the skyscraper," such a building was, actually, in contemplation; but it has also been generally understood that this matter was among those to which public reference would better not yet be made. The March *Architectural Record*, however, dissipates the professional mystery in which this scheme had theretofore been shrouded, by publishing a rather rough and unprepossessing perspective of the proposed building and making some comment thereupon. In that comment most attention seemed to be directed to the building's fire-proof qualities and to its intended use by scholars in a "School of Commerce" — which, after all, hardly seems to be adequate or sufficient reason for its being.

Our understanding is not that this skyscraper school was first suggested by those in authority; but rather the outcome of an attempt to utilize a piece of property, already in the possession of the school board, in a district where it was impossible to get other land, and where it was also impossible to dispose of this parcel (itself of very limited area) to advantage; and therefore the necessity of adopting an "office-building" solution — in case the property was to be put to any use whatever — was, in a way, forced upon those having the matter in charge.

We are not quite sure whether the publication of this design means that this structure has been accepted by the Chicago Board of Education or not, as we believe there has been considerable opposition and criticism of the scheme in that city; but while it is always easier to take an obstructive point-of-view on any novel or unusual idea, it might also be well to remember that not only is it necessary, for the safety of its pupils, for the school structure to be most absolutely indestructible; but that even this is not, in itself, enough! It is quite as essential that *all* abutting and surrounding buildings be equally incombustible; and certainly, in a case like this, the ordinary slovenly misuse of the word "fire-proof" is not to be taken as sufficient warranty for the crowding of a number of children into a building of such unusual height. By "fire-proof" should be meant an *absolutely unburnable structure*; and that term should be most rigidly interpreted, not only for the building itself, but for all those structures that at present do — or in the future may — surround it!

ANENT the statements made last month in these columns on the revision of competitions and competitive programs, we show — subjoined below — an incidental document received by one of our subscribers and intended as a further exhibit in this same case! This "program and conditions" we have reproduced in facsimile, save that we have ventured to direct especial attention by the marginal brackets to the more remarkable stipulations. While brevity is acknowledgedly the soul of wit, we doubt if this extreme is any more to be desired than such another one, for instance, as the encyclopædic document issued for the New York State Prison competition.

For full, exact, and definite information, discriminating, sententious, and comprehensive terminology; the exquisite care and judgment displayed in the selection of competitors *and* judges; and a full-hearted and judicial commitment to a method of judgment and an adoption of a design, when judged, the accompanying "program" is certainly a model of its kind!

Current Periodicals
A Review of the Recent American And Foreign Architectural Publications

View of Southeast Alcove, National City Bank of New York.
McKim, Mead & White, Architects.

Banking-room, National City Bank of New York.
McKim, Mead & White, Architects.

View of Main Entrance, National City Bank of New York.
McKim, Mead & White, Architects.

IF these columns possess any virtue at all, it is that they suggest, almost every month, numerous texts pertinent to the gradual development of our American architecture, as it flows slowly and often somewhat deviously along before us. Often, too, a month's magazines' illustrations do not bring forth anything of vital interest. In such a month's review we should be excused for pausing for retrospect or comment on some transient thought brought to us on the passing current; and that thought is this month supplied by a drawing appearing in the first issue of *The American Architect* for March.

The question of adapting or borrowing of motives in architectural design is one that is always with us. Frequently we find that men have borrowed from others ideas that they have then better developed themselves — in which case it would seem that such adaptation is excusable as performing its office in the development of an architectural style in America. When such borrowed motive is used with less success it becomes less justifiable, from any ethical point of view. There can, of course, be less criticism when a man borrows merely from himself, and repeats in new designs motives or details that he has previously used in others. The danger to his reputation then consists in that only he may be accused of lack of invention and paucity of idea. This is especially true when this repetition of motive applies to decorative details, as is the case with certain ornament used on the Y. M. C. A. building published in the magazine referred to above, where we find the same identical detail earlier employed by the same architects on the Union Trust Co.'s building in Washington — shown by us last May.

The use, on the latter building, of a similar arch and panel treatment — now employed as the principal unit of the façade's design, and somewhat more than suggesting a repetition of the arch motive of the first story of the Washington Bank — is perhaps less to be criticized. It may be that the designer would feel he had not perfectly expressed in the earlier composition the best use of

a motive such as was there employed for the base story. It may be that it was essential for his own satisfaction and development for him to try this same feature more importantly, and with a similar accompanying first-story arched opening, on a building with a wall broken only by fenestration, instead of by the articulation of a classic order — as was the case with the middle stories of the earlier design. Or it may even be taken as a definite indication that, so far as his own development is concerned, that designer has ceased further to progress; and that he has by this means expressed the best of which he is capable in the solution of a building problem demanding height as a principal dimension.

The moral is, after all, only that one is his own worst enemy either in reproducing himself, or the work of other people. Such mechanical imitative repetition is not essential to express individuality, and in fact never will be found to obtain that result. Originality is the expression of an inventive and creative personality that would naturally balk at conventional repetition of motive or idea in the creation of an art-design!

Undoubtedly the principal architectural exhibit in last month's magazines is the interior of the National City Bank — McKim, Mead & White's now somewhat well-known alteration from the old Custom House in New York. We have earlier spoken of the exterior of this building, but have not before attempted to show the majestic interior banking-rooms. The *New York Architect* for February gives us, however, the best idea that has yet appeared of this portion of the structure, — probably largely by the means of the great number of plate illustrations of the interior views reproduced, and we have made from these a selection that will, we hope, render some adequate idea of this very beautiful and monumental room. Of course, no impression of its charm of color is yet conveyed, which is much to be regretted, as this interior is effective largely because of the simplicity and unity resulting from restricting the interior walls to practically one marble and color tone, — a lesson the success of which we hope will have its effect

Union Trust Company's Building, Washington, D. C.
(From "The Brickbuilder.")

Durand Commons, Dining-Hall, Lake Forest University. Lake Forest, Ill.
Howard Van Doren Shaw, Architect.

Residence of F. W. Sutton, Kenilworth, Ill.
George W. Maher, Architect, Chicago.
(From "The Western Architect.")

Residence, E. S. Harkness, 5th Ave., N. Y.
Hale & Rogers, Architects.
(From "The Builder," London.)

Country House, George G. Benjamin, Far Rockaway.
Edward S. Shire, Architect.
(From "Architecture.")

Chancel Furniture and Decoration, Essex Church, Notting Hill Gate.
Ronald P. Jones, Architect.
(From "The American Architect.")

Elevation, Prize-winning Design, Y. M. C. A. Building, Norfolk, Va.
Wood, Donn & Deming, Architects. Russel Edward Mitchell, Associate.

upon those other practitioners who often try to obtain richness of result by the mere noise and bluster of marble contrasts. The same magazine also shows several interiors of the Hotel Meurice, Paris — a much more refined and commendable use of French classic decoration than is generally to be found in recent work in that capital of Europe.

The American Architect for March 3, contains, besides the two sets of competitive drawings for the Norfolk Y. M. C. A. that furnished the text for this month's opening paragraphs, several plates of Beaux-Arts student work, along with Part II of the article on "English Mansions" mentioned in our last issue; which is concluded in the number for March 10 — of which the plates show several public buildings and houses at Pittsburg by Alden & Harlow, March 17 there is published a school near Montreal by Ross & McFarlane, a Universalist church in Watertown, N. Y., by Horace B. Upjohn, and several plates of student work. An article entitled "Notes from Europe" illustrates some interesting recent English houses, of which several were included in the special issue of the English *Architectural Review* that we reviewed in our last issue. The plates for April 24 are given to publishing Mr. Donn Barber's Lotus Club, both exterior and interior, of which the former, another essay in the introduction of variety in texture into brickwork, was reproduced in these columns last month. Inside of Mr. Boyd's house in Pennsylvania, — another instance of the typical use of the distinctive kind of ledge stone that the locality is so fortunate in possessing, — the number for March 31 is not of any especial value. The month's frontispieces illustrate European and English work, old and new, the former predominating. The department of "Architectural Criticism" in *Architecture* for March treats of the Hendrick Hudson Apartments, the Indianapolis Post-Office, the interesting Bronx Church house by

Bosworth & Holden, and two New York buildings by C. P. Huntington. The plates include a plan and perspective by Howells & Stokes for the development of a certain section of Seattle, two designs for the Elks Club, New York City; several views of Gordon, Tracy & Swartwout's Connecticut Savings Bank, which we illustrated in these pages last month; and the rather dry and elaborate residence on Fifth Avenue and 75th Street, New York, by Hale & Rogers. A very ineffective picture of Delano & Aldrich's notable Walters Art Gallery in Baltimore is shown; and a brilliantly simple little country house at Far Rockaway, one view of which we reproduce. A brick dwelling by Charles Volz at Riverdale, N. Y., nearly escapes complete success. One is rather inclined to regard the tile adopted for the roof as a principal reason for its failure, as both in scale and texture it appears somewhat obtrusive; which defect, taken with the grouping of windows and the rather unpleasant height and proportions of the gables, prevents the building from being as successful a solution of directness in American house design as one would wish of so nearly commendable an effort.

The March *Brickbuilder* contains a further section of the articles on "Gymnasiums," and another on "Specifications." The plates show a dignified house at Lawrence, L. I., by William Adams; the rather startling and unpleasing interior of a Natatorium at Pittsburg, which is also shown in this month's *Architecture*; and Howard Shaw's dining-hall for Lake Forest University. Two plates of drawings by Mr. Magonigle for a Brooklyn Gas Company Meter House are careful studies in the variation of texture in brickwork, while one of the views, showing the garden end of a brick house by Mr. Platt at Katonah, is so attractive we can hardly forbear reproducing it. Interesting as is the brick texture adopted for portions of Mr. Schweinfurth's

(From "The Builder," London.)

Messrs. Debenham & Freebody's Premises, Wigmore Street.
W. Wallace and James S. Gibson, F.R.I.B.A., Architects.

(From "The Architect.")

Premiated Design, Primitive Methodist Church and Hall, Cousett, Durham.
J. W. F. Phillipson, Architect.

Briggs House at Cleveland when studied in detail, the composition as a whole is so bare and forbidding that it unfortunately suggests a fortress rather than a dwelling. Two or three other residences of less interest are shown, along with some Western brick factory buildings and other structures of minor importance.

The Western Architect publishes a number of plates of a new hotel at Toledo, O.; views of the Indianapolis Post-Office, a commendable instance of government architecture, but one that has been known to the profession now for a number of years; and several photographs, that are somewhat too vague to reproduce, of a house by Rutan & Russell at Cobourg, Ontario. We have therefore selected an attractive little picture of a plaster house by Mr. Maher, whose later manner we find distinctly more attractive than some of his more extreme and earlier styles. The present design is, however, marred by an extremely eccentric window, of that kind generally labeled on "archytects'" plans as "Art Glass!"

The Architectural Record, after taking official note of the regretted death of Mr. Russell Sturgis, gives considerable space to the description and illustration of the three important New York bridges recently constructed,— the Queensboro, Williamsburg, and Manhattan structures, — and to the old East River bridge. An article on "Contemporary Swedish Architecture," and several others dealing with historic architecture and furnishings, complete the issue.

Of the English magazines, *The Architectural Review* prints an engaging scheme for an improvement of the Horse Guards Parade, London, two articles dealing with the public buildings of Sicily, and an old Scotch pre-Reformation church. The article on "Architecture in the United States" treats in this issue of a number of recent banking institutions; while a large country house and an extension for the Chelsea Town Hall, both by Leonard Stokes, represent the section given to recent architecture.

The Architect publishes plates of several "Business Premises," only one of which, occupying the site of the late Crosby Hall, is to be remarked as above the general British average. The study for a

(From "The Builder," London.)

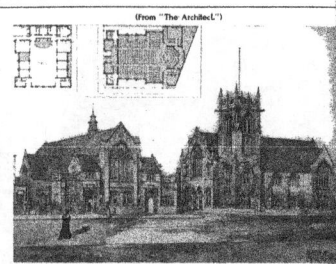

Detail of Chancel Decoration, Essex Church, Notting Hill Gate.
Ronald P. Jones, Architect.

Church and Hall on adjoining locations, and a couple of churches by J. W. F. Phillipson, from the issues of March 5 and 19, are noted as being commendable among the plates printed this month.

We reprint from *The Builder* for March 6 the altar and pulpit of a church at Notting Hill Gate. From the issue of March 20 we show a scheme for a Business Premises, illustrating in the same design both extremes of restful and restless composition of classic elements, neither conformable with the other.

The Builders' Journal prints, as usual, a number of small cottage schemes, including part of the new "Garden City" at Finchley; the drawings other than these being given mostly to work of historic rather than of modern interest, the exception proving to be the number for March 25, where there are reproduced a number of student designs from the Architectural School of Liverpool University. As these students have but two years study outside of public schools, the designs shown as representative of the general average of work compare more than favorably, both in draughtsmanship and composition, with the more mature student work with which we are familiar in this country. It is noticeable that most of these students' designs employ the simpler classic orders rather after the colder, more reserved fashions found in the work of the earlier Italian Renaissance.

The last number of *The Builders' Journal* for March tells of a Los Angeles theater building in reinforced concrete, and also gives some information as to the new chair of civic design that has been recently founded in Liverpool University, which has just been taken by Mr. Stanley Adshead.

La Construction Moderne for March 6 reproduces a number of drawings and photographs of Government Buildings at Washington, including the office building for the Houses of Congress, the Capitol, White House, Treasury, Library, and Department of Agriculture, along with some rather amusing and characteristically Gallic comments on the same; while the following number shows the Stadium at Syracuse, U. S. A.

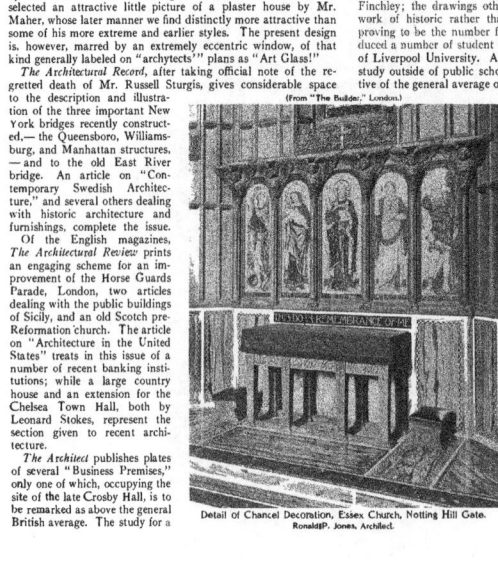

The Architectural Review

An Open-Air Exhibition of American Sculpture

By Jens Jensen

UNDER the auspices of the Municipal Art League, and with the assistance of the West Chicago Park Commissioners, was held last year in Chicago an exhibit that was, in its way, absolutely unique in ig plastic art in harmonious relation to out-of-door surroundings.

e purpose of the exhibit was to educate ublic to the proper use of sculpture in ican parks. Due allowance must be to the impossibility of selecting the ideal of sculpture for such exhibits; and from iew alone is a just criticism fairly possible. familiar with the careless selection and died distribution of sculpture in many of ity parks will realize the great importance a public exhibit, and help to promote similar exhibits in other cities. There is still room ulpture in our parks; but it must be appropriate. Certainly a war hero in fighting on is not the kind of sculpture to place on toral meadow, or burst upon in a woodpath where soul and heart have finally rest and proclaimed peace and good will men! Neither does the usual portrait ment placed directly in the center of the rive add to the effect of the landscape.

Fountain by Mr. Crunelle, Humboldt Park, Chicago.

On wandering along the rippling brook into a dark and shadowy cove where every nook teems with the mysticism of the forest, here certainly is not the place for the commemoration of heroic deeds! Or in a mirroring lake, where reflections suggesting mystic depths are cast from woodland groves — not here the bearded figure of Neptune! No; but where park and city meet — where the city extends into the park, and the park into the city, "the clasping hand"— there we may find a place for plastic forms. Or where formal lines dominate the landscape, and precision in line is the rule — there is the natural place for an appropriate group.

The park has been established in the city to represent and recall the absent country. It is the country, with its groves, meadows, brooks, and lakes, that we need; and whatever intrudes upon or disturbs the quiet and peace of the country-recalling park is out of place. The right relations between the sculpture and its surroundings must be studied as conscientiously as harmony in an opera. Sculpture lends beauty and charm to the landscape in which it belongs, and the effect of plastic forms is enhanced by being placed in the right surround-

Entrance to Rose-garden, Humboldt Park, Showing Groups by French and Potter from the Chicago World's Fair.

Copyright, 1909, by Bates & Guild Company

Rustic Figure, by Mr. Crunelle, Humboldt Park.

Curving Pergola, Rose-garden, Humboldt Park, Chicago.

Taft Groups before the Shelter in Rose-garden, Humboldt Park.

ings. Therefore, we find both sculpture and landsc... beautified by being brought into proper contrast and ... tion with each other.

The accompanying photographs of this exhibit are ... structive on these principles to as great an extent as ... be possible with any showing where the surroundings ... not especially made for each separate piece. Part of ... gardens used are of a formal nature, and part are nat... istic. This permitted a greater variety of sculpture an... better setting for the individual pieces than otherwise w... have been possible. In this way Crunelle's fountai... ceived a charming setting, and Miss Walker's "Grief"... greatly emphasized by its surroundings. The bu... French and Potter stood out well in silhouette agains... red light of the western sky as day turned into nig... the forms above the garden terrace, well backed by ... growth of woodland plantation, assured one of outli... added distinction to the gardens; while the smaller ... in the pergolas filled a perceptible vacancy, and a... terest to the pergolas themselves.

Rose-garden, Humboldt Park, Chicago, Looking toward Park Shelter.

Shelter and Pool, Humboldt Park, Chicago. Looking from Entrance.

"Afterward," by Nellie V. Walker, Humboldt Park.

Mulligan's Lincoln brought us back to the woodland, where he belongs. He stood where park and garden meet, and in this location served two purposes: the motive to what was soon to be seen, and the linking together of natural woodland and formal work. Other groups were used in a similar manner to tie the entire exhibit into an harmonious whole.

Mr. Taft's groups, a charming theme for garden work, although their relationship to the Park Shelter in the rose-garden was of an harmonious nature, yet, of course, best realized their purpose in their permanent location. Here, grouped by luxurious palms flanking a vista into the depth of the conservatory,—or, more correctly, the pillars of the gateway to the indoor pavilions,—they are rightly at home. These two groups, perhaps better than any other, emphasize the great want of the right kind of sculpture in our gardens. In their present location they must impress more or less any one entering the building; and it is hoped they will become valuable adjuncts in educating the public to the right appreciation of plastic art.

Figures around Border of Rose-garden, Humboldt Park, Chicago.

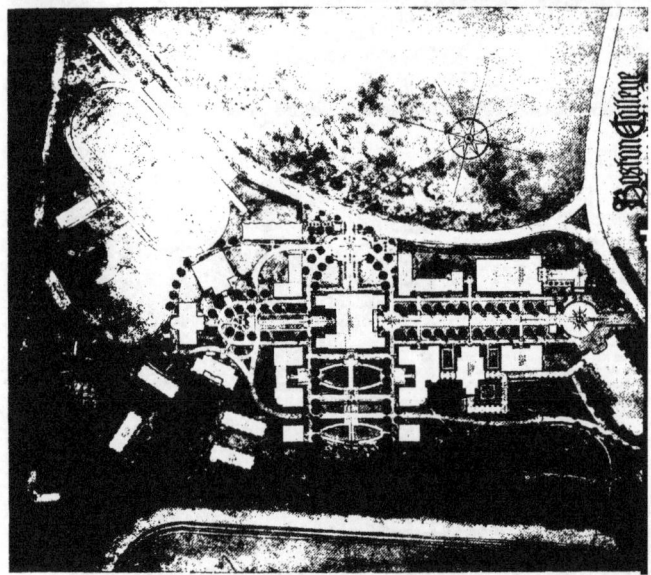

BOSTON COLLEGE COMPETITION.
FIRST AND THIRD PRIZE DESIGN.
MAGINNIS & WALSH, ARCHITECTS.

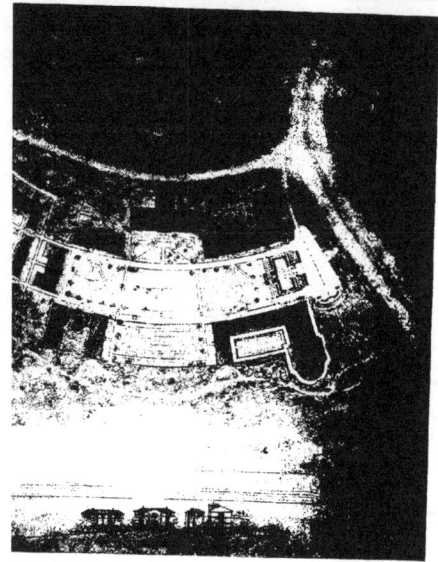

BOSTON COLLEGE COMPETITION.
SECOND PRIZE DESIGN.
ARCHITECT. WARREN H. MANNING, LANDSCAPE ARCHITECT.

BOSTON COLLEGE COMPETITION.
ALLEN R. COLLENS AND JAMES W. O'CONNOR, ASSOCIATE ARCHITECTS.

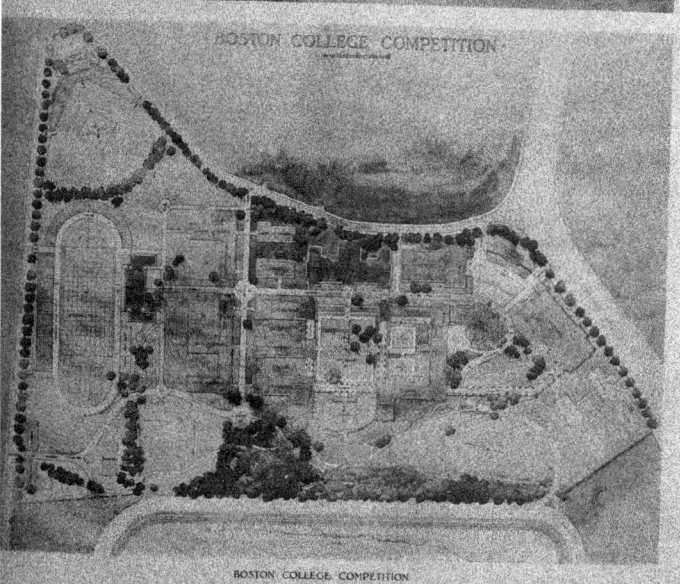

BOSTON COLLEGE COMPETITION
PEABODY & STEARNS, ARCHITECTS

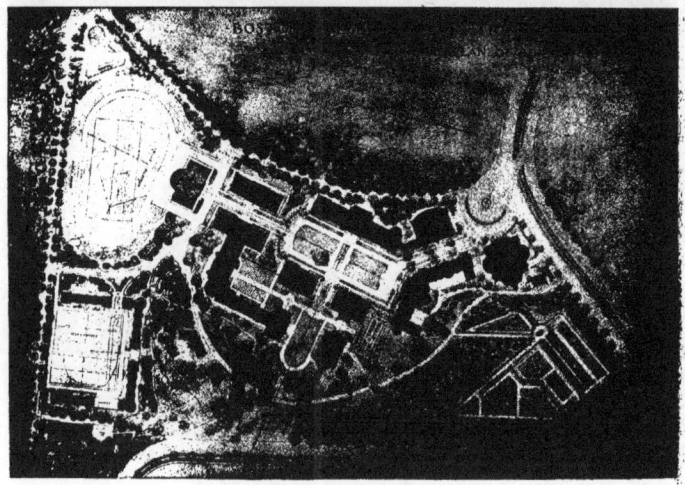

BOSTON COLLEGE COMPETITION.
COOLIDGE & CARLSON, ARCHITECTS.

MODERN ENGLISH COUNTRY HOUSES

PLATE VII

COMPTON HEY, PRESTWICH, MANCHESTER, ENGLAND.

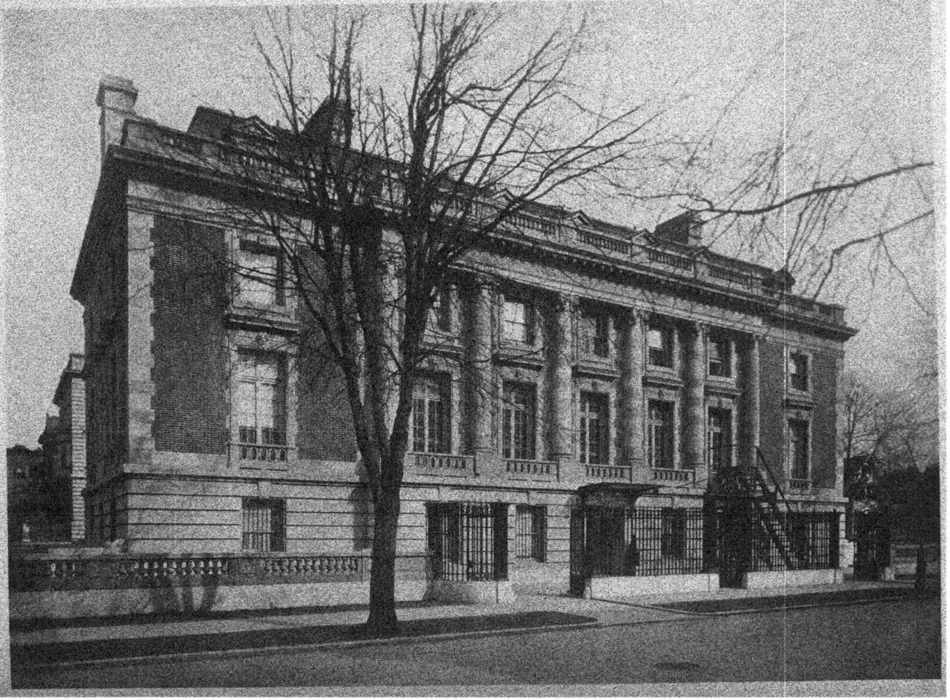

EXTERIOR DETAILS, RESIDENCE OF H. L. PRATT, ESQ., BROOKLYN, N. Y.
JAMES BRITE, ARCHITECT.

DETAILS, RESIDENCE OF H. L. PRATT, ESQ., BROOKLYN, N. Y.
JAMES BRITE, ARCHITECT.

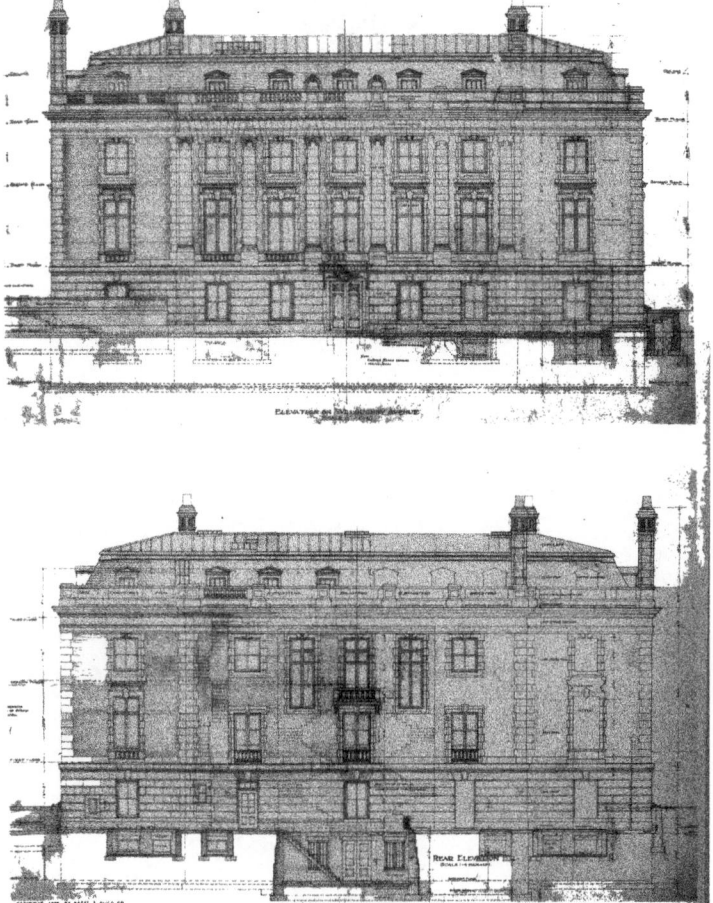

ELEVATIONS, RESIDENCE OF H. L. PRATT, ESQ., BROOKLYN, N. Y.
JAMES BRITE, ARCHITECT.

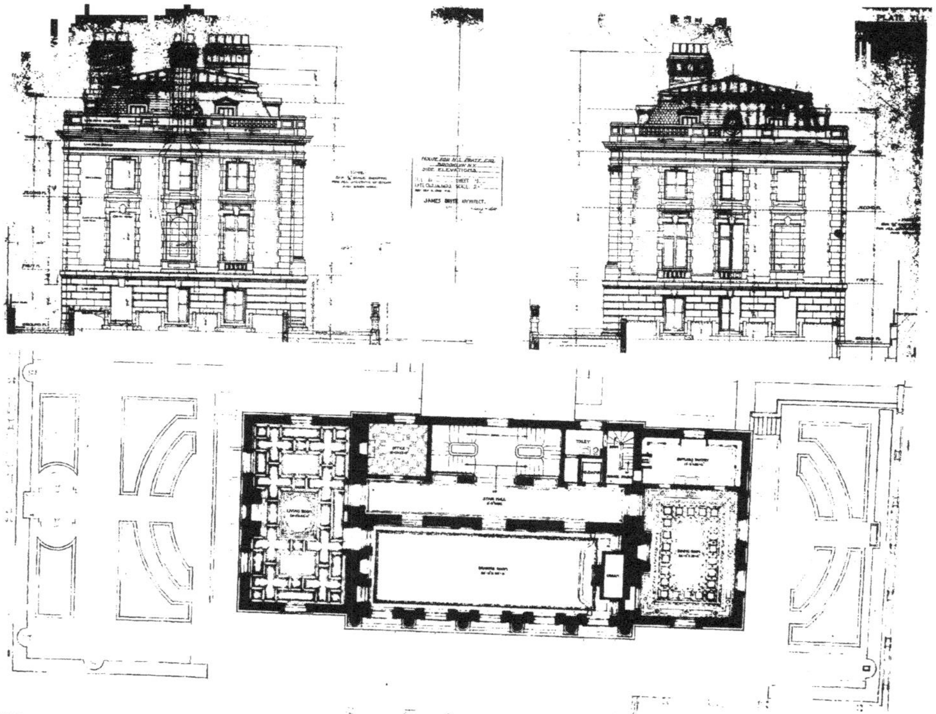

SIDE ELEVATIONS AND PLAN. RESIDENCE OF H. L. PRATT, ESQ., BROOKLYN, N. Y.
JAMES BRITE, ARCHITECT.

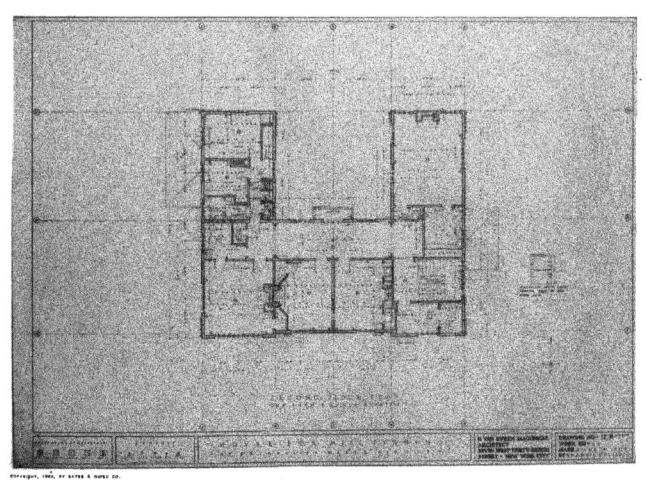

PLANS, HOUSE FOR MISS DUNNING, BRIARCLIFF MANOR, N. Y.
H. VAN BUREN MAGONIGLE, ARCHITECT.

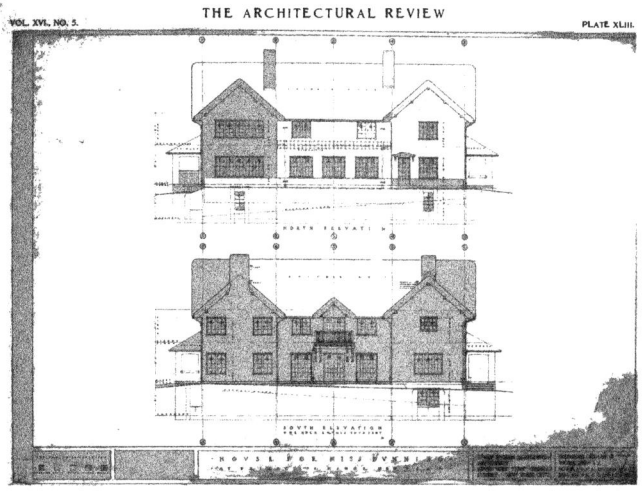

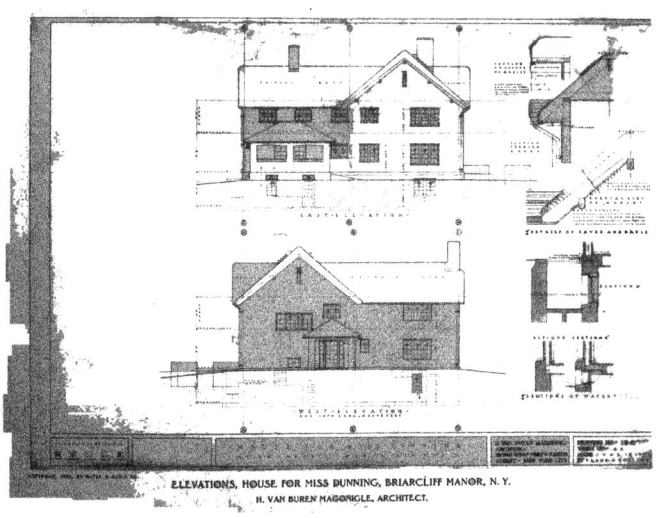

ELEVATIONS, HOUSE FOR MISS DUNNING, BRIARCLIFF MANOR, N. Y.
H. VAN BUREN MAGONIGLE, ARCHITECT.

DINING-ROOM, RESIDENCE OF H. L. PRATT, ESQ., BROOKLYN, N. Y.
JAMES BRITE, ARCHITECT

GARDEN FRONT : DENHOLME : WALTON-ON-THAMES, SURREY, ENGLAND.
WALTER F. CAVE, ARCHITECT.

COOLIDGE & CARLSON, ARCHITECTS.

ALLEN & COLLENS AND JAMES W. O'CONNOR, ASSOCIATE ARCHITECTS.

EDWARD T. P. GRAHAM, ARCHITECT.

MAGINNIS & WALSH, ARCHITECTS.

PERSPECTIVES OF RECITATION BUILDING, BOSTON COLLEGE COMPETITION.

MUSIC-ROOM

LIVING-ROOM.
RESIDENCE FOR H. L. PRATT, ESQ., BROOKLYN, N. Y.
JAMES BRITE, ARCHITECT.

ENTRANCE HALLWAY.

HALL ON PRINCIPAL FLOOR.
RESIDENCE FOR H. L. PRATT, ESQ., BROOKLYN, N. Y.
JAMES BRITE, ARCHITECT.

ENTRANCE FRONT.

TERRACE FRONT.
HOUSE FOR MISS DUNNING, BRIARCLIFF MANOR, N. Y.
H. VAN BUREN MAGONIGLE, ARCHITECT.

The Architectural Review

VOLUME XVI. NUMBER 5

MAY, 1909

BATES & GUILD COMPANY, Publishers
42 Chauncy Street, Boston

NEW YORK OFFICE, PARK ROW BUILDING

Issued monthly. Price, mailed flat to any address in the United States or Canada, five dollars per annum, in advance; to any foreign address, six dollars per annum, in advance. Subscriptions begin with the issue following their receipt. Single copies, fifty cents. Special numbers, two dollars. Entered as second-class mail-matter at the Post-office, Boston, Massachusetts, November 27, 1891.

PLATES

PLATES XXXVII — XLI. — RESIDENCE FOR H. L. PRATT, ESQ., BROOKLYN, N. Y. (PLANS, ELEVATIONS, DETAILS, AND PHOTOGRAPHIC VIEWS) — JAMES BRITE, ARCHITECT.

PLATES XLII, XLIII. — HOUSE FOR MISS DUNNING, BRIARCLIFF MANOR, N. Y. (PLANS AND ELEVATIONS) — H. VAN BUREN MAGONIGLE, ARCHITECT.

PLATE XLIV. — DINING-ROOM, RESIDENCE FOR H. L. PRATT, ESQ., BROOKLYN, N. Y. (PHOTOGRAPHIC VIEW) — JAMES BRITE, ARCHITECT.

WHEN the ethics of competitions come finally to be determined, it would be well for those having the matter in hand to attempt at the same term to "lay" the architectural "Ghost;" as it is high time that this very ubiquitous character be eliminated from gentlemen's society. Possibly there may be some members of the profession who do not realize how often, in what high architectural circles, this designing skeleton is from his closet and takes charge of competitions! If so, they should make it their business to immediately inform themselves, as we believe this canker lies near the very heart of professional honesty and business repute. It is, of course, sometimes difficult to obtain absolute evidence of this custom. It is known, nevertheless, that many of the designs submitted by competitors in several recent important competitions were done either partially or wholly outside of their offices and draughting-rooms. The competitor who, under the Tarsney Act, to compete for a small post-office offered a flood of letters from gentlemen desirous of making his plans for him. It was said that in one Government Competition the eight sets of plans submitted were worked up by persons other than the reputed designers, and that of these six, five were by one concern; and it is a fact that there is one large office noted entirely on work of this sort, picked up from all over the country!

"Grub Street" no longer exists in literature, while there is no law whatsoever of public sentiment in regard to those who to-day pass off as their own work a book that had been written by another. We see absolutely no difference between this state of affairs and its architectural parallel, whereby an architect may submit in a competition, under his own name, a design that has been worked up by another individual, and yet for which he gets entire credit — and receives the advertising — in case the competition is awarded him upon that design!

We confess to wonder" at a state of affairs that allows of an otherwise reputable firm having their (?) competitive designs and plans made entire by a brother architect; or even — as has been done in several recent competitions — "made to order," and imported direct from Paris! If the architectural competition has any reason for being at all, it is certainly to obtain work different from the conventional in type; but when so many men of high professional standing and reputation are content to let their competitive work be worked out outside their own offices, sometimes by people who do nothing else but make a business of this sort of work, it would appear that nothing else than a species of fraud was being perpetrated upon the public. While if, as so many people claim and believe, the competition is held to select an *architect* rather than a *plan*, the "Ghost" system becomes even more indefensible — if not criminal — in its results.

IT seems remarkable, with the expenditure of energy and thought that has been given the problem of filing in a readily available form the many publications that should be of interest to architects and the building-trades, that no one has yet thought of extending the "vertical file" system to include this class of published matter. To be sure, it would require a certain amount of coöperation on the part of the various manufacturers. They would have to publish their catalogs and other information in a shape that would allow them to be included in such a collection; but once the idea was adopted by a few of the leading manufacturers, there is no question but that the rest would have to come to issuing their publications in a similar form, or be placed at a great disadvantage in reaching the trade. Book publishers have already adopted a uniform size of catalog publications which, at the end of the year, are gathered together and bound in a tremendously bulky volume, that by the aid of a cross-index gives a complete publishers' trade-list of the books published that season. In the building-trades, where the amount of money every year invested in publishing valuable trade information is very large, this obvious solution never has been attempted. Its advantages are many. Each publisher is enabled to get out his catalog at as great length as he may desire. It is only necessary for him to conform, in the size of the page and — to a limited extent — in the surface of the paper, to general specifications which need not be onerous nor stringent. Once issued, it is possible to file his catalog and the extra pages occasionally required for corrections or additions — whether consisting of few sheets or many — in exactly that section where it is most easily referred to in the especial office to which it is sent. It may be arranged under an alphabetical classification, or by any subdivision of kinds of material or trades that may better suit the customs or the convenience of the persons to whom it is delivered. It can be adapted with equal facility to a vertical file system, or for the shelves of a library, or kept within covers or letter-files — in any way whatsoever, so long as it answers the needs of the recipients; and by so doing it best suits the purposes for which it was issued by the advertiser!

WE regretfully note that the standard of the dollar-sign in architecture has again been adopted, and this time by so important a publication as *Collier's Weekly*. For years, throughout the country, the architectural profession, the building-trades and the intending home-builder have suffered from widely published misrepresentations as to the costs of house-building, for which the popular magazines — and especially *The Ladies' Home Journal* — have been solely responsible. Year after year this journal persists in publishing house designs that cost two and three times the sums they claim. No person with knowledge of the situation but would instantly agree that *The Ladies' Home Journal* has done more to permanently injure the development of domestic architecture in America than any other single influence that has been exerted upon its progress.

It was with considerable trepidation that we read the announcement of *Collier's* intention to take up, in the section of their magazine entitled "Outdoor America," the subject of "Home Building and Furnishing;" especially when it appeared that this department was not under the control of a person of any knowledge whatsoever in this important and specialized field, but merely of a "Sporting Editor!" It hardly seems dignified or just for a magazine of this reputed standard to treat a profession of the importance of architecture so slightingly; but we confess to much greater disappointment at finding, as the first sample of their intentions, an article — entitled "The Economical Cottage; What We Can Do with $2,500" (*sic!*) — purporting to deal with homes for people who cannot afford servants and do their household work themselves, containing poetic references to silver candlesticks and tea-services, as well as such strength-producing viands as "Finnan-Haddie'á la Newburg!" This *is* out-Boking Mister Bok with a vengeance!

(From "The American Architect.")

The Columbia Theater, San Francisco, Cal.
Bliss & Faville, Architects.

Current Periodicals
A Review of the Recent American And Foreign Architectural Publications

(From "The Western Architect.")

Masonic Temple, Brooklyn, N. Y.
Lord & Hewlett, Architects.

(From "Architecture.")

The Elks Club, Washington, D. C.
B. Stanley Simmons, Architect.

THE architectural magazines for April are rather notably lacking in material of value to the profession, the single important published design being Lord & Hewlett's Brooklyn Masonic Temple, which further serves as another example of the distinctive modern use of Greek architectural forms that we have recently remarked. Even as shown in the single view published in *The Western Architect*, it must be regarded as a building of undoubted monumental intent. In the same April magazine are several dwellings, among them Albert Kahn's Walker residence at Walkerville, Ontario; which is by now sufficiently familiar to the profession not to require reproduction here. Of the other houses, but one demands mention: an attractive "bungalow"— of which our only criticism would be confined to the title! — by Green & Green at Pasadena. From a textpage we cull a dwelling that, while ocularly a cement house, we are assured, in the accompanying context, is of tile. As it expresses considerable variation from the usual type, we reproduce it here without further comment.

Architecture for April prints Marshall Fox's Miller house at Barrington, Ill. (which we reproduced here month before last); B. Stanley Simmons's design for the Elks Club at Washington, that we reprint and a number of views of Mr. Platt's formal garden on the Larz Anderson estate in Brookline, a garden that — already rather too much-confused, especially in the planting — apparently has been still further elaborated since it was last illustrated. We believe the entrance-structure and pergolas — architecturally, the most interesting features of the garden — have not before been as well shown as in these illustrations. There can be no doubt but that the most interesting dwelling shown in this month's magazines is that by Bosworth & Holden. If we are not mistaken, this is one of the best country houses of the classic type so far achieved in America. We certainly reproduce nothing better this month than the view of this design. The details of Palmer & Hornbostel's Education Building

(From "The Western Architect.")

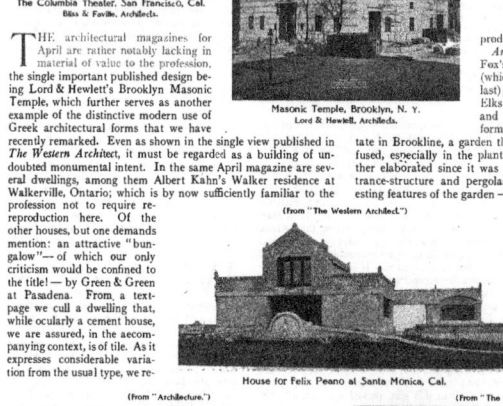

House for Felix Peano at Santa Monica, Cal.

(From "Architecture.")

Entrance Front, Country House, E. D. Godfrey, Oceanic, N. J.
Bosworth & Holden, Architects.

(From "The American Architect.")

Stable for Charles S. Brown, Esq., Mt. Kisco, N. Y.
Albro & Lindeberg, Architects.

(From "The Brickbuilder.")

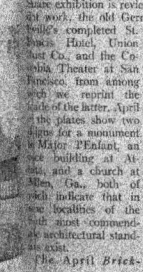

Building for the Women's Baptist Home Mission Society, Chicago, Ill.
Pond & Pond, Architects.

(From "The Brickbuilder.")

Dining-hall, Wheaton Seminary, Norton, Mass.
Ripley & Russell, Architects.

(From "Architecture.")

Subway Entrance, Queensboro Bridge.
Palmer & Hornbostel, Architects.

(From "The Builder's Journal.")

The Façade at Pall Mall.
Mewès & Davis and E. Keynes Purchase, Associate Architects.

Albany, show a somewhat surprising character of ornament for a structure of the design expressed in the original drawings. One rather wonders, from these documents, if the entire scheme has not been considerably modified from the original competitive design. The gigantic columns and order there employed could scarcely be carried out in the terra-cotta details here shown. By themselves they are, nevertheless, extremely interesting records, illustrating a considerable fertility in the rather profuse use of ornament of a distinctively original architectural type. Other illustrations show the architectural sections of the Queensboro bridge, by the same designers, including the charmingly brilliant little subway station of brick and terra-cotta reprinted from the magazine's text-pages — which should certainly be placed third in interest among the architectures illustrated this month, as one of the most appropriate, original, and satisfying designs yet produced by so modern a problem.

The American Architect for April 7 contains another instalment of the distinctive work of Albro & Lindeberg, showing a picturesque stone and half-timber house at Mt. Kisco, with its interiors, and the drawings for a New Jersey version of the Mt. Vernon type of residence by the same designers. For April 14 both leading article and plates illustrate a concrete dam and power-house by Lockridge & Ackerman; and the completed Chicago University Club, — a perspective of which we printed in these columns in May. This is shown in a couple of photographs. April 21 the T-Square exhibition is reviewed, and the plates reproduce some studio work, the old Germantown house "Stenton," and Bliss & Faville's completed St. Francis Hotel, Union Trust Co., and the Columbia Theater at San Francisco, from among which we reprint the façade of the latter. April 28 the plates show two designs for a monument to Major l'Enfant, an office building at Atlanta, and a church at Macon, Ga., both of which indicate that in some localities of the South most commendable architectural standards exist.

The April Brick-

builder has a Piranesi frontispiece of Roman architectural details, and well-illustrated articles dealing with the housing problem and the plan and equipment of gymnasiums. The plates show Ripley & Russell's new buildings at Wheaton Seminary, of which we reprint the dining-hall, Stratton & Baldwin's Orphans' Home at Detroit, and another building in Pond & Pond's characteristic style, which may be seen in the view we reprint. Pell & Corbett's School of Applied Design for Women, printed last month in these columns, is illustrated in this same magazine; and a High School at Madison, Wis., is surprisingly similar to Parker & Thomas's John Greenleaf Whittier School for the city of Boston, the principal difference being in the addition of a third story, which was evidently required in the Western problem.

The Architectural Record publishes with its first article a number of houses illustrating some quite remarkable architectural misuses of the so-called "mission style." The illustrated article on New Rochelle is, with the exception of two or three instances, disappointing; but the article showing by illustrations and text a parallel between Mr. Platt's Palmer house and Westover is worthy of some note. We have only to regret that these — along with the other illustrations of the number — are so indistinct that it is quite impossible to reproduce from them here. Other articles of historic or more general interest that do not require specific mention in these columns are contained within the number.

The New York Architect for March prints additional illustrations of the Hotel Meurice, the remainder of the number being given up to Donn Barber's now familiar Lotus Club, — the principal interest lying in the details of exterior brick, texture provided by the line plates, — and a very beautifully rendered drawing advertising the "furnishers of the Club-house."

Before turning to the English magazines we pause to call attention to the interesting interchange of thought now in process between the domestic architecture of England and of America. In this country we have now for some years been utilizing modern

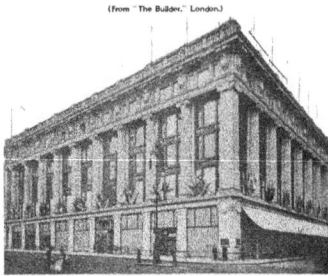

Messrs. Selfridge's Premises, Oxford Street.
Mr. R. Frank Atkinson, F.R.I.B.A., Architect.
(From "The Builder," London.)

The Victoria Station, S. E. & C. Railway.
Principal Frontage, Facing Forecourt.
(From "The Architect.")

Dodford Church, Worcestershire, from the Southwest.
Arthur Bartlett, Architect.
(From "The Architectural Review," London.)

The Queen Victoria Memorial Hall, Calcutta.
Sir William Emerson, F.R.I.B.A., Architect.
(From "The Builder," London.)

English domestic architectural forms, modifying their detailed members often but very slightly. Now England has begun to take her revenge; and there has recently arisen in that country a notable and distinctly evident tendency on the part of the younger men to derive detail—and, somewhat rarely, composition—from the American Colonial period. This evidences rather an interesting reversal to type, and, as proof that such a movement has actually already expressed itself, we call attention to the interior details of Mr. C. H. Reilly's house in the January English *Architectural Review* (referred to in these columns in the February issue), as well as to various other work reproduced in current English architectural magazines.

It is, in a way, typical of English country-house design that they have found only Colonial *details* worthy of borrowing. The classic composition, and repetition and balance of feature so noticeable in Colonial work, does not appeal to the English designer. He has passed through that stage of development, basing his work upon his own earlier and sturdier Georgian precedent, which he has modified by introducing Gothic — or, more strictly speaking, Elizabethan — detail forms. He has since, by using the larger Elizabethan or Gothic motives, and grafting upon them detail of a distinctly Colonial type, progressed a further step! The result is always interesting, although somewhat inclined rather to effeminacy (as was also true of much Colonial work, where the material had over-much influenced the modifications of classic detail that took place in the endeavor to adapt distinc[tive] stone-designed forms to woo[d].

Of the English magazine[s] *The Architectural Review* sta[rts] the first of what is apparent[ly to] be a series of articles on Ca[m]bridge College, that we hope w[ill] make these somewhat little[-re]garded buildings better kno[wn] to the profession. For curr[ent] architecture, a new library [of] somewhat extravagant Engl[ish] architectural type, and a chu[rch] in Worcestershire, carried o[ut] apparently in slap-dash [way with] stone trimmings, are of princ[ipal] interest. We reproduce on[e of] the illustrations of the buil[ding] last mentioned. We note [in] this number contains a s[ection] dealing with "Current Pe[riodi]cals, a Review of Some Recent Publications" evidently to b[e a] department similar to this that we have run in this paper for [over] a dozen or more years. We are pleased that Mr. Ross's Colum[n] Library, published in our last November issue, is apprecia[ted] by the English at somewhat more nearly its true value than [is] the case with some of our American contemporaries!

The Architec[t] April 9 contains a [view] of Victoria Sta[tion,] Southeastern and C[hat]ham Railway, tha[t we] show in a reproduc[tion] of the main façade.

The Builder's Jo[urnal] publishes, on April [9,] buildings from [the] Alaska-Yukon Expo[si]tion — that have n[ot] received recognition [in] the American magaz[ines.] From the same pap[er we] reprint the Royal A[uto]mobile Club; and [in] *The Builder* for A[pril 9,] two imposing for[eign] structures — Me[ssrs.] Selfridge's Premise[s and] the Queen Victori[a Me]morial Hall at Cal[cutta.]

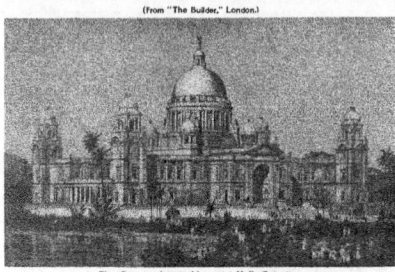

The Architectural Review

Volume XVI June, 1909 Number 6

The Berlin "Underground"

By Julius Grundmann

AGAIN a new stretch of the ever-extending net of elevated and (even more up-to-date) underground railways has been completed in the German capital. In 1902 the first line was built to connect the extreme eastern part of the city with the most densely populated section, around the Leipziger Platz. But as Berlin had not as yet a direct line running north and south, a branch from this central point, the Leipziger Platz, to the most northern section of the State steam railway was also started. This new line has at last been completed, after more than two years of hard work; and as it is by far the most important, interesting, and difficult section of the general scheme for intramural transportation, some data may now — since the scope of the architect has been widened to include problems of city planning and details of "Subway" and "L" stations and ironwork — not be out of place.

The course follows, generally, the existing surface streets, as the tunnel is built just beneath the pavement; — not as in London, where one has to go down several stories, and where, of course, the tunnel can proceed beneath houses and streets without much regard being paid to either. At one section of the work, the present terminal, — which is lighted from openings placed in the stone river-embankment, — the line runs along beside the River Spree, and here considerable precaution had to be taken to keep back the underwater. A continuous sheet piling was put into the river-bed, and a space about one yard wide by nine yards deep filled with waterproofing. And finally, for the protection of several large adjacent business buildings, which might otherwise have sunk or settled, another sheet piling, consisting of heavy steel girders, was put in parallel to the other formation.

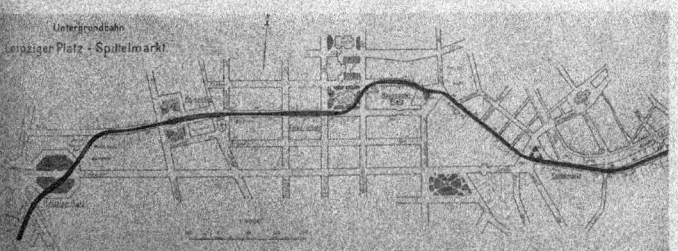

As is usual in the German empire, arrangements for the public safety were exceptionally well designed and executed, and in this respect the new stretch of railway compares more than favorably with foreign roads, — especially those in the United States, — where human life is cheap and accidents are likely to be more frequent than elsewhere.

Ironwork of Typical Station Entrance.

Plan Showing Location of New Section of Berlin Underground Railway and of Stations.

Copyright, 1909, by Bates & Guild Company

Typical Station Treatment of Supports.

Station Underneath Spree Embankment.

The electric current for lighting has been arranged entirely independent from that for the train service, so that the stations and shaft will be lighted even if anything goes wrong with the power-stations, or with the trains. The stations and street-entrances are real masterpieces of artistic design; and the wonderfully well-executed portals of forged iron, the stairways leading to the streets and their monumental adornments, are really beautifying the streets and squares in which they occur — which is certainly not the case in many other foreign cities! The walls of the stations are entirely of well-patterned mosaics, with light colors always predominating, white tiles being mostly used, sometimes with trimmings or panels of marble or majolica. Great precautions were also taken to ensure a constant supply of fresh air by means of a very complete ventilating-plant and the windows overlooking the river, opening along the Spree embankment.

Windows Along the Spree Embankment, from Without.

A special feature of the whole line is that it cuts through the most ancient part of Berlin, where there are many narrow and sharply curving streets. At three points buildings had to be undermined just beneath the pavement, which of course presented far greater difficulties than were encountered in London, where the tunnel runs a number of feet below the street-levels. In those places it was necessary to put in new pillars, and greatly to enlarge the old foundations; while the tunnel was so laid that it did not come into contact with any important part of the house standing above. Owing to the very unfavorable soil, the undermining of some houses, and the fact that the line cuts through the principal business section of the city, the expenses were very high; and although this stretch of road is only two thousand meters long (6,562 feet — about a mile and a quarter), it has cost about two million marks (about $480,000) to build!

Offices for Ticket Sellers and Collectors.

Tile Wall Treatment Along Station Platform.

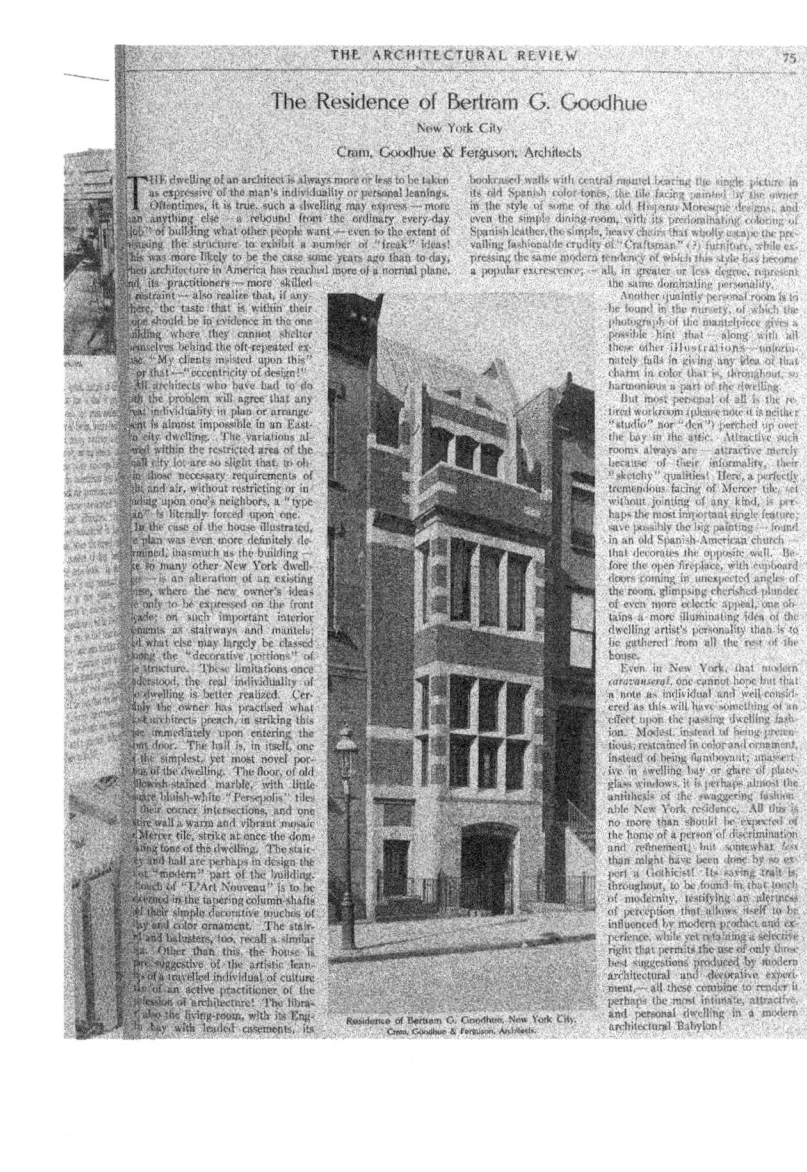

The Residence of Bertram G. Goodhue
New York City
Cram, Goodhue & Ferguson, Architects

THE dwelling of an architect is always more or less to be taken as expressive of the man's individuality or personal leanings. Oftentimes, it is true, such a dwelling may express — more than anything else — a rebound from the ordinary every-day job of building what other people want — even to the extent of investing the structure to exhibit a number of "freak" ideas! This was more likely to be the case some years ago than to-day, when architecture in America has reached more of a normal plane, and its practitioners — more skilled and restraint — also realize that, if anywhere, the taste that is within their scope should be in evidence in the one building where they cannot shelter themselves behind the oft-repeated excuse, "My clients insisted upon this", or that — "eccentricity of design!" All architects who have had to do with the problem will agree that any real individuality in plan or arrangement is almost impossible in an Eastern city dwelling. The variations allowed within the restricted area of the small city lot are so slight that, to obtain those necessary requirements of light and air, without restricting or intruding upon one's neighbors, a "type plan" is literally forced upon one. In the case of the house illustrated, the plan was even more definitely determined, inasmuch as the building is due to many other New York dwellings, is an alteration of an existing house, where the new owner's ideas could only be expressed on the front façade; on such important interior elements as stairways and mantels; and what else may largely be classed among the "decorative portions" of the structure. These limitations once understood, the real individuality of the dwelling is better realized. Certainly the owner has practised what most architects preach, in striking this note immediately upon entering the front door. The hall is, in itself, one of the simplest, yet most novel portions of the dwelling. The floor, of old yellowish-stained marble, with little square bluish-white "Persepolis" tiles at their corner intersections, and one entire wall a warm and vibrant mosaic of Mercer tile, strike at once the dominating tone of the dwelling. The stairway and hall are perhaps in design the most "modern" part of the building. A touch of "L'Art Nouveau" is to be discerned in the tapering column-shafts of their simple decorative touches of inlay and color ornament. The stair-rail and balusters, too, recall a similar idea. Other than this, the house is more suggestive of the artistic leanings of a travelled individual of culture than of an active practitioner of the profession of architecture! The library — also the living-room, with its English bay with leaded casements, its bookcased walls with central mantel bearing the single picture in its old Spanish color tones, the tile facing painted by the owner in the style of some of the old Hispano-Moresque designs, and even the simple dining-room, with its predominating coloring of Spanish leather, the simple, heavy chairs that wholly escape the prevailing fashionable crudity of "Craftsman" (?) furniture, while expressing the same modern tendency of which this style has become a popular excrescence, — all, in greater or less degree, represent the same dominating personality.

Another quaintly personal room is to be found in the nursery, of which the photograph of the mantelpiece gives a possible hint that — along with all these other illustrations — unfortunately fails in giving any idea of that charm in color that is, throughout, so harmonious a part of the dwelling.

But most personal of all is the retired workroom (please note it is neither "studio" nor "den") perched up over the bay in the attic. Attractive such rooms always are — attractive merely because of their informality, their "sketchy" qualities! Here, a perfectly tremendous facing of Mercer tile, set without jointing of any kind, is perhaps the most important single feature; save possibly the big painting — found in an old Spanish-American church that decorates the opposite wall. Before the open fireplace, with cupboard doors coming in unexpected angles of the room, glimpsing cherished plunder of even more eclectic appeal, one obtains a more illuminating idea of the dwelling artist's personality than is to be gathered from all the rest of the house.

Even in New York, that modern *caravanserai*, one cannot hope but that a note as individual and well considered as this will have something of an effect upon the passing dwelling fashion. Modest, instead of being pretentious; restrained in color and ornament, instead of being flamboyant; unassertive in swelling bay or glare of plate-glass windows, it is perhaps almost the antithesis of the swaggering fashionable New York residence. All this is no more than should be expected of the home of a person of discrimination and refinement; but somewhat less than might have been done by so expert a Gothicist! Its saving trait is, throughout, to be found in that touch of modernity, testifying an alertness of perception that allows itself to be influenced by modern product and experience, while yet retaining a selective right that permits the use of only those best suggestions produced by modern architectural and decorative experiment, — all these combine to render it perhaps the most intimate, attractive, and personal dwelling in a modern architectural Babylon!

*Residence of Bertram G. Goodhue, New York City,
Cram, Goodhue & Ferguson, Architects*

LIBRARY FIREPLACE.   DINING-ROOM FIREPLACE.
RESIDENCE OF BERTRAM G. GOODHUE, NEW YORK CITY. CRAM, GOODHUE & FERGUSON, ARCHITECTS.

WORKROOM, FIREPLACE END. WORKROOM, SEAT END.
RESIDENCE OF BERTRAM G. GOODHUE, NEW YORK CITY. CRAM, GOODHUE, & FERGUSON, ARCHITECTS.

ENTRANCE HALLWAY, GROUND FLOOR.

LIBRARY.
RESIDENCE OF BERTRAM G. GOODHUE, NEW YORK CITY. CRAM, GOODHUE & FERGUSON, ARCHITECTS.

MODERN ENGLISH CHURCHES

ST. SWITHIN'S CHURCH, LEWISHAM, KENT, ENGLAND.

PLATE XV.

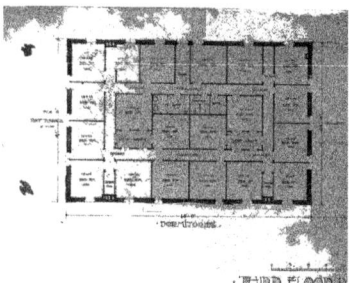

ELEVATION ON MAMARONECK AVENUE.

THIRD FLOOR PLAN.

ELEVATION ON MARTINE AVENUE.

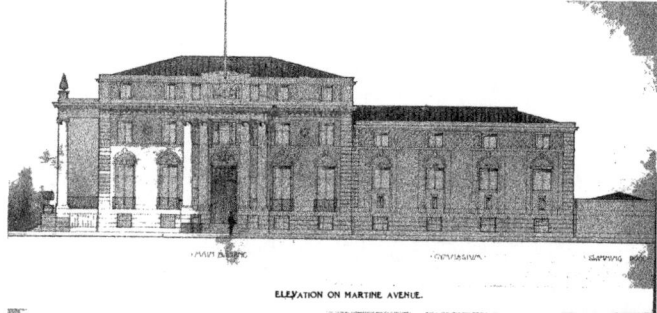

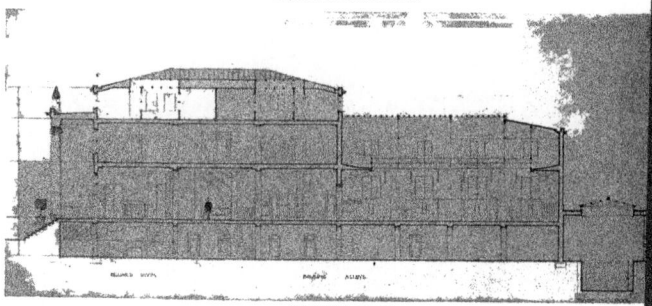

LONGITUDINAL SECTION.

Y. M. C. A. BUILDING, WHITE PLAINS, N. Y.
ALBRO & LINDEBERG, ARCHITECTS.

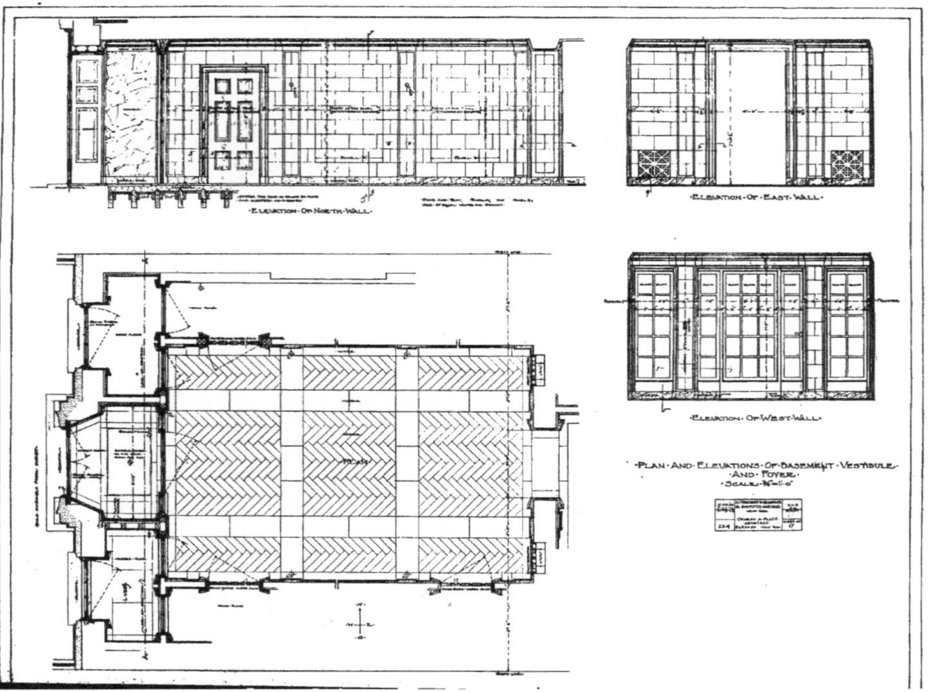

·PLAN·AND·ELEVATIONS·OF·BASEMENT·VESTIBULE·
·AND·FOYER·
·SCALE·⅜"=1'-0"·

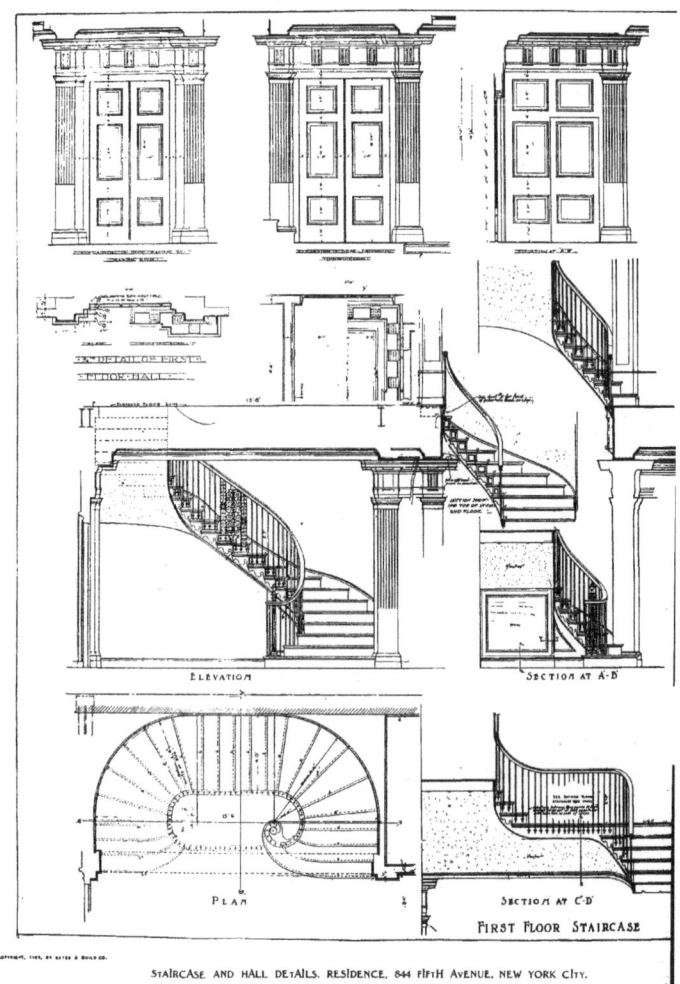

STAIRCASE AND HALL DETAILS. RESIDENCE, 844 FIFTH AVENUE, NEW YORK CITY.
CHARLES A. PLATT, ARCHITECT.

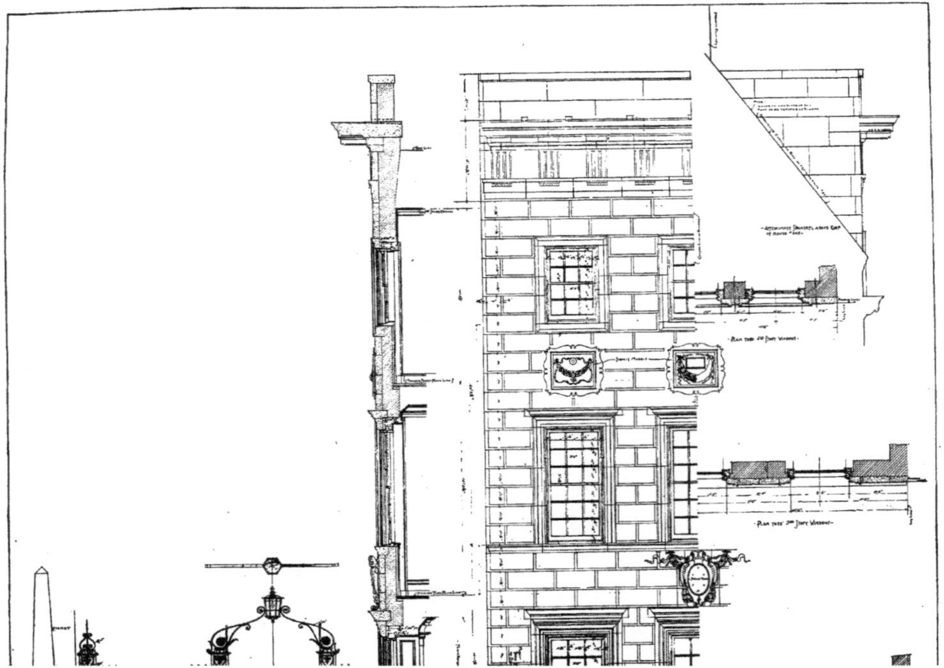

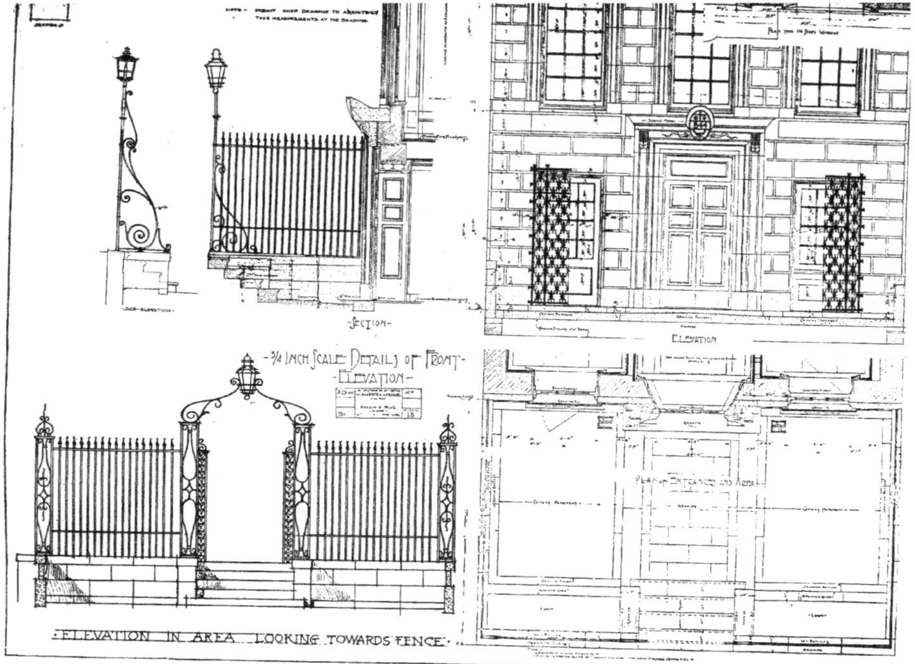

SCALE DRAWING OF FACADE, SHOWING IRONWORK DETAILS. RESIDENCE, 824 FIFTH AVENUE, NEW YORK CITY.
CHARLES A. PLATT, ARCHITECT.

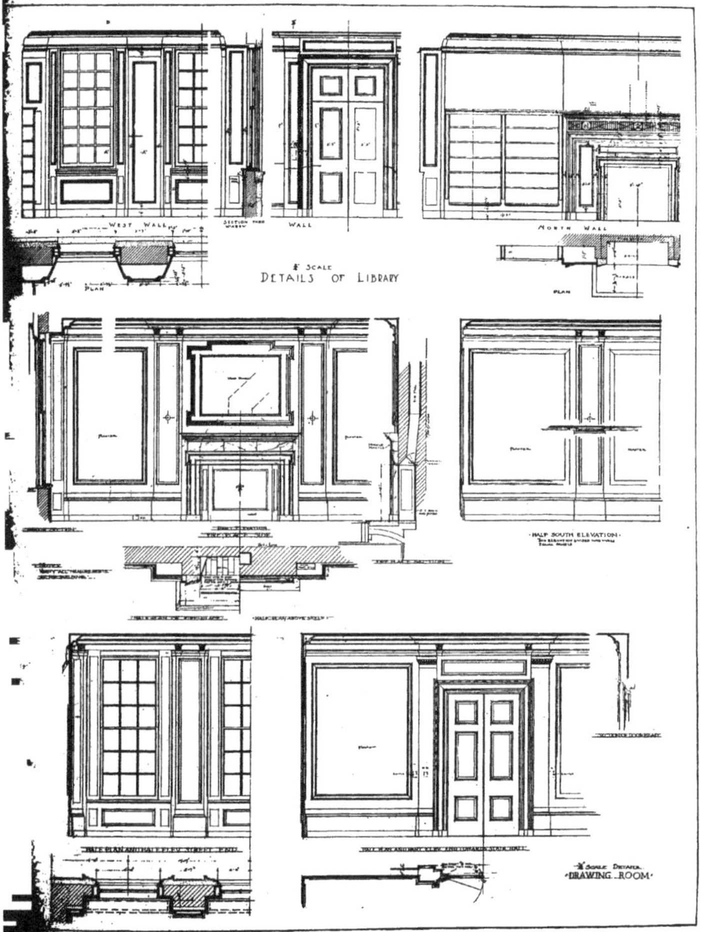

DRAWING-ROOM AND LIBRARY DETAILS. RESIDENCE, 844 FIFTH AVENUE, NEW YORK CITY.
CHARLES A. PLATT, ARCHITECT.

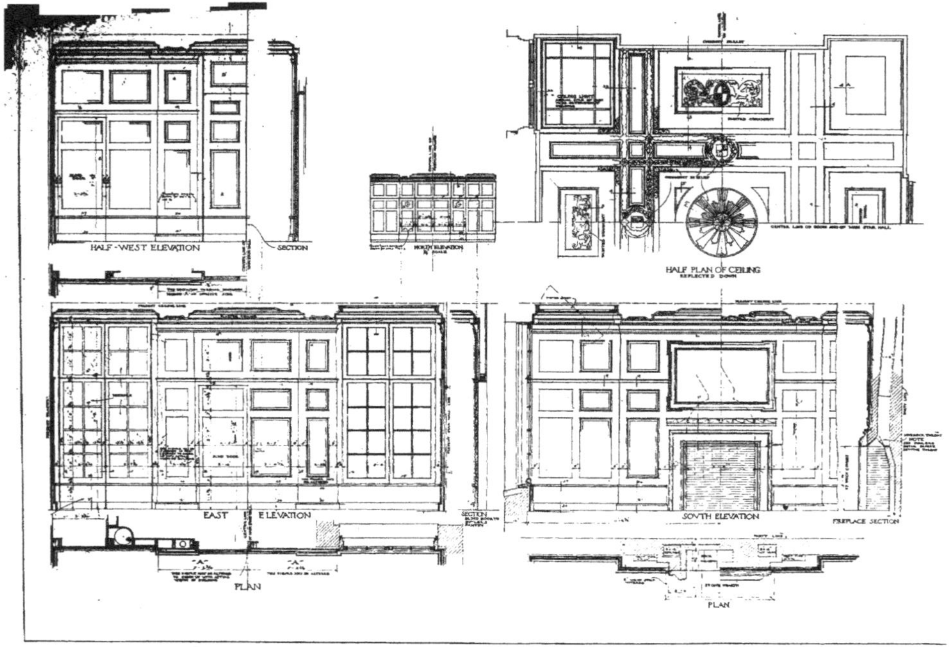

DINING-ROOM DETAILS. RESIDENCE, 844 FIFTH AVENUE, NEW YORK CITY.
CHARLES A. PLATT, ARCHITECT.

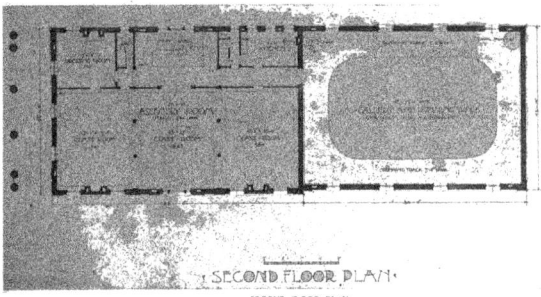

SECOND FLOOR PLAN.

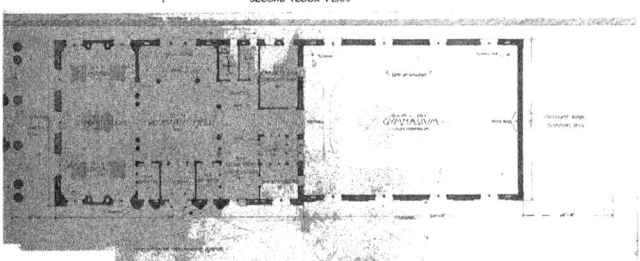

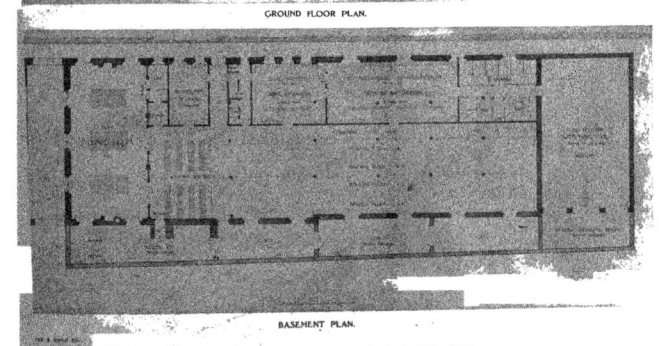

GROUND FLOOR PLAN.

BASEMENT PLAN.

FLOOR PLANS, Y. M. C. A. BUILDING, WHITE PLAINS, N. Y.
ALDRO & LINDEBERG, ARCHITECTS.

MODERN ENGLISH CHURCHES

INTERIOR, LOOKING EAST, ST. SWITHIN'S CHURCH, LEWISHAM, KENT, ENGLAND.
ERNEST NEWTON, ARCHITECT.

PLATE XVI.

MANTEL IN BEDROOM.  MANTEL IN NURSERY.

HALL, LOOKING TOWARD DINING-ROOM.  DETAIL OF ENTRANCE GATES.

RESIDENCE OF BERTRAM G. GOODHUE, NEW YORK CITY. CRAM, GOODHUE & FERGUSON, ARCHITECTS.

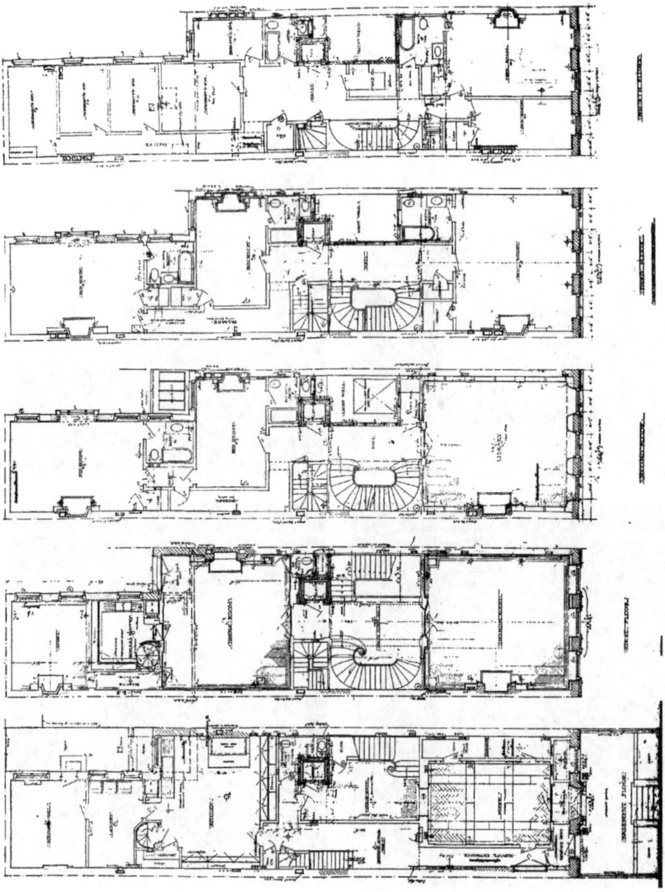

The Architectural Review

VOLUME XVI. NUMBER 6

JUNE, 1909

BATES & GUILD COMPANY, Publishers
42 Chauncy Street, Boston

NEW YORK OFFICE, PARK ROW BUILDING

Published monthly. Price, mailed flat to any address in the United States or Canada, five dollars per annum, in advance; to any foreign address, six dollars per annum, in advance. Subscriptions begin with the issue following their receipt. Single copies, fifty cents. Special numbers, two dollars. Entered as second-class mail-matter at the Post-office, Boston, Massachusetts, November 27, 1891.

PLATES

PLATE XLV.— Y. M. C. A. BUILDING, WHITE PLAINS, N. Y. (ELEVATIONS, PLAN, AND SECTION) — ALBRO & LINDEBERG, ARCHITECTS.

PLATES XLVI.—LI.— RESIDENCE, 844 FIFTH AVENUE, NEW YORK CITY (ELEVATION AND INTERIOR FINISH DETAILS) — CHARLES A. PLATT, ARCHITECT.

PLATE LII.— Y. M. C. A. BUILDING, WHITE PLAINS, N. Y. (FLOOR PLANS) — ALBRO & LINDEBERG, ARCHITECTS.

BY right of the first President of the United States having been a graduate of the University of Pennsylvania, Washington's Birthday is observed in that institution as "University Day," and it is the custom each year then to confer an honorary degree upon a few distinguished individuals. On Feb. 22, 1909, there were selected to receive this distinction a Professor of Literature, a Doctor, and an Architect. The latter was Mr. C. F. McKim, who was in such poor health at the time, that he was able to appear for only a few moments and was forced to leave immediately after he had received his degree of LL.D. in person. The University of Pennsylvania rendered something more than a mere mark of respect to individual merit in thus publicly recognizing, and for the first time, the architectural profession. May it not quite rightly be taken to indicate a considerable and growing respect on the part of the public for the profession of architecture in America? If so, a long-hoped-for and deeply cherished dream on the part of a few — including among the first of them, Mr. McKim himself, — is that much the nearer to being realized!

In conferring this honorary degree, the highest that Mr. McKim has received, Prof. Warren Powers Laird, in his address of presentation, aptly expressed some part of both the professional and public feeling for its recipient when he said: "During your career architecture has advanced in this country from obscurity to its rightful position as the Master Art. In this development, sir, your influence has been supreme, by reason of a noble purity of style, exalted professional ideals, and passionate devotion to the cause of education. Therefore, by request of the Trustees, I have the honor to ask the Provost to confer upon you, Charles Follen McKim, native of Pennsylvania and foremost American architect, the honorary degree of Doctor of Laws."

THAT we cannot have good architecture in this country until the general public acquire an understanding of and appreciation for what is best in the work given them by the profession is a fact that is slow in being generally recognized. It is the more encouraging, then, to find a client of Mr. Root's standing so enlightened as to take the point of view adopted by him in the statement quoted below, from *The Washington Star* of April 1 last. It happened, in working out the Bureau of American Republics in Washington, that some of the sculptural adornments proved, when well along toward completion, to be below the

standard that the architects and the Government were desirous should prevail in this building, intended for the exercise of the country's hospitality to her sister republics on this continent. In this dilemma Mr. Root, desirous to obtain the very best results possible, did not hesitate to abandon models and work already well advanced, and to authorize the additional expenditures necessary to replace it.

It should be a signal of hope and encouragement to all sincere members of the profession that Mr. Root, himself one of the rarely few men in public life of sufficient education to realize, and of artistic feeling enough to appreciate and understand, something of the artistic side of architecture, is quoted as saying, "An architect who does not change and improve his design as it is being executed, and who does not ask for extras [when necessary to be expended for that purpose], must be dead."

It is unfortunate for the general public, as well as for the progress of the profession and the advancement of the art of architecture, that this breadth of view-point belongs only to an individual representing the still infrequent pioneer in artistic development. When the greater proportion of American clients have attained an equal amount of enlightenment our architecture will have adopted a much higher standard than is possible at present. In working under such appreciative conditions the individual designer is perforce put to his best endeavors and, in case the result is not in every way unimpeachably satisfactory, he cannot then blame any part of his failure upon his client!

THE architect should have enough interest in many of the items in the tariff schedule now being discussed at Washington to concern himself rather more importantly than he does with the actions there being taken by his *mis*representatives. While many of the profession will regard the advanced price of lumber likely to result from the proposed increase of the tariff as not an unmixed blessing, inasmuch as it will bring that much the nearer the arrival of the day when fire-proof materials will be used universally — instead of only occasionally, as is at present the case — yet, if the increases contemplated are effected, it will undoubtedly mean much less activity in building-operations for the next year or two, so immediately and substantially affecting the incomes of the contractor and the architect.

Many other even more important building-trade products, such as iron and glass, are also under discussion. For years the price-list of the plate-glass salespeople has been a most farcical exposition of the absurdities of "protecting" a trust of this proportion under the all-embracing cloak of an "infant industry"! The tariff stipulates definite advances, based upon the areas of sheets of glass, which has resulted in the price-lists following these advances so closely as to jump the price of a sheet of glass from $3.15 for a light 60 inches long to $6.20 for a light *one inch longer!* A light 16 x 44 inches costs $7.35; one 16 x 45 inches, $12.30! A light 18 x 80 inches costs $24.00 and one 18 x 81 inches $33.30!

If it were not for our "protective" tariff, one fairer wonders if we would have to pay an extra eight or ten dollars for a piece of glass *a few inches* more than another sheet in area!

WE are creditably informed that a number of well-known universities, abroad and at home, are establishing departments in Aërial Architecture. We have already departments of architecture devoted to the science of building on land and on the water; and now comes aërial architecture, devoted to "Aëreostatics," the science of building in the sky. Certainly, other times, other customs!

Not only has a new departmental name been created, but a new science as well. The building of houses was an accomplished fact long before the builders discovered they were doing "architecture;" of transport on the seas, before the makers of boats labeled the trade of their design as "marine architecture;" the study of natural land contours a practised trade long before these simple gardeners suspected they had created a new profession in "landscape architecture;" but now we discover that we can navigate the air,— and we must therefore have, almost simultaneously, an architecture of "aëreonautics"! So much as evidence of the rapid progress of the Anglo-Saxon Yankee!

(From "Architecture.")

Country House, Peapack, N. J.
Edward S. Hewitt, Architect.

Current Periodicals
A Review of the Recent American And Foreign Architectural Publications
(From "The New York Architect.")

The McKinley National Memorial, Canton, Ohio.
H. Van Buren Magonigle, Architect.
(From "The New York Architect.")

Gates Avenue Court-house, Brooklyn, N. Y.
H. Van Buren Magonigle, Wilkinson & Magonigle, Architects.
(From "The New York Architect.")

Music-room.
H. Van Buren Magonigle, Architect.

(From "The American Architect.")

Country House, Cynwyd, Pa.
Mellor & Meigs, Architects.

THE May architectural magazines have begun to evidence their annually recurring attack of "that spring feeling." Their thoughts would appear to have quite completely turned to some other domain than architecture. Among such a poor field the "one best bet" for the month is easily placed on a rather infrequent favorite, *The New York Architect*, which, for April, illustrates work by Mr. Magonigle, beginning — and somewhat prematurely — with his McKinley Memorial; as, when the surroundings of that impressive monument have had opportunity to grow up, it should appear to far better advantage. The selections made from the magnificent working drawings for this structure but whet the appetite for more, although, if we are not mistaken, one or two of these documents have been previously published. Other illustrated work by the same architect includes the cast bronze A. P. C. A. fountain, the Piccirilli Studio Building, Miss Dow's School at Briarcliff Manor, the very simple, yet sturdy design for the Gates Avenue Court-house at Brooklyn, and a very elaborately designed and decorated private music-room, of which we reproduce one view that gives a general idea of its treatment and decoration.

While there may be some who will be inclined to cavil at decorative architecture as elaborate as this, yet, once granting its necessity — or, rather, its inevitability! — one cannot but acknowledge that the architectural handling of the decorative treatment given this room is much more to be desired than results obtained by other and less restrained means. We can easily recall a number of interiors where the decorator has been given an unlimited hand, with results far more to be regretted; or still other instances where architects, offered the same opportunity, have plunged into the most abysmal depths of modern French extravagances, producing interiors of a bombast of scale and vulgarity of decoration such as were much more to be condemned. If clients *will* insist upon rooms intended principally for "show," it undoubtedly presents an interesting problem to the architect to give them the desired results, while still remaining within the vicarious boundaries of good taste. It remains, of course, doubtful if such an interior could ever really be considered "livable," either from its overstrong ornament or color, or — as we feel to be the case in the present instance — from its somewhat over-formal architectural balance and arrangement, a defect that must be conceded as probably inseparable from an apartment as "set" and stately as this.

"Second place" can be given to this month's *Architectural Record*. All of a half-dozen articles of this issue present different aspects of the Permanent Dwelling, dealing with the history of earlier concrete buildings, the construction of dwellings built of terra-cotta and of concrete, and the architectural development of these types of design. This issue ought to help toward popularizing "the fire-proof house" — the more general use of which we believe should bring an era of public and building prosperity to America. The articles are the more definitely valuable from being accompanied by many examples of attractive dwellings built in these constructions described, including several houses by Louis Boynton and Robert Gardner — with the work of the latter of whom the profession is already well acquainted — and a number of picturesque house-designs by Squires & Wynkoop. It is unfortunate that these latter had mostly had to be pictured by sketches, instead of the much more convincing photographs showing the executed work. Among the houses illustrated are dwellings for Mr. Matthew Sullivan, for William Borland (illustrated in our August number), and some of the buildings by Fernekes & Cramer of the Pabst Farm near Milwaukee.

The Western Architect for May prints a number of text cuts from the recently held Minneapolis Architectural Club Exhibition. The plates give, for the first time, a New York residence by Harry Allen Jacobs, the recently completed Plymouth Church in Minneapolis, and a number of house designs; from among which we note Howard Shaw's Veeder House, Chicago, a residence in Los Angeles by Hudson & Munsell, with a rather novel gable treatment and a "concretish" bungalow at Dallas, Tex. The first last named of these we reproduce.

We find in *Architecture* a

THE ARCHITECTURAL REVIEW 83

(From "The Brickbuilder.")

Excelsior Club-house, Cleveland, Ohio.
Lehman & Schmitt, Architects.

(From "The Western Architect.")

Residence, C. S. Guggenheim, N. Y.
Harry Allen Jacobs, Architect.

(From "Architecture.")

Accepted Design, U. S. Post-office and Court-house, Denver, Col.
Tracy, Swartwout & Litchfield, Architects.
(From "Architecture.")

Competitive Design, U. S. Post-office and Court-house, Denver, Col.
Arnold W. Brunner, Architect.
(From "Architecture.")

Competitive Design, U. S. Post-office and Court-house, Denver, Col.
H. Van Buren Magonigle, Architect.

(From "The Western Architect.")

Residence, Henry Veeder, Chicago, Ill.
Howard Van Doren Shaw, Architect.

(From "The Western Architect.")

Residence, Colonel J. T. Trezevant, Dallas, Tex.
Edward Overland & George Willis, Architects.

(From "The American Architect.")

House for George R. Stearns, Summerville, Ga.
Kemp & Wendell, Architects.

interior cottage at Peapack, N. J., by E. S. Hewitt, and a selection of the designs submitted in competition for the Denver Post-office and Court-house, including those by Tracy, Swartwout & Litchfield, given first place, H. Van B. Magonigle, and Arnold W. Brunner. We omit the façade of Trowbridge & Livingston's design, as it is so nearly like the elevation accepted in another recent competition that it does not seem necessary to again reproduce it here. Those who so desire may find its substantial equivalent in these columns in our issue for June last.

The Brickbuilder for May prints another plate of Roman details by Piranesi, further instalments of the articles dealing with Gymnasiums, the Housing Problem, and the first of a series on Warming and Ventilation. The plates illustrate a club-house at Cleveland, that we reprint; a Toledo hotel (and, by the way, our American hotels seem to be approaching in conventionality to the uniformity of the now established post-office type); the working drawings of an exceedingly well-considered and dignified church at Chattanooga by McKim, Mead & White; and a couple of residences,— one in Milwaukee, another in Los Angeles.

The American Architect for the month has illustrated articles dealing with the Portland Architectural Exhibition (May 5); the Minneapolis Architectural Exhibition (May 12), notes from Europe (May 19), and (in the number of May 26) an article on

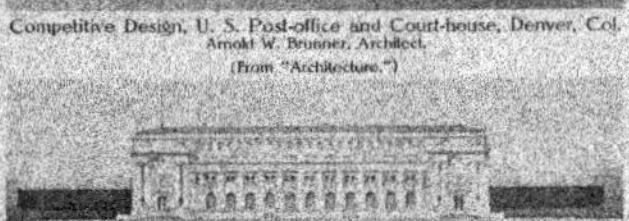

Augusta, Ga. The frontispieces are — with a single exception — reproductions of foreign architectural subjects.

Among the plates of current American work, the only things of especial note are a country house of excellent and simple proportions at Cynwyd, Penn., by Mellor & Meigs (May 12); the same drawings of McKim, Mead & White's church at Chattanooga (May 19) as were published in *The Brickbuilder* for this same month; and a couple of individual houses at Summerville, Ga., by Kemp & Wendell (May 26), from which we reproduce a view of one. We regret that the photographs of the other house were taken at a time when the surroundings — landscape and gardening — were so raw that it would do only extreme ill-justice to that dwelling to reprint them here.

Of the English magazines, *The Architectural Review* publishes an article on Constantinople Mosques, with some photographs and unusually crisp and decisive pencil drawings showing the "soap-bubble architecture" that these domical structures always recall. Part the Sixth of the articles on American Architecture — still dealing with "Commercial Buildings," and in this issue specializing on banks — includes much material known to the profession in America, and ends with two notably modern designs: one — built only last year — being Mr. Sullivan's Owatonna Bank, and the other a design, sufficiently old to appear above lutely new, for a projected but unexecuted building for a Minneapolis bank that nevertheless appears,— in a drawing done by Harvey Ellis a dozen or more years ago,—equally with Mr. Sullivan's design, modern. The section dealing with Current Architecture reproduces some views of the recently fitted interior of Dunkeld Cathedral by W. Dunn & R. Watson, and a single view of Mr. John Belcher's completed Ashton Memorial at Lancaster.

The *Builder's Journal and Architectural Engineer* prints (May 5) some photographs showing the still incomplete Château de Rochfort-en-Voelins, by Charles F. Mewès, that, as a frankly modern reworking of so well-known a model as the *Hôtel de Salm* on the Seine at Paris — better known as "The Legion of Honor Building"— is so good as to instantly recall the original at the same time that it must be recognized as more than equaling it in many details. The owner and the architect are both to be congratulated at securing so distinguished a design. The interiors for the Steamship *Kauserin Auguste-Victoria* of the Hamburg-American line, by the same architect, are notably refined and attractive; while doubly welcome as testifying that a new period in the treatment of steamship architecture is at hand!

Two other issues provide unusually well-rendered perspectives, one (on May 12) of a dwelling by Guy Dawber; the other (May 26) a sketch, almost as interesting, of a group of houses at Hampstead, by Geoffry Lucas.

The *Architect* for May 14 illustrates some rather nervous and unpleasing new buildings at Cambridge by T. G. Jackson, a rather astonishing design for a building in London City for the Government of Victoria, Australia, and Ashton Webb's *Italianate* offices the Grand Trunk Railway, prin several months ago in these colum

The *Builder* publishes, May some very charming cottages by Curtis Green; May 8, a laboratory for ford, by Mr. T. G. Jackson, that is somewhat less interesting than the same chitect's designs for the Cambridge buil just mentioned above; again reproduc as is also the Victorian Government Buil — in another view in this magazine. May 22 we note a factory building of plicity and inherent "style" construction, and from the la sue for the month we reprint Paul Waterhouse's design fo Prudential Insurance Offic Aberdeen.

A perspective of A. Gi Scott's remarkable and asto ing design for Glamorgan Co Hall is reprinted from *Builder* for its architect moral in contrast with Mewès' columnar portic ment in the Château de Roch en-Voelins. We regret that Mewès' exceptionally happy of the order cannot be consid as always typical of mo French practice! A recolle of the current architectur lished in that country's maga recalls it to be far and awa rare exception! Neither d quite dare to state that the lish treatment is represent of the use of the order in country! — as the colum sometimes employed Renaissance effectiveness.

La Construction Moder lishes (May 15) a private" that is about the best des a façade for a moving theater (American archi please take notice!) that w member to have seen recen

The Architectural Review

Volume XVI   July, 1909   Number 7

Amusement Architecture

By Frederic Thompson

Founder and Designer of the New York Hippodrome, Founder, Designer, and Proprietor of Luna Park, "the Heart of Coney Island"

ALL of the usual and most of the unusual architecture is conventional. Everything pertaining to the carnival spirit must be unconventional. Because of this indisputable fact every architect who religiously adheres to his Vignola is, and will continue to be, unsuccessful in designing buildings intended to amuse the public. This has been demonstrated repeatedly in expositions. The occasion of every great American fair has been that of a celebration, but the majority of our architects have designed structures as seriously as if theirs was the business of providing a State capitol or a temple of law, which in itself should suggest all seriousness, every suggestion of which must be absent from a composition designed for the inspiration of the carnival spirit.

In building for a festive occasion, there should be an absolute departure from all set forms of architecture. The design must not take the form of the residential, for that suggests quietness; nor of the commercial, for that suggests work; nor of the ecclesiastical, which suggests religious devotion. It must not be on the pattern of law, government, or education, for they are all things indicative of serious thought; and if these more serious forms of architecture are not subservient on a carnival occasion the crowds will be absent. If you accept my premise you must agree that an architect who engages in the business of providing temples of amusement for a pleasure-loving, midsummer populace should depart from all set rules of architecture except those which have to do with proportion and good taste. The schemes of such a man must be fantastical, even sometimes to an extreme; for his is more like the undertaking of an artist with imagination than of a craftsman whose efficiency is restricted by his subservience to a triangle and a T-square.

He must dare to decorate a minaret with Renaissance detail or to jumble Romanesque with *l'art nouveau*, always with the idea of keeping his line constantly varied, broken, and moving, so that it may lead gracefully into the towers and minarets of a festive sky-line. His task is a matter of solving the problem of a large picture composition; not of remembering and practising the set formulæ of correct architecture. He must learn to use the same license as does the scenic artist who paints the background for

Entrance to the "Dragon's Gorge," Luna Park.
One of the best "fronts" on the Island, and showing the scale of the architecture.

An Early Morning View in Luna Park, looking from Entrance toward Japanese Tea Garden.

Copyright, 1909, by Bates & Guild Company

Main Dining-room, Murray's Restaurant, New York City.

Fountain in Main Dining-room, Murray's Restaurant, New York City.

a fantastic spectacle with the very implements which have invested properly the forum scene in "Julius Cæsar." The work of an architect should, by its proper variations, influence the mood of the public — just as does that of an artist; and the difference between an amusement design and a more conventional problem should be as noticeable as that between Doré's illustrations to Dante's "Inferno" and to the "Paradise Regained."

I have been both criticized and complimented on the pictorial impression made by Luna Park, as well as by the many buildings which I have designed for some of the chief American Expositions within the last ten years. Most of the criticisms came from people who asserted that my output was not architecture, and all of the professional appreciation came from celebrated architects who weighed the value of a final effect. At the criticisms I have learned to smile, and I now accept them as emanating from nothing more potent than a T-square architect — a man who, if he is ever to be successful in this line of ac-

The Hippodrome, looking across Auditorium at the Box Tiers.
Thompson & Dundy, Designers.

tivity, must first learn the lesson which I have been taught by experience: to throw away the Vignola, to trust to his own sense of form, for his proportions, and to gather his ideas of the beautiful from his own good taste.

Too much of our architecture is being produced by the T-square triangle fellow. Generally speaking this man does not recognize the reason or the intent of the thing he is doing. The fact that the Flatiron Building is an exceedingly effective piece of New York architecture — not only effective, but, in its environment, beautiful — does not carry with it the suggestion that a similar structure would be similarly effective or similarly beautiful among the Berkshire Hills or in a bayou village of Louisiana. Any architect knows this, and yet nine out of ten of them put Flatiron buildings in the Berkshires whenever they start to design edifices intended to harmonize with the spirit of freedom. When I built Luna Park I did not seek to create a thirty-eight-acre architectural enclosure which might be visited with pleasure by people

"Curves and Circles," the "Helter Skelter" at Luna Park.

"Electric Architecture," Sky-line and Towers around Central Court at Luna Park at Night.

Towers, Minarets, Rides, Slides, etc. at Luna Park.

who obtain enjoyment from spending an entire afternoon in admiring chaste lines and correctly conventional decorations. My idea was that of every showman — to erect a park where people would laugh, enjoy themselves, and would spend money while being amused. I knew that no one had ever laughed at a beautifully conventional architectural design! I had never heard of a man who felt like a spendthrift as a result of gazing at a magnificent home of Justice. I could not remember of ever hearing or seeing any evidence of hilarity as a result of admiring a cathedral. So I decided to eliminate these and other serious forms from Luna; and by a negative process of reasoning I arrived at the conclusion that, if conventional lines interfered with my purpose, I must fall back on the unconventional, which should assist it!

I threw away my Vignola and all my architectural handbooks because they interfered with the working out of this scheme, and I accepted in their place ideas which I believed would foster rather than hinder the growth of the thing I was bending every effort to develop — the world's greatest carnival-place, which could succeed only when inhabited by men and things which did not interfere with the carnival spirit.

I remember well the days when I followed from a tracer up to a draughtsman, and I am duly acquainted with the importance of an adherence to the mathematical details of set rules, which is infinitely better than the independent meandering of the untrained man who builds monstrosities. An architect, no matter what his field may be, should have a thorough command of classical detail; but he should also be given the license of the trained artist to make full use of his conception of the mission of the particular building he is designing. And he must also understand that no structure which jars on its neighbors realizes completely its mission. He must have an eye for the pictorial as well as for the correctly architectural. A great deal of human pleasure arrives at the seat of our intelligence through the eye, and if the things we see do not fit in their surroundings and qualify with the general *raison d'être* of the whole picture, they do not please as they should; therefore they fail in their mission. That is the reason why Luna Park does not look like the average exposition or world's fair. It is also one of the chief reasons why it is more successful than any other amusement-place in history. But I am getting away beyond my field. The ideas which I am attempting to set down here are only those which pertain to the carnival spirit in architecture. Before returning to my argument, let me say that I would like to see a competition on any given architectural subject, arranged with the idea of showing the value of *artistic* rather than mechanical equipment and endeavor.

What architect designed the buildings of Fairyland — of Picture-Book Land? None. He was an artist who knew nothing of T-squares and triangles, or one who cleverly disguised his knowledge. Amusement-parks and expositions are nothing more than Fairy Picture-Books — Toy-Lands elaborated by adult hands; which statement brings me to the very pith and meat of my short excursion into architectural literature.

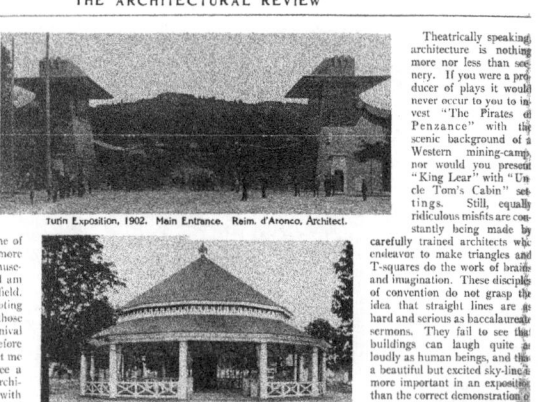

Turin Exposition, 1902. Main Entrance. Raim. d'Aronco, Architect.

Dance-Hall in Amusement Park, Munich. Franz Zell, Architect.

The Large Restaurant in Amusement Park, Munich.
Franz Zell, Otto Dietrich & Orlando Kurz, Architects.

Turin Exposition, 1902. Automobile Building. Raim. d'Aronco, Architect.

Turin Exposition, 1902. Principal Building. Raim. d'Aronco, Architect.

Theatrically speaking, architecture is nothing more nor less than scenery. If you were a producer of plays it would never occur to you to invest "The Pirates of Penzance" with the scenic background of a Western mining-camp, nor would you present "King Lear" with "Uncle Tom's Cabin" settings. Still, equally ridiculous misfits are constantly being made by carefully trained architects who endeavor to make triangles and T-squares do the work of brains and imagination. These disciples of convention do not grasp the idea that straight lines are as hard and serious as baccalaureate sermons. They fail to see that buildings can laugh quite as loudly as human beings, and that a beautiful but excited sky-line is more important in an exposition than the correct demonstration of any man's recollection of the fine points in Sir Christopher Wren's handiwork! If the carnival spirit is a necessity in an amusement-park, why not make everything promote rather than retard its development? In the show business "bally hoos" are a considerable means to success, and there are various usual and unusual "bally hoos." Every one, I take it, knows that a "bally hoo" is a device calculated to attract the attention of people and to guide them into a show — a brass band, an automaton, lightning calculator, among dervish, anything which can collect a crowd and hold it until the "barker" can get in his fine work. All showmen use them, but I think I am one of a very few who have ventured to make architecture about my wares. I have tried hard to make it as much a part of the carnival spirit as the bands, flags, rides, and lights. I have tried to keep it active, mobile, free, graceful, and attractive; and I have always preferred the remark, "What is that?" or "Why is that?" to "Is n't that a beautiful building?"

A correct conception of the mission of a prospective architectural work should be a basic stock in trade of every architect, and I think it is possessed and utilized in nearly every line of work except the one which has to do with outdoor amusements. A dramatist and a writer of fiction must have a plot and a purpose before he starts any effective literary or dramatic work, and the same truth obtains in art and architecture. At the Pan-American Exposition in Buffalo, I, with my late partner, Elmer S. Dundy, had the illusion show "A Trip to the Moon" as a principal attraction on the so-called Midway. The exposition started unsuccessfully, and was not placed on a paying basis until August, when, through a plan of which I happened to be the author, enough of the carnival spirit was injected into the mass of severely beautiful architecture, praiseworthy sculpture, and well-arranged landscapes to make it inviting to the crowds. The story of this sudden and rather spectacular change has been told several times, and has no place in this article. However, one detail of my interview with the Board of Directors, when the plan was first broached, illustrates the above statement regarding the value of a mission. My plan was to create a "Midway Day," on which nothing but fun and frolic should exist throughout the open spaces of the exposition; and in proposing it I told the distinguished committee that they were unsuccessful because there was not a showman in the lot. I told them about the carnival spirit, and I explained to them the value of a laugh. They came back at

me by insisting that the Pan-American Exposition was a colossal educational institution, instructive of the best in all the arts and trades and sciences.

"But what's the use of a college if there are no students?" I asked. "Before we talk of educational benefits let's get a crowd to educate."

Then I told them that an exposition was a celebration, a festival, a carnival; and I explained my reasons for believing it would fail so long as people came only to admire the buildings and went away without having laughed until their sides ached. I thought then, and I think now, that even the Pan-American had too much architecture — architecture which did not fulfil its mission — and too little of what makes for gaiety and good nature. The same thing is true of amusement parks. There are some of the latter in the eastern United States which, so far as conventional lines, surfaces, and layouts are concerned, have Luna Park easily beaten. But they are financial failures. Luna Park is not. Design sweetly beautiful buildings for a popular amusement place if you will, but do not let them be conventional.

The very word "amusement" should bring up ideas that are unconventional. The toys of our childhood were exaggerated, so far as lines and proportions were concerned; but they will ever be beautiful, although they were not architecturally designed. Grotesquely delightful, the picture-book buildings of the Golden Yesterday have become the amusement edifices of Iron Gray To-day. They were things of imagination, and so are the successful carnival spots which cater to our midsummer populaces. Only by making grown-ups children again (and they are really only boys and girls grown tall) can an amusement park be successful. To do this a spirit of frolic must be manufactured, and it cannot dwell where straight lines, dignified columns, and conventional forms predominate. Just as men and women are only elongated youngsters, so amusement parks are only adult toy-shops.

And who ever heard of T-squares in a toy-shop?

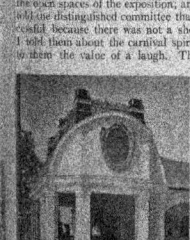

Entrance Arcade from Exposition Hall to Theater Café, Munich. Wilhelm Bertsch, Arch't.

Main Entrance, Dresden Exposition. Oswin Hempel, Architect.

Example of "Popular" Theater Architecture.

First Exposition Hall, Munich. Wilhelm Bertsch, Architect.

Artist Theater, Munich. Max Littmann, Architect.

Restaurant in Munich Exposition Park. Emanuel von Seidl, Architect.

Restaurant Building.

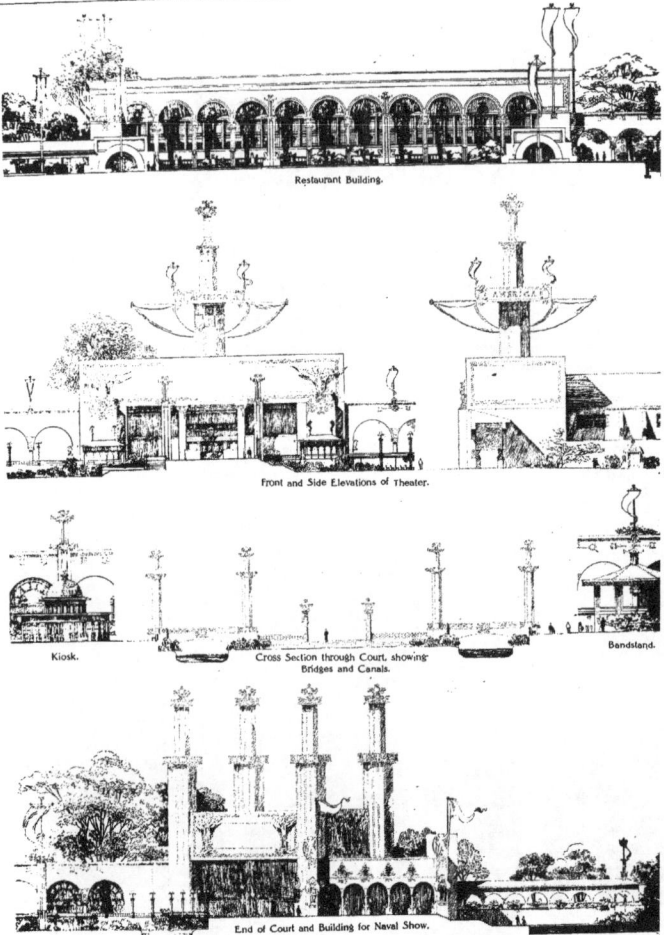

Front and Side Elevations of Theater.

Kiosk. Cross Section through Court, showing Bridges and Canals. Bandstand.

End of Court and Building for Naval Show.

ORIGINAL SKETCHES FOR BUILDINGS IN "ISLAND CITY," AN AMUSEMENT PARK NEAR PHILADELPHIA, PA.
LOUIS H. SULLIVAN, ARCHITECT.

MODERN ENGLISH CHURCHES

INTERNAL VIEW OF CHANCEL, CHURCH OF ST. COLUMBA, WANSTEAD SLIP, STRATFORD, E., ENGLAND.
EDWARD P. WARREN, ARCHITECT.

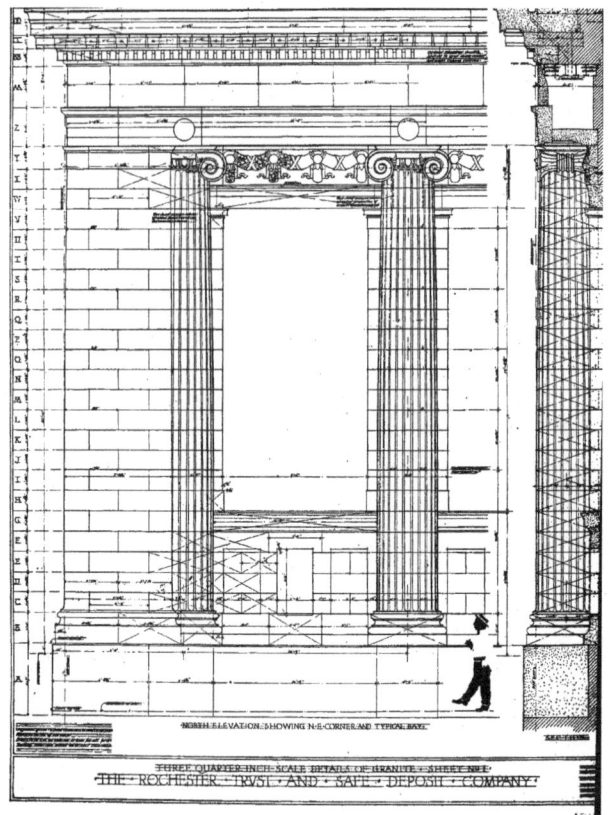

DETAIL OF EXTERIOR, ROCHESTER TRUST AND SAFE DEPOSIT COMPANY, ROCHESTER, N. Y.

YORK & SAWYER, ARCHITECTS.

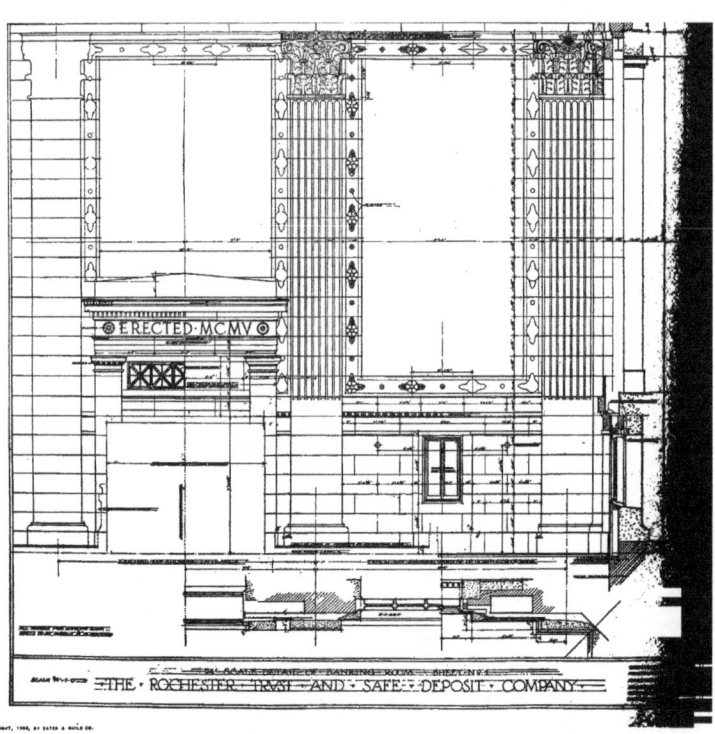

INTERIOR DETAILS, SHOWING PILASTERS, ROCHESTER TRUST AND SAFE DEPOSIT COMPANY, ROCHESTER, N. Y.
YORK & SAWYER, ARCHITECTS.

CEILING DETAILS, ROCHESTER TRUST AND SAFE DEPOSIT COMPANY, ROCHESTER, N. Y.
YORK & SAWYER, ARCHITECTS

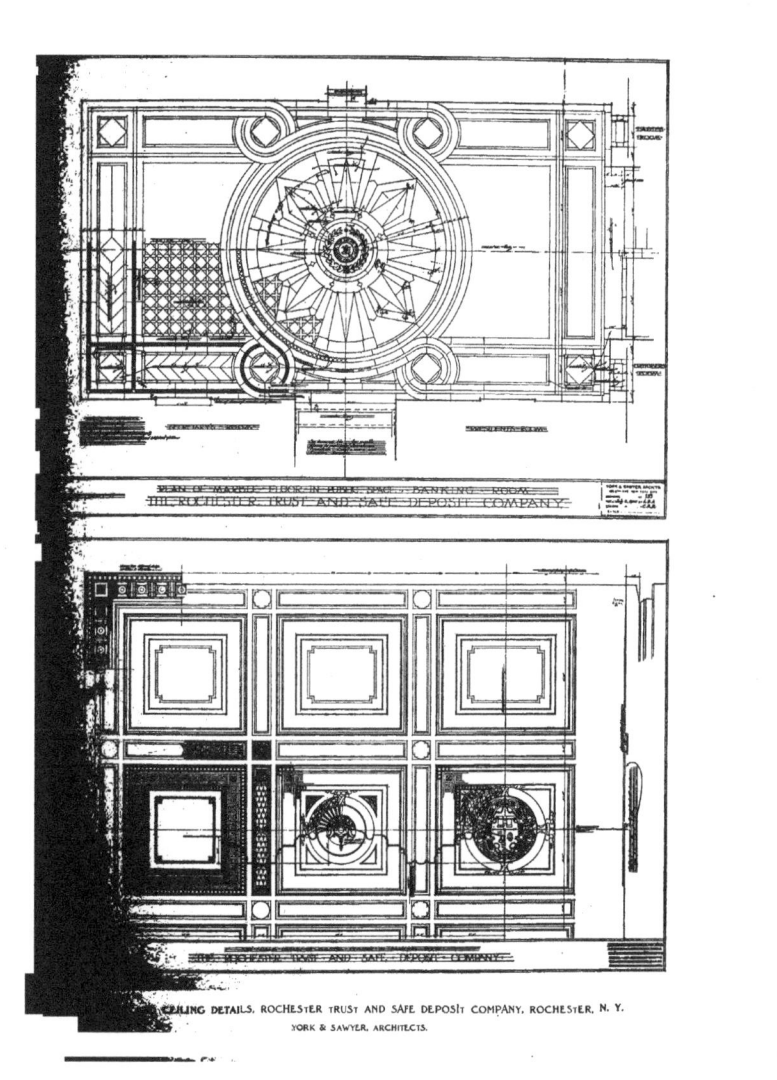

INTERIOR VIEW OF BANKING-ROOM, ROCHESTER TRUST AND SAFE DEPOSIT COMPANY, ROCHESTER, N. Y.
YORK & SAWYER, ARCHITECTS.

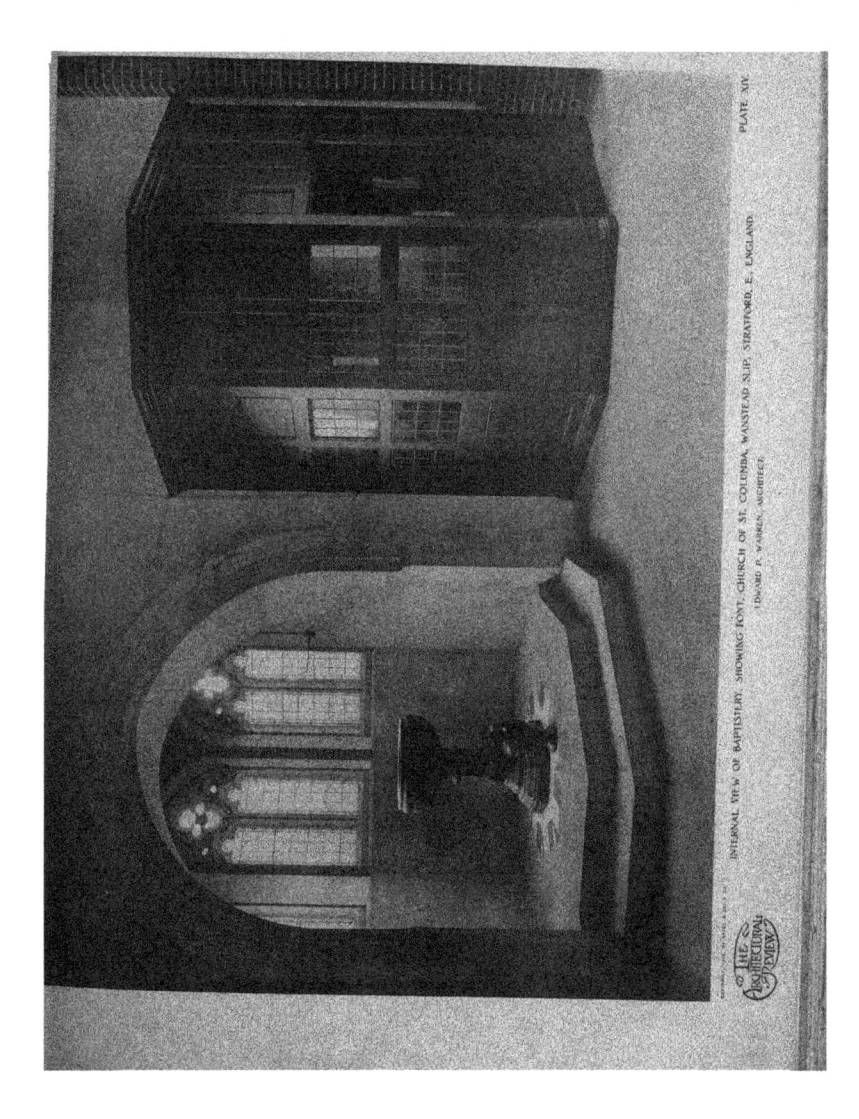

INTERNAL VIEW OF BAPTISTERY, SHOWING FONT, CHURCH OF ST. COLUMBA, WANSTEAD SLIP, STRATFORD, E., ENGLAND.
EDWARD P. WARREN, ARCHITECT.

PLATE XIV.

APARTMENT BUILDING, 925 PARK AVENUE, NEW YORK CITY. DELANO & ALDRICH, ARCHITECTS.
For typical floor plans see next page.

Current Periodicals
A Review of the Recent American And Foreign Architectural Publications

(From "The Brickbuilder.")
St. Catherine's Church, Somerville, Mass.
Maginnis, Walsh & Sullivan, Architects.

(From "The Western Architect.") 
Rosita Villa, Seattle, Wash.
Harlan Thomas, Architect.
(From "Architecture.")

(From "The American Architect.") 
First Congregational Church, Danbury, Conn.
Howells & Stokes, Architects.

"Studio Building," 44 E. 77th St., New York City.
(From "The Brickbuilder.")

"Front" on Streets.

"Inside View," Pavilion for Am. League Baseball Club, Philadelphia, Pa.
William Steele & Sons Co., Architects and Builders.

THE month of June will long be remembered in architectural circles as having witnessed the American publication of the choicest candidates that have yet appeared for our architectural " Chamber of Horrors." Where we have generally to go abroad to find really satisfying illustrations of what *not* to do in architecture, we can now point with a thrill of patriotic pride to these two examples of the real home-grown product. The first of these " Architectural Marvels of the New World " is, unfortunately, prominently located upon an open square in New York City, where its incrustated stalactical façade — yclept a " Studio Building," but that might be, as well, a Brobdingnagian reredos — would, we are sure, appear as amazing and exuberant to the builders of Canterbury, of Amiens, or of Cologne and Milan, as it does to us of these degenerate days. It is, of course, possible that some purists would prefer a return to conventional mediocrity and classic precedent rather than medieval and unconventional originality such as this! The remainder of the June issue of *Architecture* falls into comparative insignificance. We do recall, however, a rather crude appearing Y. M. C. A. building at Stamford, Conn., and Walker & Gillette's accepted design for the Golf Club at Greenwich, Conn., which we reproduce, along with the beautifully composed and rendered Envoi of the McKim Fellowship for " A Proposed School of Art and Archæology in Rome."

With considerable regret we find that the department of "Architectural Criticism," which started out so well in this same magazine a few months ago, has untimely fallen into the mediocre and conventional hands of a fully accredited, or common, " critic." No longer do the architects of the illustrated buildings criticize their own work, and the unnamed individual now performing that labor perforce sees the problem not from within, but from without. We can easily see this column next deteriorating into merest journalistic " puffs " of the buildings and architects concerned.

The Brickbuilder fathers the other ning example,— a really illuminating architectural dramatization of our native American phrase of " putting up a front"! the Baseball Park building that we refer shown in two views on this page, Philadelphia can now boast of a truly amazing architectural illustration of the word " sham." We digress to recall an historic incident occurring in a Massachusetts Town Meeting when, in a discussion of the town's attempt at municipal architecture, a citizen arose and characterized two of Brookline's well known architectural experiments as being in the one case (the Town Hall) " all back and no shirt " and in the other (a High School) " all shirt and no front"! The building just referred to belongs undoubtedly to the former of these two classifications.

The articles on "Gymnasiums," and " The Warming and Heating of Hospitals" continue. The plates illustrate — as it seems to us rather inadequately — Maginnis, Walsh & Sullivan's very notable Church of St. Catherine at Somerville. We reproduce a view that our readers may compare with the working drawings published in our issue for April, 1908. Certain of the designs reproduced in the "Terra-Cotta House *is cast-iron* Competition" (to which the remainder of the number is devoted) are artistically interesting, if occasionally somewhat " mannered." Two — or possibly three — of the houses printed might be built for upwards of $15,000; the remainder are residences impossible of construction by this time except at varying costs above $100,000. Apparently few competitors had even a bowing acquaintance with this type of problem. In our opinion it is hardly dignified, but a competition conducted in an age

House at Birmingham, Ala.
Warren & Welton, Architects.
(From "The American Architect.")

Accepted Design, Fairfield County Golf Club, Greenwich, Conn.
Walker & Gillette, Architects.
(From "Architecture.")

...magazine, to award prizes or mention designs so outrageously violating ...dition that, if established at all, ...be supposed to receive at least a ...moment's consideration at the ...of contestants *and* judges! Modestly hidden away on the last page ...same issue may be discovered a ...cut of an attractive schoolhouse in ...by Jenney, Mundie & Jensen — ...to the Somerville church, the best ...architecture illustrated.

...*Architectural Record* seems to ...drifting from the field of architec... magazines and giving its attention ...more popular (and, probably, more re...ative) field. The June number con...articles of such general interest as ...Selection of a Suburban Home ...Famous Châteaux of the Sarthe," ...ity's Architecture" — this latter ..., too, have been architecturally inter...if the photographs had been repro...at a less diminutive size! — and ...reproduction and criticism, as another ...series of "Architectural Aberra... of the same New York Studio ...ing we have just been admiring. An ... on the Boston ...politan Park Sys... fails to receive the ...it deserves from ...miniature size of the ...company...ing illustra..., apparently of a ...of picturesque ...attractive buildings ...bridges built for ...park purposes. ...ormer, particu...by Stickney & ...are certainly

deserving of better consideration in an architectural magazine. Mr. Claude Bragdon's series on "Architecture in the United States" is represented by "The Birth of Taste," and again the context suffers from the inadequate size and reproduction of the illustrations.

The American Architect during June still lingers southward, showing, June 2, a number of attractive cottages, including a charming house at Columbia, S. C., by Edwards & Walter; June 9, illustrating several more houses and an attractive and informal design by Warren & Welton, that we reproduce; on June 19, a number of schoolhouses in Atlanta and South Carolina, and several plates of Beaux-Arts student work; June 23, a new church at Danbury, Conn., by Howells & Stokes is illustrated, and, further, described under the somewhat ostentatious caption, "The Development of the Meeting-House." A comparison with "the real thing" in Colonial churches thus being invited, we feel no compunctions in criticizing, in this design, such jarring anachronisms as the French Renaissance interior treatment, the rock-face ashlar underpinning, the low and narrow course of marble at the spring of the window-arches, and (most of all to be regretted) the over-tall and "spindly" columns under the portico, the more notable by contrast with the too sturdy shafts upon the stories of the spire — all defects not to be found in good English Georgian or Colonial precedent!

Entrance in Courtyard, Ponce de Leon, St. Augustine.
Carrère & Hastings, Architects.
(From "The New York Architect.")

Residence of Robert K. Cassatt, Rosemont, Pa.
Cope & Stewardson, Architects.
(From "The New York Architect.")

Residence at Germantown, Pa.
Thomas, Churchman & Molitor, Architects.

Residence at Chestnut Hill, Pa.
Charles Barton Keen, Architect.
(From "The New York Architect.")

House at Bromley, Kent.
T. P. Figgis, F.R.I.B.A., Architect.

"Dormers," Bovingdon. Walter E. Hewitt, Architect.

House at Bromley, Kent.
T. P. Figgis, F.R.I.B.A., Architect.

June 30, a New York City house alteration with some rather painfully stiff Italianate interiors is illustrated. The frontispiece for June 9 shows a detail of Carrère & Hastings's Hotel Ponce de Leon at St. Augustine, that, seen in the company of its European associates, might easily pass as a real view in Granada — an illusion that the careless profusion of foliage growth helps to confirm. The series of "Notes from Europe" — seemingly now become a monthly department in this magazine — occurs on June 16.

The Western Architect publishes views of a dignified Court-house at White Plains, N. Y., by Lord & Hewlett; Peabody & Stearns' Union Trust Bank at Springfield, Mass.; the Senate Office Building at Washington, and some Washington and Seattle houses. From these we select a rather unusual type of apartment-house at Seattle.

Is it only a coincidence or an expression of the workings of the Law of Average that sees the publication of the Baseball Pavilion just mentioned (again reviving Philadelphia's reputation for having the ugliest architecture in the world!) and, in the same month, the number of *The New York Architect*— dated May — devoted to suburban residences of that same city? They include four individually successful — if somewhat over-familiar — houses by Wilson Eyre, Frank Miles Day, Charles Barton Keen, and Field & Medary. Less well known are houses by Thomas, Churchman & Molitor, Horace Wells Seller, and last — but certainly not least — Cope &

School of Art at Rome (Envoi of the McKim Fellowship).
Lucian E. Smith, Holder, 1905-07.

Stewardson's house for Mr. Cassatt at Rosemont. The latt along with Cram, Goodhue & Ferguson's John Nicolas B house at Newport — is the best French Mansart *Châteauesque* sign we know. All in all, this issue is doubly welcome as publication's first declaration for American ideals in architect

The English *Architectural Review* prints the new Self "American Department Store" in London — exteriorly show these columns in May — and an attractive group of cottage Silcock & Reay, that gests one means of viding for working that might be advan in semi-suburban tions in America.

The Builder's prints some of th portions (recently veiled) of the Victoria Memorial (on July 9), at scale, drawings o Middleborough Schools comp This magazine, as *The Builder*, duces various att cottage sketches, an latter some of the plans for the National Library of Wale on June 12 a notable drawing of "a bridge for a commercial

The Architect for June 4 prints a competitive design f Cornwall Country Offices, several buildings at Khartoum the very attractive perspective of Walter E. Hewitt's "Dor that we reprint. On June 18 appear some individual studi houses in the Hampstead Garden Suburb by different well-l English architects; and (on June 12) *La Construction Mode* prints some Bourneville cottages.

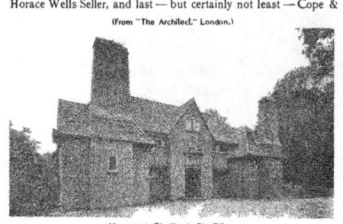

House at Chalfont, St. Giles.
Forbes & Tate, Architects.

Quadrangle, Churchill Cottage Homes, Somerset.
Silcock & Reay, Architects.

Study for Coykendall Mausoleum.

Study for Coykendall Mausoleum.

Sketch for Office Bldg., Buffalo, N.Y.

Sketches for Candelabra.

will be bettered or improved upon. The plan is invariably as thoroughly studied as the façade; and so it always accords with the architectural expression of the structure rising above it. Always it is simple, always it is direct; always, too, it offers effective opportunity to realize the spaciousness and architectural scale of the interior. The two or three President's and Directors' rooms illustrated are quite as dignified in scale, and quite as reserved and simple in expression, as the more important public portions of these same banking institutions.

The Riggs Bank in Washington we published some time ago, and therefore show it only in its newer relation to the American Security and Trust Building,—perhaps the best expressed banking structure in America,— to which, having been already partially illustrated, we do not give the space it otherwise worthily deserves.

Besides those banks where the order has been used with a magnificence truly Roman, and with a restraint as truly Greek, the sturdy simplicity of such brick buildings as the Settlement House and the New York Juvenile School are even more widely interesting for their fresh and individual use of a material that has become, merely by its universal employment, banal and commonplace.

Sketch Elevation for Bank, Babylon, L. I.

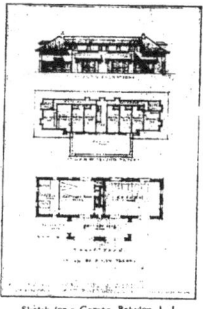

Sketch for a Garage, Babylon, L. I.

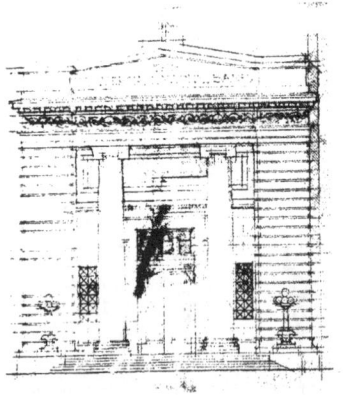

Study for the National Commercial Bank, Albany, N. Y.

Study for the National Commercial Bank, Albany, N. Y.

Study for a Two-story Bank Building.

Study for a Three-story Bank Building.

INTERIOR VIEW FROM BEHIND RECEPTION-ROOM SCREEN, ROCHESTER TRUST AND SAFE DEPOSIT COMPANY, ROCHESTER, N. Y.
YORK & SAWYER, ARCHITECTS.

Preliminary Sketch for Broadway Savings Bank.

Perspective View, Office Bldg. for General Electric Co., Buffalo, N. Y.

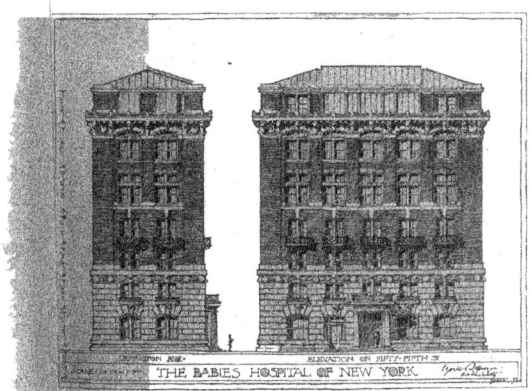

Preliminary Elevation, The Babies' Hospital of New York.

Study for a New York House.

Riggs Bank, Washington, D. C.

Broadway Savings Bank, New York City.

Provident Savings Bank, Baltimore, Md.

National Commercial Bank, Albany, N. Y.

BRONZE LAMP STANDARDS, YORK & SAWYER, ARCHITECTS.

Detail of Entrance, National Commercial Bank, Albany, N. Y.    Detail of Entrance, Provident Savings Bank, Baltimore, Md.

Doorway in Screen, Rochester Savings Bank, Rochester, N. Y.    Entrance Grille, Broadway Savings Bank, New York City.
BRONZE DOORS AND DOORWAYS, YORK & SAWYER, ARCHITECTS.

Entrance Front.

Rear View.

CATHEDRAL SCHOOL, WASHINGTON, D. C.   YORK & SAWYER, ARCHITECTS.

General View.

Detail of Entrance.

Detail of End Gable.

SCHOOL BUILDING, N. Y. JUVENILE ASYLUM, DOBBS FERRY, N. Y.   YORK & SAWYER, ARCHITECTS.

RIGGS NATIONAL BANK AND END OF AMERICAN SECURITY AND TRUST COMPANY, WASHINGTON, D. C.
YORK & SAWYER, ARCHITECTS

MODERN ENGLISH CHURCHES

SOUTHEAST VIEW, CHURCH OF ST. MICHAEL AND ALL ANGELS, BASSET, NEAR SOUTHAMPTON, ENGLAND.

PLATE XVII.

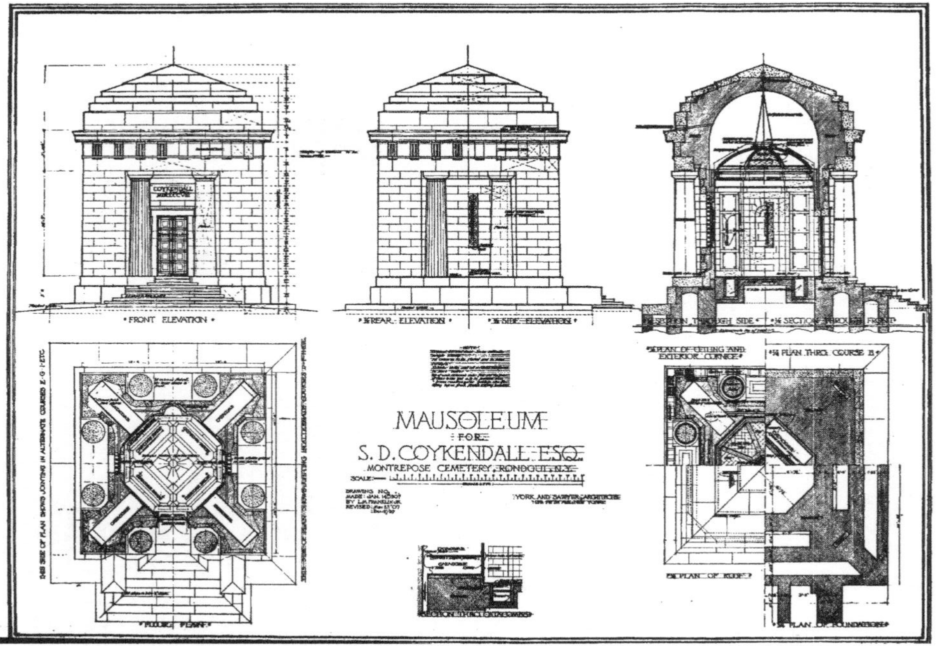

FRONT ELEVATION
REAR ELEVATION
SIDE ELEVATION
SECTION THROUGH SIDE
SECTION THROUGH FRONT
PLAN OF CEILING AND EXTERIOR CORNICE
PLAN THRO. COURSE B
PLAN OF ROOF
PLAN OF FOUNDATIONS
FLOOR PLAN
THIS SIDE OF PLAN SHOWS JOINTING IN ALTERNATE COURSES E-G-I-ETC.
MAUSOLEUM
FOR
S. D. COYKENDALL ESQ.
MONTREPOSE CEMETERY, RONDOUT, N.Y.
SCALE
YORK AND SAWYER ARCHITECTS
COYKENDALL

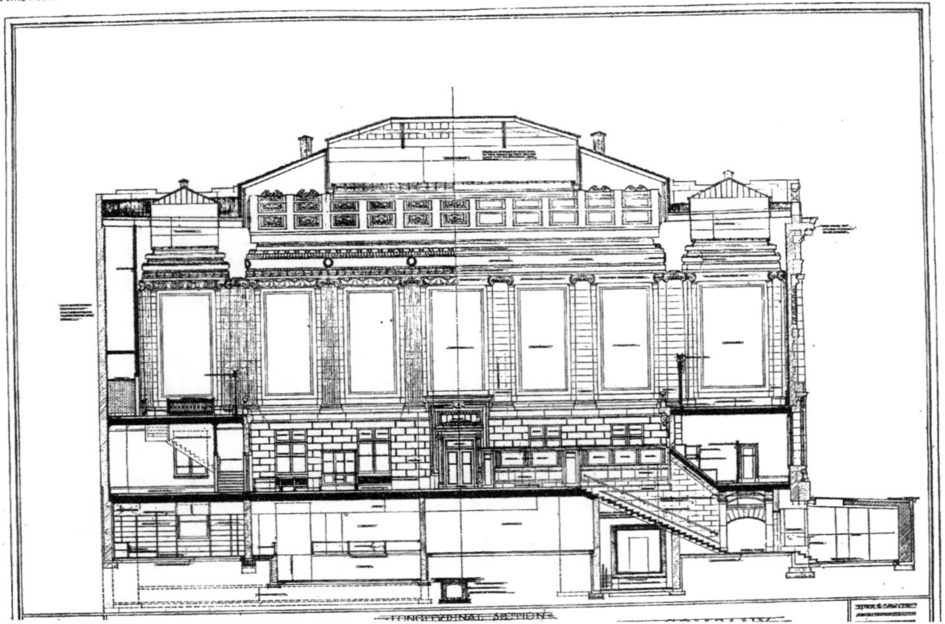

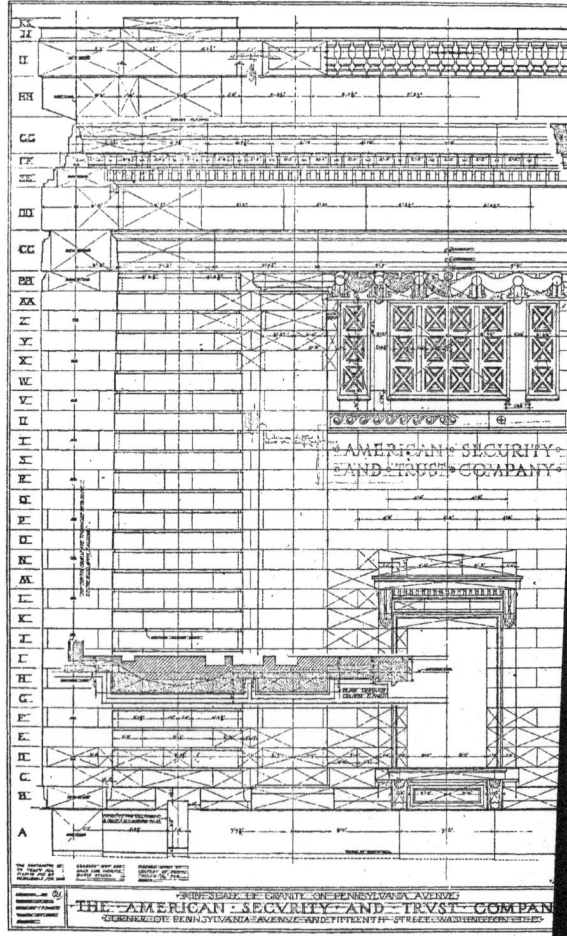

SCALE DRAWING, CORNER BAY, AMERICAN SECURITY AND TRUST COMPANY, WASHINGTON,
YORK & SAWYER, ARCHITECTS.

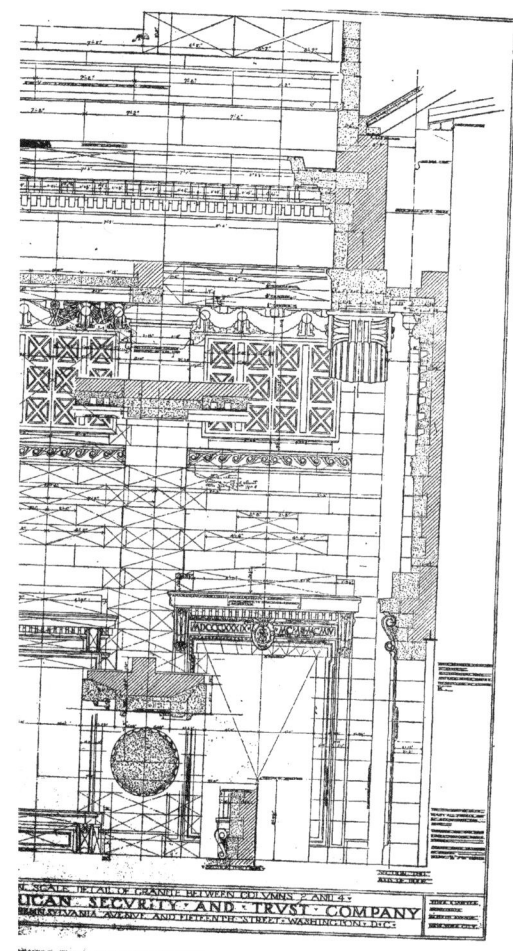

CENTER BAYS, AMERICAN SECURITY AND TRUST COMPANY, WASHINGTON, D. C.
YORK & SAWYER, ARCHITECTS.

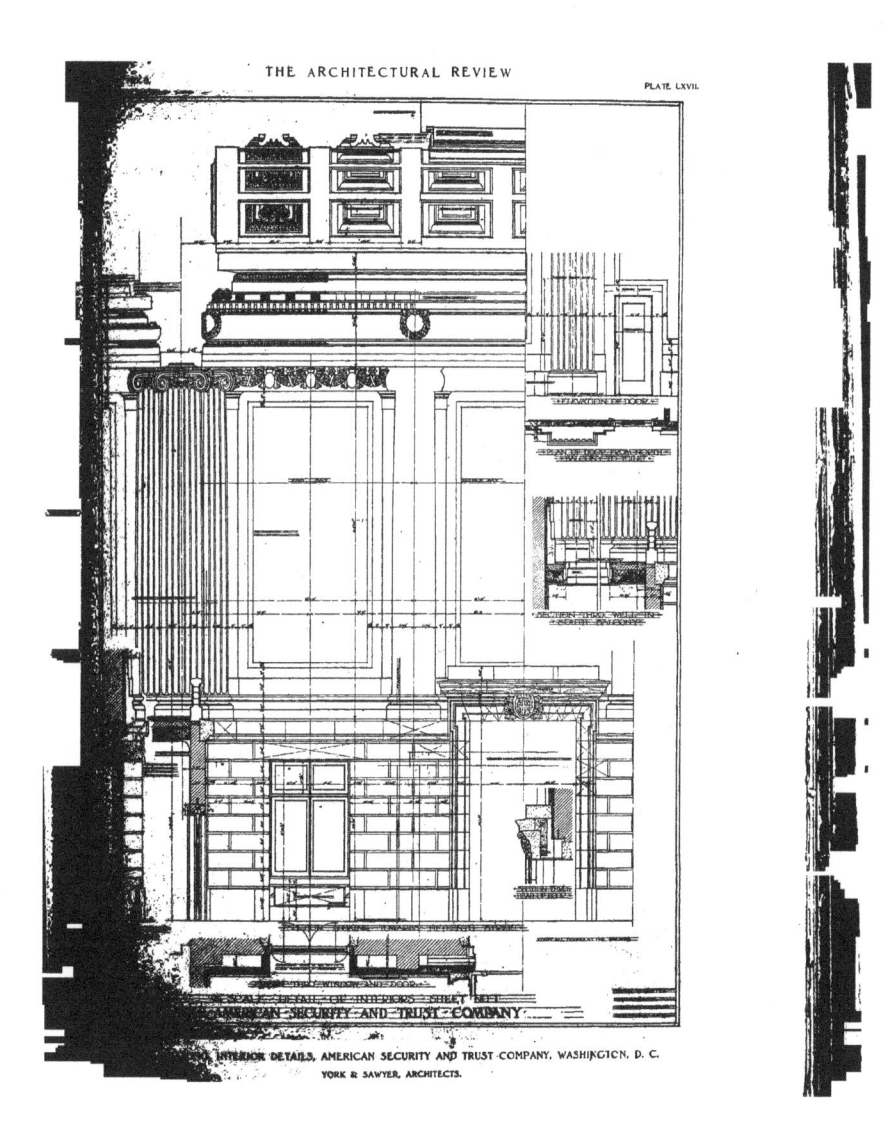

INTERIOR DETAILS, AMERICAN SECURITY AND TRUST COMPANY, WASHINGTON, D. C.
YORK & SAWYER, ARCHITECTS.

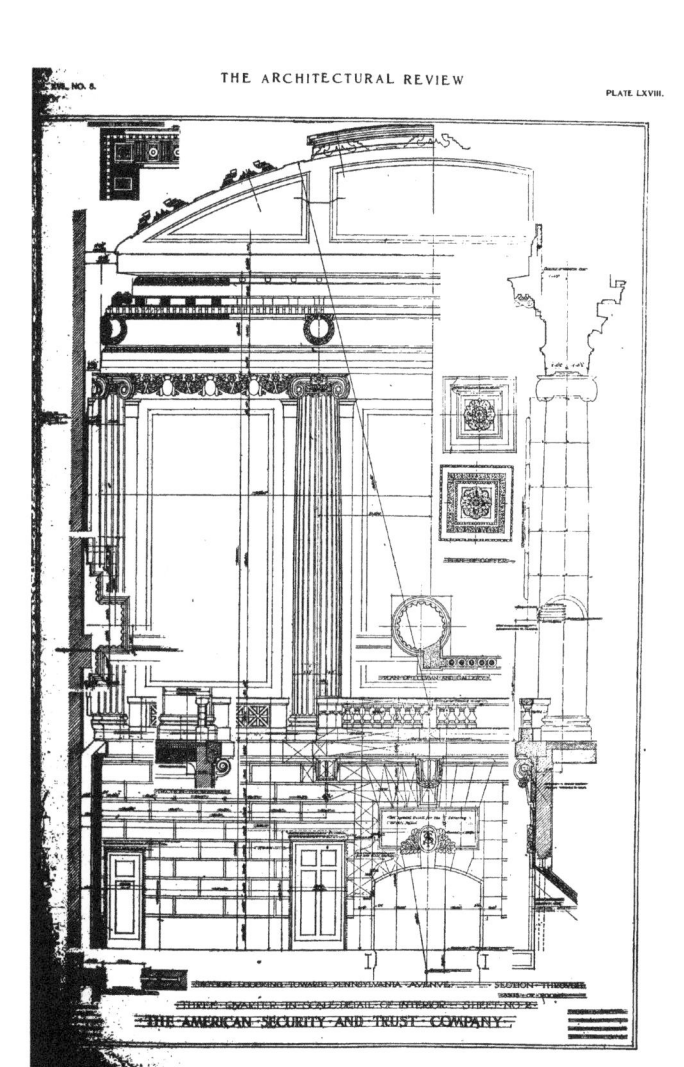

SCALE DRAWING OF END, AMERICAN SECURITY AND TRUST COMPANY, WASHINGTON, D. C.

YORK & SAWYER, ARCHITECTS.

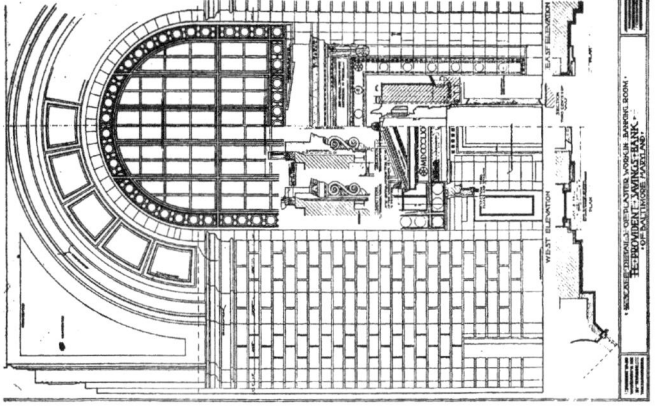

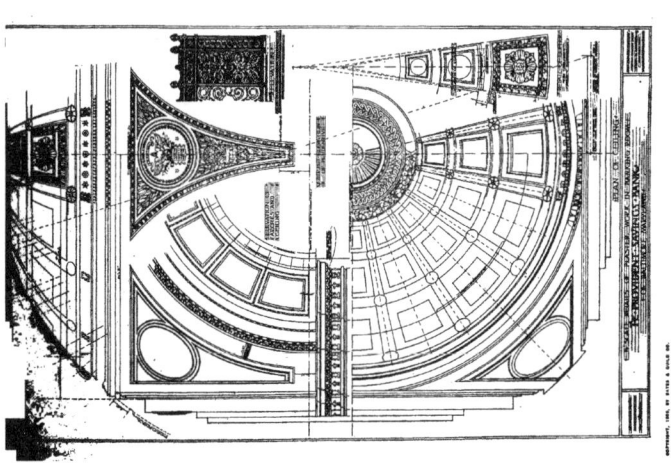

DETAILS, INTERIOR AND CEILING, PROVIDENT SAVINGS BANK, BALTIMORE, MD.
YORK & SAWYER AND JOSEPH EVANS SPERRY, ASSOCIATE ARCHITECTS.

MODERN ENGLISH CHURCHES

CHANCEL, LOOKING TOWARDS ORGAN, CHURCH OF ST. MICHAEL AND ALL ANGELS, BASSET, NEAR SOUTHAMPTON, ENGLAND
EDWARD P. WARREN, ARCHITECT

PLATE XVIII.

EXTERIOR, AMERICAN SECURITY AND TRUST COMPANY, WASHINGTON, D. C.
YORK & SAWYER, ARCHITECTS

DETAIL, END PAVILION AND ORDER, AMERICAN SECURITY AND TRUST COMPANY, WASHINGTON, D. C.
YORK & SAWYER, ARCHITECTS.

PROVIDENT SAVINGS BANK, BALTIMORE, MD.
YORK & SAWYER AND JOSEPH EVANS SPERRY, ASSOCIATE ARCHITECTS

INTERIOR, LOOKING TOWARD ENTRANCE OF SAFE DEPOSIT VAULTS, AMERICAN SECURITY
AND TRUST COMPANY, WASHINGTON, D. C.
YORK & SAWYER, ARCHITECTS.

INTERIOR, NATIONAL COMMERCIAL BANK, ALBANY, N. Y.
YORK & SAWYER, ARCHITECTS

INTERIOR AND VESTIBULE, ENTRANCE DOORWAY, PROVIDENT SAVINGS BANK, BALTIMORE, MD.
YORK & SAWYER AND JOSEPH EVANS SPERRY, ASSOCIATE ARCHITECTS

ENTRANCE AND VESTIBULE TO SAFE DEPOSIT VAULTS, AMERICAN SECURITY AND TRUST COMPANY, WASHINGTON, D. C.
YORK & SAWYER, ARCHITECTS

MANTEL IN PRESIDENT'S ROOM NATIONAL COMMERCIAL BANK, ALBANY, N. Y. DIRECTORS' ROOM
BOSS & SAWYER, ARCHITECTS

SETTLEMENT HOUSE, TENTH AVE. AND FIFTIETH ST., NEW YORK CITY.
YORK & SAWYER, ARCHITECTS.

The Architectural Review

VOLUME XVI. NUMBER 8

AUGUST, 1909

BATES & GUILD COMPANY, Publishers
42 Chauncy Street, Boston
NEW YORK OFFICE, PARK ROW BUILDING

Published monthly. Price, mailed flat to any address in the United States or Canada, five dollars per annum, in advance; to any foreign address, six dollars per annum, in advance. Subscriptions begin with the issue following their receipt. Single copies, fifty cents. Special numbers, two dollars. Entered as second-class mail-matter at the Post-office, Boston, Massachusetts, November 27, 1891.

PLATES

PLATE LXI.— FAÇADE OF THE NATIONAL COMMERCIAL BANK, ALBANY, N. Y. (RENDERING IN COLOR BY P. J. ROCKER)— YORK & SAWYER, ARCHITECTS.

PLATE LXII.— MAUSOLEUM FOR S. D. COYKENDALL, ESQ., RONDOUT, N. Y. (PLANS AND ELEVATIONS)— YORK & SAWYER, ARCHITECTS.

PLATES LXIII.-LXVIII.— BUILDING FOR THE AMERICAN SECURITY & TRUST COMPANY, WASHINGTON, D. C. (ELEVATIONS, SECTIONS AND DETAILS)— YORK & SAWYER, ARCHITECTS.

PLATE LXIX.— THE PROVIDENT SAVINGS BANK, BALTIMORE, MD. (DETAILS, INTERIOR AND CEILING)— YORK & SAWYER, AND JOSEPH EVANS SPERRY, ASSOCIATE ARCHITECTS.

PLATE LXX.— THE NATIONAL COMMERCIAL BANK, ALBANY, N. Y. (PHOTOGRAPHIC VIEW)— YORK & SAWYER, ARCHITECTS.

WHAT'S in a name, indeed? Even the prehistoric genius who first invented this conundrum might have had cause to wonder had he been in attendance at the last convention of the Architectural League in Detroit; where many, many words were given to a discussion as to whether or no the League should accept the "atelier system," in conjunction with the Beaux-Arts problems, for its educational work. Pray, why all this waste of energy and time? Of what, in its essentials, does the "atelier system" consist? Merely in the study of similar problems, by beginners as well as by men advanced in design, working side by side in groups or studios — neither more nor less than this! Certainly, these requirements are all met by the conditions that actually exist in the office of any architect of importance. If a lack of atmosphere, of prestige, or of precedent is still to be bewailed, this, too, can be provided in notable and individual instances. H. H. Richardson, for example, had an office where many future architects were bred and schooled, chief among them being F. McKim and Stanford White, who in their turn have conducted an "atelier" where further scores of architects have been and are being taught and schooled; for, lo, these many years, to-day the office of McKim, Mead & White, for instance, would provide all the above necessary accessories; with the addition of a practical experience in schooling in the handling and solution of American problems that could never be obtained in years of residence and study abroad. Already the best recognized architects practising throughout the country are proud to claim any affiliation with this American "atelier"! If it is the name rather than the method that offends our loyal western-Americans, they have but to suggest an acceptable Anglican synonym. Cannot the existing system, practised under any other name, be made to sound as well?

PROBABLY neither of the two principal factions who have carried on so long the merry war of words in regard to the advantages of the various methods of architectural instruction destined to achieve an immediate victory; yet of the many rivals arguing pro and con, how many stop to realize the radical differences in the conditions existing in France and in America? In France it is practically impossible to obtain any recognized architectural education save at the one Government School. Graduates of this school, as they enter into the practice of the profession, do so under customs diametrically different from those customary in England, and from those that have become established in America. The practice of the French architect, no matter how distinguished he may be, is restricted to a few buildings, and he has under way at the same time probably only one or, at the most, two important structures.

There is no opportunity in France for an untrained draughtsman to obtain a good position in an architect's office of established reputation, and learn by practical experience the practice of the profession. There is no office in France — or for that matter in England — of the size of any one of a score of firms that could be named in this country who, probably any one of them, carry out in a year an amount of work that would suffice to last their continental colleague for the space of his business life.

The American School of Architecture, as such, does not exist. Nor do the numerous colleges where the art of the designing of buildings may be formally studied as a part of the regular curriculum in any sense take the place of the French School of Fine Arts, although such is their evident ambition and intent. The American school for the study of architecture has been, and doubtless long will remain, in those architectural offices throughout the United States where the practice of building-design is regarded as an art rather than a mere business.

An architect has to be born; he cannot be manufactured by any machinery yet known. But any method of study — called by whatever name — tending to develop a latent artistic sense will be the more valuable to the student and the more successful by its teachers the nearer it parallels the conditions existing (or the ideal conditions that may exist) and the methods employed in the offices of the best architects of the country. This fact is so obvious that the Architectural League would better "get together" on practical ways and means, instead of fighting windmills and bogies that do not exist outside their excited and supersensitive imaginations!

IT is possibly one of the defects of architectural schooling, as current in this country and abroad, that a perhaps too exclusive attention is given to educating the eye at the expense of the mind, to acquiring a merely manual dexterity instead of an ability to analyze clearly and comprehensively from the real basic facts of a problem. One result is to be noted in the architect depending almost altogether on the pictures in the current professional magazines, rather than bothering to read thoroughly the accompanying text.

It is useless to make a flippant and utterly obvious retort. The fact remains that, from constant custom, the architect has adopted the standpoint of the child, and prefers a "picture-book" to almost any other toy. One evidence is in their preference for studying the elevation rather than the plan — the one being a merely pictorial presentation, the other expressing the very bases and groundwork of the entire problem and the means of its solution. While that purely practical sense that is fortunately lacking in few of Anglo-Saxon heritage has so far prevented our architecture from going far astray, yet it is an undoubted danger in the practice of the profession to disregard practical considerations and too exclusively consider everything from a purely æsthetic point of view. This is as short-sighted as it is injurious to constant growth and development. Progress in the study of plan arrangements, definite advance in the knowledge of practical accessories, are disregarded for the study of what are, after all, but transitory and passing decorative fads. Ornamental moldings and other purely decorative non-essentials are rapidly assimilated into our local architecture throughout the country, while more practical improvements remain disregarded, or are passed by unseen. Instead of the architect being first a well-developed and thoroughly balanced individual of culture, he is more likely to be an unbalanced eccentric whose personality has been developed in one direction at the expense of that sanity of view-point that has become most essential for the right solution of the purely commercial problems that are yearly assuming more importance in the architectural growth of America.

Current Periodicals
A Review of the Recent American And Foreign Architectural Publications

Stafford Little Hall, Princeton University.
Cope & Stewardson, Architects.

View down the Proposed Campus Axis, Princeton University.
Ralph Adams Cram, Supervising Architect.

Seventy-Nine Dormitory, Princeton.
Cram, Goodhue & Ferguson, Architects.

THE *American Architect*, dean of the American architectural magazines, and conducted for years with an independent and definite editorial policy, has fallen at last into the innocuous desuetude of that sincerest flattery— imitation of these poor columns; hitherto, at least, all our own! THE ARCHITECTURAL REVIEW inaugurated its department of "Current Periodicals" twelve years ago this month. Last October we were flattered — somewhat measurably! — to find this same magazine had borrowed from us that part of these columns given to the review of the foreign architectural magazines. Not satisfied to stop there, this imitation has now been extended to include the remainder of this department; and — in the issue for July 7 — it has gone to such heights of sincerity as attempting employment of the identical and characteristic vocabulary here familiar to our readers. But even this was not enough! Not only were we complimented by imitation; but we were also, and in this very same issue, damned by misrepresentation; — our name being misplaced (with the most careful assumption of carelessness imaginable!) under one of *The Architectural Record's* typical illustrations. This final straw breaks not our back, but our silence; until we protest, with Marc Antony, "This was the most unkindest *cut* of all!"

Besides "borrowing the 'Knocker Department' of THE REVIEW," as one architect in writing us has phrased it, *The American Architect* for

Governor's Room, New York City Hall.
Restoration by Grosvenor Atterbury, Architect.
(From "The New York Architect.")

July 7 illustrates the restored Governor's room in the New York City Hall, and a number of views of St. Augustine architecture by Carrère & Hastings. While the majority of this work has been illustrated many times, it is instructive to see it once again gathered together in this way, and to find now that the lapse of some years has provided the proper natural surroundings, how permanently effective it has become.

July 14 Mr. P. Thornton Marye's Birmingham terminal station is illustrated by working drawings and photographs. We reprint a general view of the exterior. One of the most interesting details of this structure is the concrete train-sheds.

July 21 appears an article on the development of Princeton University, by Ralph Adams Cram, supervising architect for the institution. It appears from the photographs (from which we select a couple as particularly interesting views for reproduction) that this University is fortunate in having already acquired a number of buildings sufficiently in the same style to add a considerable cumulative architectural effect when viewed from the University grounds. The plan shows the individual quadrangular development customary in English colleges in place of the common campus ordinarily adopted in American institutions.

The last issue for the month (July 28) contains "Notes from Europe" (the review of "Foreign Periodicals" referred to!), and the plates show several buildings at Atlanta, Ga., from which we

Building for Hon. Hoke Smith, Atlanta, Ga.
Harry Leslie Walker, Architect.

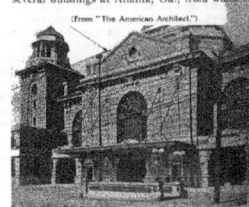

Milbank Bldg., New York City.
Geo. B. Post & Sons, Architects.

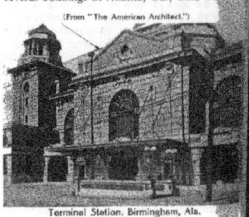

Terminal Station, Birmingham, Ala.
P. Thornton Marye, Architect.

Central Court, Alaska-Yukon-Pacific Exposition, Seattle, Wash.
Howard & Galloway, Architects. Olmsted Bros., Landscape Architects.

Central Court and Geyser Basin, Alaska-Yukon-Pacific Exposition.
Howard & Galloway, Architects. Olmsted Bros., Landscape Architects.

select the design for a commercial building by Harry Leslie Walker that accompanies these remarks.

The Western Architect, appropriately enough, is the first architectural paper to properly illustrate the Seattle Exposition, the illustrations of which it accompanies by other work in the same city. Besides the several photographs of exposition work, we note, as of particular interest, an apartment hotel by Somervell & Coté.

The July *Architectural Record* illustrates the completed building for the Chicago University Club by Holabird & Roche. With the exterior our readers should be familiar from its previous illustration (in May, 1908) in these columns. The interiors are, in the main, more successful in such similar rooms as the library, or the second-floor reception, and private rooms, where Gothic forms have been largely cast aside, than in such other interiors as the lounging and main dining rooms, where they become nervously predominant. Far and away the best interior shown is the rather naively titled — as though attempting rather to forestall criticism on the last count — "typical bedroom of the club, completely furnished"! This room, in restraint in treatment and furnishing, is a model for house-holders to study. The furniture is, throughout, commendably simple, and conservatively based on English motives, while most thoroughly to be commended is the very excellent series of decorative treatments by Mr. Frederick Clay Bartlett, whose window-designs in the great dining-hall are particularly to be remarked.

The Seattle Exposition is again described, and illustrated (?) so inadequately that we can only reprint one from the number of buildings shown. The house at Santa Monica that we published last month in these columns is de-

Manufacturers' Bldg. and Formal Garden, Alaska-Yukon-Pacific Exposition.
Howard & Galloway, Architects. Olmsted Bros., Landscape Architects.

California Building, Alaska-Yukon-Pacific Exposition.
Sellon & Hemind, California State Architects.

scribed, and its architectural style here courageously labeled as "the style of Felix Peano"!

Mr. Claude Bragdon's second article on "Architecture in the United States" deals with "The Growth of Taste," the beginnings of which the author credits to the World's Columbian Exposition in Chicago, in 1893. An article on Italian Gothic in New York lacks interest from inadequate illustration, and the final paper deals with the architect during the dark ages in history.

The July *Brickbuilder* contains an interesting article by Mr. Lindeberg, of Albro & Lindeberg, explaining, by photographs and diagrams, how the effect of a thatched roof may be obtained in shingles. We only fear that this exposition is too likely to be followed by a "flood of roofs" of this extremely picturesque character that, in the overwhelming majority of cases, will be most consistently misapplied.

The articles on "Warming and Ventilating of Hospitals" and "The Housing Problem" continue. The plates illustrate Lord & Hewlett's Masonic Temple at Brooklyn (which we reproduced in these columns from *Architecture* three months ago) that here show in detail the means by which an exceptionally effective monumental structure has been produced. One is rather inclined to remark that, if the effect of scale obtained by grouping the brick courses in pairs by means of an exceptionally wide joint between each two rows of brick was worth while, the same treatment should have been continued — at the cost of a little further ingenuity — in the arch courses occurring over the window-openings behind the colonnade (we presume we should say the "fourth story window-openings," but the matter of stories in this structure is so effectively obscured that it is difficult to determine on what

Agricultural Bldg., Alaska-Yukon-Pacific Exposition.
Howard & Galloway, Archts. Graham & Myers, Associate Archts.

Knickerbocker Trust Co., New York.
McKim, Mead & White, Architects.

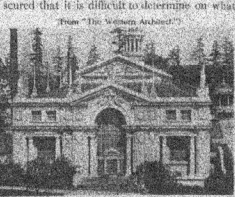

Oriental Bldg., Alaska-Yukon-Pacific Exposition.
Howard & Galloway, Archts. Bebb & Mendel, Associate Archts.

floor these arches actually occur!).

The attempt by Wood, Donn & Deming at a building for similar purposes, published in the same number, suffers by contrast. Where the one is virile, bold, and commanding of attention, the other appears cold, featureless, and conventional. None of these latter adjectives can be truthfully applied to Messrs. Olds & Puckey's Jewish Synagogue at Wilkesbarre, Penn. Starting with a distinctively Persian doorway in terra-cotta, and the lofty "minaret" so inseparable from Eastern religious architecture, the architects have designed a building of considerable originality in the handling of brickwork that makes for variety and for interest; although we feel that the minarets are not properly in scale with the remainder of the design, nor are they properly joined onto or combined with it. Newhall & Blevins' Malden Odd Fellows Building has two upper stories of such considerable interest that it is to be regretted that inspiration did not last long enough to cause the lower two better to conform with them, when an unusually successful commercial building might result.

Architecture for July still continues its department of "Architectural Criticism," though now fallen from its former high estate. A number of attractive "bungalows" (*sic!*) by Aymar Embury, II; several buildings for the Jewish Protector and Aid Society at Hawthorne, N. Y.; the officers' rooms and exterior of the Knickerbocker Trust Co. 60 Broadway, by McKim, Mead & White, architects; Lord & Hewlett's Masonic Temple; and Westchester County Court-house, White Plains, N. Y., both the latter of which have been published in other magazines within the last two or three months, are the most interesting plates in the number. We reprint a detail of the lower stories (or first completed portion) of the Knickerbocker Trust Co. The old Hunnewell Gardens at Wellesley are also shown by several text photographs.

The New York Architect (for June) publishes views of the Paris Opera Comique, the remainder of the number being given to buildings (both old and new) by George B. Post & Sons. Of the work illustrated in the plates nothing now demands reproduction here; but from one of the advertising pages we reprint an attractive study for a New York office building.

In the English *Architectural Review*, the articles on "Constantinople Mosques" continue. The department of "Current Architecture" prints a country house at Whitfield, Derbyshire; and Sir Aston Webb's additions to the Victoria and Albert Museum, of which we reproduce the most interesting portion, the main entrance on Cromwell Road. We also find room for a charming alteration to obtain an appropriate entrance for a small banking institution in an old house on Euston Road. Prof. Beresford Pite's attractive use of color in this design is to be noted. It is also in other ways an unconventionally brilliant little *tour-de-force*.

The last number of *The Builder* for June prints several of the designs submitted in competition for the National Library of Wales. July 3 it also prints a number of views of the new Victoria and Albert Musum and (on July 10) several Montreal buildings. We reprint McKim, Mead & White's additions to the Bank of Montreal and the façade for the Mount Royal Club. On July 24 appeared the perspective for the quaint church at Lythe by Walter J. Tapper, that we reproduce.

The Architect for July 2 and 9 also prints views of the Victoria and Albert Museum. The latter issue contains competitive designs for the Middlesbrough Public Library, which showing is continued in the issue for July 16. H. P. Burke Downing's Wimbledon school is illustrated July 16 and 23.

The Builder's Journal prints, July 7, some views of Birmingham University, by Sir Aston Webb and E. Ingress Bell; July 14, an article on work of Ernest Newton and July 30, the Victoria and Albert Museum and designs for the National Library of Wales.

A glass marquise, by M. R. Binet, and a "Hôtel" on the Rue Raynouard, Paris, by M. G. Bellettre, are illustrated in *La Construction Moderne* for July.

Bank of Montreal, Montreal, Canada.
McKim, Mead & White, Architects.
(From "The Builder," London.)

Mount Royal Club, Montreal, Canada.
McKim, Mead & White, Architects.

New Bank Front, Euston Road.
Prof. Beresford Pite, Architect.
(From "The Architect," London.)

Main Entrance, Victoria and Albert Museum.
Sir Aston Webb, R. A., C. B., Architect.

Pelham School, Wimbledon.
H. P. Burke Downing, F. R. I. B. A., Architect.

Lythe Church, Yorkshire.
Walter J. Tapper, A. R. I. B. A., Architect.

EXTERIOR, THE NATIONAL COMMERCIAL BANK, ALBANY, N. Y.
YORK & SAWYER, ARCHITECTS.

The Architectural Review

Volume XVI   September, 1909   Number 9

The Hotel Meurice, Paris

By George B. Ford

THERE is one hotel in Paris which is intended exclusively for Americans, and though it is only recently completed, yet true to its intention, ninety-five per cent of its guests thus far have been Americans.

This hotel was built by a French architect, Monsieur Nenot, for a French company, and as such it should be interesting to see how a French architect would cater to American taste. We might expect to find a hotel which savored somewhat of the architecture of the better known New York hotels, but when we come to examine this hotel — the Hotel Meurice on the Rue de Rivoli in Paris — we find a building very distinctly French in its whole interior treatment. The exterior has, of course, to conform to the style set for the façades of the Rue de Rivoli, and therefore gave the architect no play whatsoever. In the interior, however, we find, as the photographs will show, a great deal of interest in the decorative treatment of the various rooms. The general style of its treatment is Louis XVI, handled in a free and large manner.

The building opens through from street to street, a depth of some two hundred fifteen feet, between party-walls some hundred feet apart, in a series of large salons, halls, and galleries.

The two interior halls — one on the Rivoli side, called Rivoli Hall, and the other toward the rear street, called the Mont-Thabor Hall — are lighted by skylights. All the other rooms receive borrowed or artificial light.

On entering from under the Rue de Rivoli Arcade we find ourselves in a large octagonal vestibule in white limestone. The photograph of this shows one side, containing a white marble statue. The floor is also of white marble, with y-green strips dividing it into three-foot squares, all with a red Verona border. In the center is a large yellow and red rug. This room is lighted by a central brass chandelier.

To the left we pass into the stair-hall, which, similarly to the vestibule, is in white limestone. In the well of the stairs is a plunger elevator upholstered in gray. This is gilded bronze, as is also the stair-rail and balcony-rail on the Mezzanine floor above. A feature is made of potted palms in the corners of the room.

A stair leads down to the American bar in the basement, this bar being a special and popular feature of the hotel, though architecturally of no great interest.

From the stair-hall we pass directly ahead into a writing-room which is lighted only by artificial light, or by borrowed light coming through great windows set in brass, opening into the Rivoli Hall. The room is treated uniformly in a Louis XVI gray, with no gilt except on the doors and the lamps and luster. The three decorative panels of a fête at Fontainebleau are in soft gray blues, with a little orange. The whole tone of the room is chaste and refined and in excellent taste.

We pass out from this into the Rivoli Hall — a room some forty-five by forty feet. This is all in white limestone, with a ceiling of sanded glass in a frame of white iron with gilded leaf ornament about the border. At many points of this, and grouped especially in the corners and center, are small electric lights. The floor is of small white marble mosaic, with a pale blue gray-green pattern supplemented with ocher, red, and violet mosaic running through it. The rugs are a soft red and yellow; the furniture of a pale olive brown. A fountain on the south side is the attractive feature of the room, especially in the way it lends itself to the massing of flowers and plants. It is of white marble, beautifully sculptured, against a background of yellow Sienna marble, about which is a narrow border of white marble and then a wider border of Cipollino. On all sides of this room are great glass doors set in brass.

On the Rue de Rivoli side we pass out into the main dining-room, the walls of which are again of white limestone, with a ceiling of plaster of the same tone. The pilasters are of the gorgeous Brèche d'Alep; the bases and capitals are of brass. All of the ornament over the openings, in the cornice, in the frame of the ceiling, etc., are of plaster

Statuette in Vestibule from Rue de Rivoli.

Copyright, 1909, by Bates & Guild Company

gilded. The two elliptical Boucher medallions over the mantels and the large oval in the ceiling were painted by Theodore Poilpot. The furniture is of a light yellowish red, with olive leather seats and backs. The carpet is of a similar yellowish red, harmonizing with the marbles and stonework. The general impression of the room is one of great richness, in good taste, and at the same time of coziness, making the room what it is intended to be, a most attractive place in which to dine. The dimensions, thirty-seven by forty-five feet, assure ample accommodations for the guests of the hotel.

Leading off of this room at the rear is the restaurant, which receives all its light from the large glass openings into the Rivoli Hall. This room is treated in a Louis XVI gray white, against which the ornament is picked out in dull gold. The four wall-paintings are in soft autumn colors. The screen in front of the serving-door is in tones to harmonize. The carpet is of rose and pale yellow. The ceiling is similar to the walls, except that it is without gilt. The room is lighted by three handsome Louis XVI lusters, with glass pendants. We may note in passing that this room, similar to most of the other rooms, is heated from floor registers.

We may pass from this room directly into the central room of the hotel, known as the Salon. This receives its light from the Rivoli Hall from one end and from the Mont-Thabor Hall at the other end. It is again of the Louis XVI drab white, with the moldings and ornament gilded and five chandeliers are similar gilded and further enriched with glass pendants. The mantel is of a white marble, with ornament applied in brass. In order to give as much openness to the room as possible, the false doors are exactly similar to the other doors except that the panes are of mirror glass. The floor is of small white marble mosaic, with a blue gray-green pattern running through it. The rug is of old rose and olive green of charming design. The furniture is all Louis XVI, with some beautiful tapestry backs and seats to the chairs, added to which the many potted plants and flowers make this room most attractive in its effect.

Fountain, Side of Rivoli Hall.

We may pass from the side of this room into the gallery which connects the Rivoli Hall and the Mont-Thabor Hall. This gallery is again of white limestone, with a Hauteville base. Two lustres in the ceiling provide for the lighting, in addition to which there are some beautiful Louis XVI wall-brackets. Large mirrors divided into panels by narrow brass strips, similarly to the treatment in the *Galerie des Glaces* at Versailles, give this room the greatest of spaciousness. The floor is of white marble, with gray marble bands, with a heavy red rug in the center.

The Mont-Thabor Hall is in white limestone, with a ceiling full of sanded glass. The floor is of white and sage marble blocks covered by a sage and salmon rug. The furniture is all of mahogany, with leather of a similar tone. In architectural treatment this room has nothing of especial interest.

This gives us a general idea of the interesting features of this hotel from a decorative standpoint, the chambers and sitting rooms in the upper floors being of a very simple Louis XVI treatment, all in excellent taste. In general we must be impressed with the hospitable openness of it all, an openness obtained by the use everywhere of great openings of glass framed in brass; an openness which cheerily invites one to wander from room to room, yet which does not in any sense preclude privacy — a feature particularly desirable in a hotel.

As to the arrangement of the service portions of the hotel we probably have very little to learn, as this same sort of thing is so much better done with us, though a surprising feature of this hotel, in consideration of the French custom, is the number of private bathrooms connected with suites or individual rooms.

The plans of the three principal floors reproduced upon the next page explain themselves. With the exception of a greater number of fireplaces, the typical upper floor plan expresses the arrangement of all the sleeping floors. In the main, they do not much vary from American custom, the principal differences being found in details of the arrangement of the kitchens and working space in the basement.

The upper parts of the two street fronts are sloped back to the curve necessary to make them

Gallery between Rivoli and Mont-Thabor Halls.

Restaurant beside Rivoli Hall.

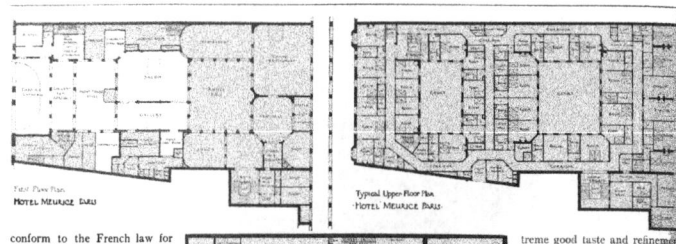

First Floor Plan
HOTEL MEURICE PARIS

Typical Upper Floor Plan
HOTEL MEURICE PARIS

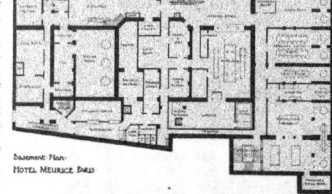

Basement Plan
HOTEL MEURICE PARIS

conform to the French law for streets of the respective width of the Rue de Rivoli and Rue Mont-Thabor.

The story heights are as follows: the ground floor, twenty feet in the clear; the first floor, thirteen feet in the clear; the second floor, eleven feet six inches; the third floor, ten feet six inches; and those above, ten feet in the clear. A great majority of the upper rooms have fireplaces in them.

As we readily see, the main interest of this hotel lies in the extreme good taste and refinement in the handling of the decorations — a refinement which adds immensely to the pleasure and comfort of the guests. At the same time, however, the treatment is one of great richness and variety, each room being quite suitable to its purpose; and the excellent harmony of all the details entering into the rooms — of furniture, carpets, screens, fixtures and hangings — give them an air of well-being and satisfactoriness that could be obtained in no other way.

Grand Staircase, showing Balcony and Elevator.

Mantel in Salon.

HÔTEL MEURICE, PARIS. H. NENOT, ARCHITECT.

CORNER OF SALON. HOTEL MEURICE, PARIS. H. SENOT, ARCHITECT. MAIN SALON.

MODERN ENGLISH COUNTRY HOUSES

GREENE HOUSE, LECKLEY WOOTTON, WARWICK, ENGLAND

THE ARCHITECTURAL REVIEW

PLATE LXII

DINING HALL, HOTEL MEURICE, PARIS, FRANCE

PLAN, ELEVATIONS, AND DETAILS. ST. PAUL'S CHURCH, BUTLER, PA.
JOHN T. COMES, ARCHITECT.

One Half inch Scale Details
St Pauls Church
Butler Pa.
Rev J. F. Collins Rector
John T. Comes Architect
Pittsburgh Pa.
Method of Laying Stone Wall
Section
Front Elevation
Plan
Detail Entrance at Side

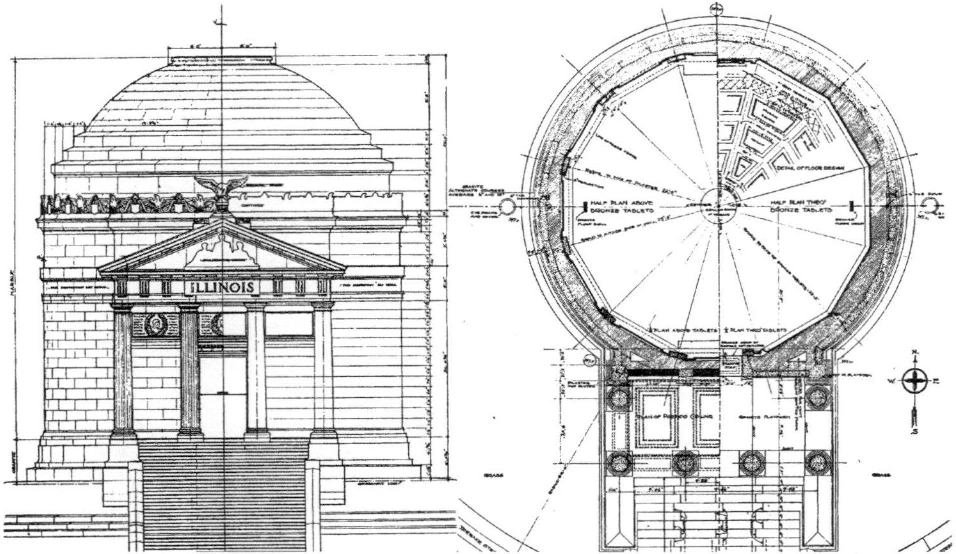
ILLINOIS
HALF PLAN ABOVE
BRONZE TABLETS
HALF PLAN THRO'
BRONZE TABLETS
DETAIL OF FLOOR DESIGN
½ PLAN ABOVE TABLETS
½ PLAN THRO' TABLETS
PLAN OF PORTICO CEILING
GRANITE PLATFORM
MARBLE
GRANITE
GRASS
N.
S.
E.
W.

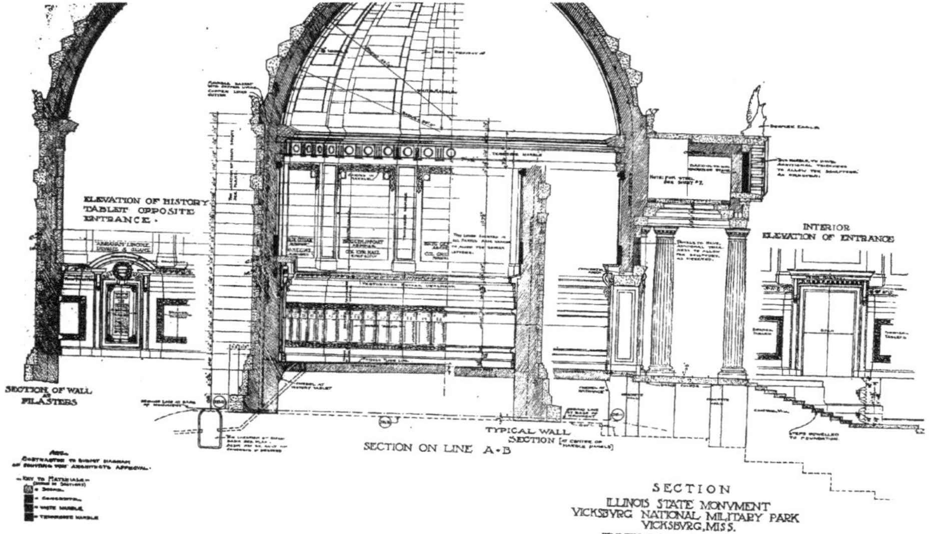

SECTIONS, ILLINOIS STATE MONUMENT, NATIONAL MILITARY PARK, VICKSBURG, MISS.

JENNEY & MUNDIE, ARCHITECTS.

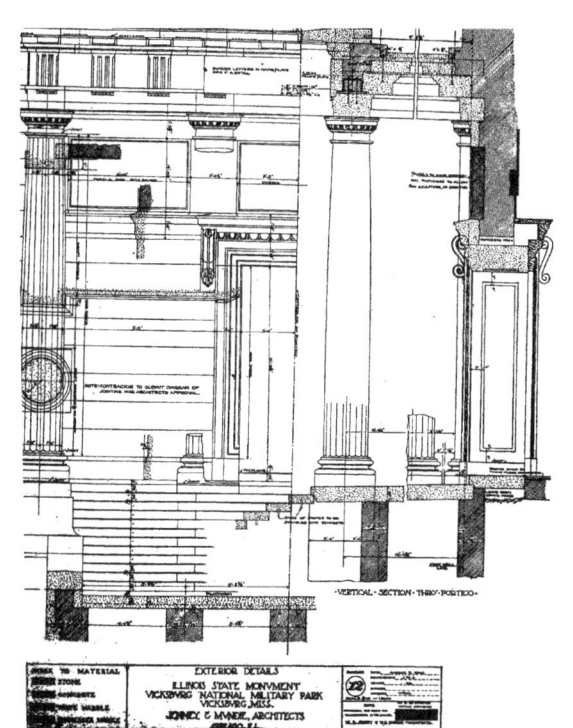

DETAILS, ILLINOIS STATE MONUMENT, NATIONAL MILITARY PARK, VICKSBURG, MISS.
JENNEY & MUNDIE, ARCHITECTS.

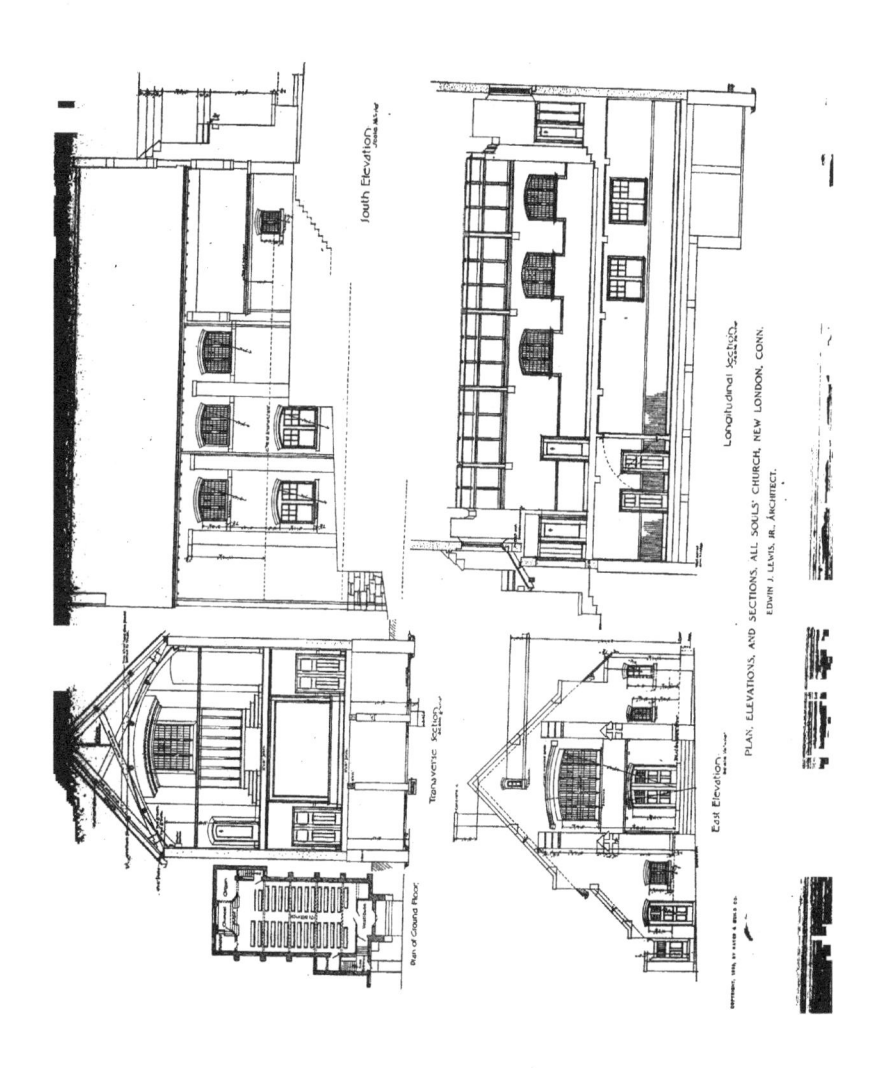

PLAN, ELEVATIONS, AND SECTIONS, ALL SOULS' CHURCH, NEW LONDON, CONN.
EDWIN J. LEWIS, JR., ARCHITECT.

GENERAL VIEW, MAIN DINING-ROOM, HÔTEL MEURICE, PARIS, FRANCE.
M. NÉNOT, ARCHITECT

MODERN ENGLISH COUNTRY HOUSES

DETAIL OF GARDEN FRONT, LUCKLEY, WOKINGHAM, BERKSHIRE, ENGLAND
ERNEST NEWTON, ARCHITECT

PLATE X

ILLINOIS STATE MONUMENT, NATIONAL MILITARY PARK, VICKSBURG, MISS.
JENNEY & MUNDIE, ARCHITECTS.

128

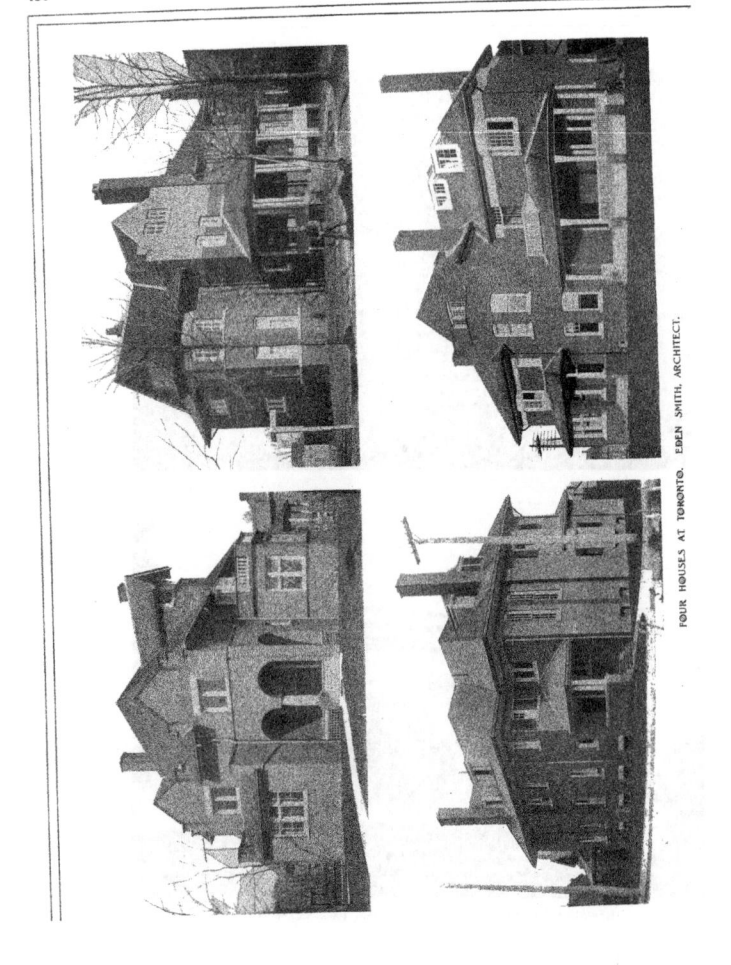

FOUR HOUSES AT TORONTO. EDEN SMITH, ARCHITECT.

The Architectural Review

VOLUME XVI. NUMBER 9

SEPTEMBER, 1909

BATES & GUILD COMPANY, Publishers
42 Chauncy Street, Boston
NEW YORK OFFICE, PARK ROW BUILDING

Published monthly. Price, mailed flat to any address in the United States or Canada, five dollars a year, in advance; to any foreign address, six dollars per annum, in advance. Subscriptions begin with the issue following their receipt. Single copies, fifty cents. Special numbers, two dollars. Entered as second-class mail-matter at the Post-office, Boston, Massachusetts, November 27, 1891.

PLATES

PLATE LXXI. — RIVOLI HALL, HOTEL MEURICE, PARIS (PHOTOGRAPHIC VIEW) — M. NENOT, ARCHITECT.
PLATES LXXII, LXXIII. — ST. PAUL'S CHURCH, BUTLER, PENN. (PLANS, ELEVATIONS, AND DETAILS) — JOHN T. COMES, ARCHITECT.
PLATES LXXIV — LXXVI. — ILLINOIS STATE MONUMENT, NATIONAL MILITARY PARK, VICKSBURG, MISS. (PLANS, ELEVATIONS, SECTIONS, AND DETAILS) — JENNEY & MUNDIE, ARCHITECTS.
PLATE LXXVII. — ALL SOULS CHURCH, NEW LONDON, CONN. (PLANS, ELEVATIONS, AND SECTIONS) — EDWIN J. LEWIS, JR., ARCHITECT.
PLATE LXXVIII. — GENERAL VIEW, MAIN DINING-ROOM, HOTEL MEURICE, PARIS (PHOTOGRAPHIC VIEW) — M. NENOT, ARCHITECT.

THE death, on Sept. 14, 1909, of Charles Follen McKim, senior member of the firm of McKim, Mead & White, means a permanent loss to the architecture of America. Although, on account of poor health, he had for some time been unable to take an active part in the work of his office, his interest and his inspiration were as great as ever; and his death at the age of sixty-two years, while not a surprise, was a shock to all who knew him. In order to begin to estimate the effect his work and influence have had upon architecture in America, it is necessary to recall that, at the time he started to practise, most of the architecture we call as the allied arts in this country were under the influence of H. H. Richardson, whose distinctive style, great as it undoubtedly was in the hands of its master, had greatly degenerated in the hands of his imitators. Mr. McKim was one of the first to realize this, and set for himself the task of discovering a type of architecture that had both the strength and the refinement necessary for the expression of the best American ideals. This style he found in the buildings of the Roman and Italian Renaissance; and the skill with which he expressed himself in his chosen language is amply illustrated by his work. Few who were not personally associated with him at the time can appreciate the magnitude of his task. It involved not only teaching his draughtsmen how to express themselves in a different and more refined architectural language than that to which they had been accustomed, but the detailed training of all the craftsmen employed in carrying out his ideas, as well. In the beginning it was difficult even to find modelers capable of producing acceptable Renaissance ornament without betraying a touch of the crudity inherent in the then prevailing style.

Mr. McKim always stood uncompromisingly for the highest ideals; and to his insistence that only the best in art and architecture was worthy of acceptance in this country the American people owe the great improvements that have been made in the designing of our public works.

Mr. McKim's interest in architectural education was fully equal to his devotion to his work. He endowed scholarships in the architectural departments at Harvard and Columbia Colleges; and it is owing almost alone to his earnest effort and his personal generosity that the American Academy at Rome was founded and has been maintained. The number of young men in the profession who have been inspired by his kindly help and criticism and who have received from him generous pecuniary assistance to enable them to travel and study abroad will probably never be known. Nothing gave him greater pleasure than the success of the younger men who went out from his office, and the undying love and loyalty of all those whose privilege it was to be brought into association with Mr. McKim will add as much to his fame, both as artist and man, as the public recognition and honors which, at the end of his life, were heaped upon him.

MR. McKIM'S death makes it more or less timely at this moment to point one direction in which his record may inspire the younger practitioner in his chosen profession. To one starting the practice of architecture there inevitably occur many trials and temptations that, if not rightly controlled, will forever militate against his obtaining great eminence in his profession. Given great training and ability, he must nevertheless possess integrity of character as well, in order to rise to the best opportunities that lie latent before him. Besides talent, training, and opportunity, absolute integrity, individual honesty, sincerity, and enthusiasm of purpose are all required to produce lasting and commensurate results. Any departure, however slight, from the highest ideals not only lessens individual prestige, but renders it the more difficult to continue to practise on that highest plane on which alone the greatest results are to be expected. The great — and to some people sudden and inexplicable — rise to popularity of the firm of McKim, Mead & White can be explained only by a realization of the inherent traits composing the personality of its individual members and to their continual adherence to only the highest ideals in architecture. Their great repute came to be accepted by the public only after it had been first freely granted them by brother members of the profession. Where lesser concerns have endeavored to obtain popularity by various attempts at doing what would impress the Man-in-the-Street, they steadfastly have adhered to doing only those things that would be of the highest artistic standard of which they were capable at the moment in which they were brought into being, and to this end no expense or pains were ever spared.

The Boston Library, for instance, one of the most noted monuments to their genius, was worked over and over and studied and restudied without any regard whatever to the cost to them of doing the work; they being satisfied if only the desired results were eventually attained. While building — and after the entire structure had been designed and laid out — Mr. McKim spent many additional months in Europe with one of the Trustees, working up once again the more important and monumental interiors. As one result, it may be stated that Bates Hall has long been known to his intimates as one of his favorite rooms; and it remains, to-day, unique among impressive monumental American interiors.

IN this month's Current Periodical Columns we twice have occasion to note the publication of architectural work where sculpture had borne an important part in the design, and where no credit had been given by the architect to his associate. Last March we commented on a view of the Cleveland Federal Building, showing sculptural groups placed against plain pier faces, where only the architect was mentioned, and no hint of the sculptor's name was given. While a more flagrant instance than either of those mentioned this month, yet, as we can recall the matter, the occasions when such proper credit is given are few and far between.

The architect has himself such frequent occasion to complain as to his own treatment on this very score by the public press that he should certainly be willing to see that adequate mention is made of his collaborating sculptors — individual creative artists, who frequently add considerable distinction to an architectural design by means of sculptural decorations. It becomes not only a matter of ethics, but of honesty and fair play, for the architect to give such credit where it belongs, instead of attempting to absorb it all for himself, as would appear to be the case in the several instances specifically noted.

Current Periodicals
A Review of the Recent American And Foreign Architectural Publications

(From "Architecture.")

First National Bank, Cleveland, Ohio.
J. Milton Dyer, Architect.

Entrance Detail, First Nat'l Bank, Cleveland, Ohio.
Carl Bitter, Sculptor.
(From "The Western Architect.")

View from Seven Corners, Approach to Capitol.
Cass Gilbert, Architect.
(From "The Western Architect.")

Bird's-eye Perspective, Approach to State Capitol, St. Paul, Minn.
Cass Gilbert, Architect.

George L. Rives's Residence, New York City.
Carrère & Hastings, Architects.

ALL the August architectural magazines are almost equally unexciting, *Architecture* being the single possible exception; as that number contains a rare instance of the appropriate use of some quite exceptional architectural sculpture by Mr. Carl Bitter. This occurs on J. Milton Dyer's First National Bank at Cleveland, a building that — excellent in proportion and detail, and successfully as it conforms to all the rules of the conventional classic game — forces recognition largely because of its unusually distinctive sculpture; and yet no hint of the sculptor's name is given on any of the reproduced illustrations! The architect is to be congratulated in his selection of so skilful an associate; but he is to be the more censured for not assuring that associate proper credit when reproduction was made from their combined work.

It is difficult to associate D. H. Burnham & Co. with the First National Bank in Pittsburg! Although lacking in homogeneity, and awkward in composition, yet the structure expresses an excellent *parti* that is, too, in the prevailingly popular *Italianate* fashion. Frank E. Wallis's country-house at Montclair would have been more interesting had the window treatment been consistently successful. In Squires & Wynkoop's very dashing sketches, particularly the Borough Hall, one is somewhat concerned to know what happens to the perspective lines that, even before they leave the extreme nearest apex of the roof, are apparently "outward bound" on a circular "round trip" back to their vanishing-point!

The columns of "Architectural Criti-

cism" continue on the downward path, disseminating in this issue such remarkable misinformation as the "pronounced Greek origin" of a mantel (only the slightest modification of the well-known Roman Doric chimney-piece in the Henry the Second Gallery at Fontainebleau!) in the Cleveland Bank.

In *The Western Architect* we again find Mr. Dyer's Cleveland Bank, with insult added to injury by giving full credit to the photographer, while still utterly ignoring the sculptor! One of Mr. Ittner's St. Louis schools is noted, and a well-considered design for a church at Montclair, N. J., by Watson & Huckel; but far and away the most interesting plates are those showing Cass Gilbert's suggested approach to the new Minnesota Capitol at St. Paul, of which we reproduce two views, along with what appears to be a concrete house at Detroit by Albert Kahn, quite different from the usual type of that architect's designs.

The Architectural Record for August is temporarily reformed, so far as to give illustrations of a size adequate to the importance of the article and the dignity of the structures illustrated, for the third part of Mr. Bragdon's "Architecture in the United States," dealing with "The Sky-Scraper." The author has, further, selected these illustrations with an exceptional discrimination. Mr. Sullivan's Buffalo Office Building, McKim, Mead & White's Gorham Building, Cass Gilbert's West St. Building and Broadway Chambers, Carrère & Hastings's Blair Building, and Robert Kohn's Evening Post Building are all notable expressions

(From "The American Architect.")

House for A. L. Schaefer, University Hts., N.Y.
Squires & Wynkoop, Architects.

(From "The American Architect.")

House for H. J. Kemor, Esq., Sea Gate, N. Y.
Squires & Wynkoop, Architects.
(From "The Brickbuilder.")

House at Cleveland, Ohio.
Watterson & Schneider, Architects.
(From "Architecture.")

(From "The American Architect.")

House for Edw. D. Page, Mountain Station, N. J.
Squires & Wynkoop, Architects.

First National Bank, Pittsburgh, Pa.
D. H. Burnham & Co., Architects.

House at Lake Forest, Ill.
Robert D. Kohn, Architect.

Country House at Montclair, N. J.
Frank E. Wallis, Architect. Wm. J. Rogers, Associated.

e commercial sky-scraper of America. he Metropolitan Life and Singer Build- g towers are "freaks" of a size that nders it impossible not to treat of them any article dealing with this topic. The me thing is largely true of Mr. Burn- m's "Flatiron," and possibly could be tched even to include the Chicago Railway Exchange," which we opine be one of the most pernicious and rtistic office buildings in the world. r. Bruce Price's American Surety uilding appears with dignity beside e Broadway Chambers, than which little higher praise can be given; of the New York Times Building oses to less advantage from the pic- rest point of view than it actually es in reality. Particularly in the ht of early morning or the twilight late afternoon, seen from far up or own Broadway, this structure, un- leasing as it may be in detail, then ars above the city streets in much the ay that we can imagine did the tow- of Florence in the days of the uelphs and Ghibelines.

We reproduce a view of Carrère & astings's Rives House on East 79th treet, New York City, one of the most endid of recent New York dwellings, ith an interior that has been carried it by the designers with great care nd particularity. A number of gro-

tesque European shop-fronts are also illus trated, along with another of the articles dealing with "The Architect in History."

The Brickbuilder for August is princi pally interesting for its leading article dealing with "The Architectural Uses of Burnt Clay," with illustrations substan tially confined to arch or dome construc tions of tile or colored terra-cotta. In the text-pages we find another instance of the individual use of brickwork (that seems, of late months, to be largely confined to expression in syna gogue architecture) in a New Orleans Synagogue by Emile Weil. An instal ment of "The Warming and Ventilating of Hospital Buildings" appears; and a great number of brick residences — sixteen in all. We confess to find the showing made by these residences most disappointingly mediocre. With two exceptions, there is hardly a new idea in the lot! The same conventional forms, the same attempts to reproduce pretentious historical styles at less than a possible cost (resulting in a very apparent thinning and cheapening of all the members), are their principal characteristics — characteristics that are coming too importantly into evi dence in American residence architec ture, and that can only be blamed upon the architect, who, unable to approach the problem in a simple, direct, and obvious manner, instead attempts to reproduce dignified and noble precedents in ignoble forms and materials. The exceptions noted refer to an attractive small house at Cleveland by Watterson & Schneider and Robert D. Kohn's house at Lake Forest, Ill. (which we reprint)—the only one in the group where any attempt has been made to express the material.

(From "The Western Architect.")

Residence of A. L. Stephens, Grosse Pointe, Mich.
Albert Kahn, Architect.

The New York Architect for July publishes exteriors and interiors of that very excellent station on the banks of the Seine known as the *Gare d'Orléans*, an elaborate dwelling on Riverside Drive containing some very marvelously carved interior woodwork, *and* the Metropolitan Life Insurance Building. It hardly seems necessary to give space to reproduction of the latter; the interiors, we regret to say, being quite as old fashioned as in the old building next door.

The American Architect for August 4 deals with what is editorially announced as the first of a series of articles on Professor Goodyear's hobby, "Architectural Refinements;" a title that has a strangely familiar sound! The "Current Architectural Press" reappears in the same reminiscent form as last month. The plates illustrate some attractive houses at Tarrytown by Ewing & Chappell.

The August 11 number treats of "The Fire-proof House," and the plates illustrate dwellings by Squires & Wynkoop that in most part have been previously published in *The Architectural Record*. We reprint one or two of the more interesting types suggested.

August 18 deals with the architecture of Atlanta, Ga. The drawings for the Forsyth Theater appear sufficiently interesting to cause one to wonder whether its peculiarities of design will justify themselves in execution. There is also illustrated a classic church by Haralson Bleckley.

On August 25 there is an article on "The Grotesque in Gothic Ornament," illustrated by a number of bosses, of which the best are certainly those from the College of the City of New York and the West Point Military Academy. Despite the fact that no mention is made of either sculptors or modelers, we suspect that, in each case, these gentlemen had rather more to do with the success of the results obtained than did the architects who have blandly absorbed unto themselves all of the credit!

The plates show working drawings of a New York church, apparently another essay in that "cast-iron" Gothic that results

(From "La Construction Moderne.")

Fencing School, Paris, France.
M. G. Farcy, Architect.

from the mechanical employment of a grammar of forms whose meaning and spirit are obsolete and forgotten. It otherwise seems impossible to imagine employing two towers so exactly alike, when so many historic examples illustrating the charm of variation in detail, if not also in proportion and shape, exist to guide observers in the right direction. An equally conventional bit of religious (?) architecture is the Classic Renaissance memorial altar for the Church of St. Paul the Apostle illustrated in this same issue.

The English *Architectural Review* contains the third article on "Lecce" and Part II. on "Cambridge Colleges," showing the Renaissance King's College, Trinity Library, Clare, Pembroke and Queen's Colleges. "Current Architecture" ("*et tu, Brute!*") illustrates interiors of the additions to the Glasgow Central Station Hotel and of a Parish Church in Berwickshire, along with some further details of the Victoria and Albert Museum, which was partially published in this same magazine last month.

The first number of *The Builder's Journal* for August publishes additional work of the Liverpool School of Architecture and, on August 11, a brick Georgian house by Mr. Mervyn Macartney.

The Builder for July 31 contains an interesting school. August 7 is published a typical "Business Premises" in London. August 14 appears another group of excellent sketches made on the annual Architectural Association excursion, which continue on August 21 with Russell & Cooper's depressing structure for a Municipal Building at Burslem.

The Architect for August 6 contains further illustrations of Birmingham University, and the attractive houses by Cossins, Peacock & Bewlay; for August 13 Boys' School at Bromley, Kent, by H. P. Burke Downing, and some Art Nouveau buildings for an Exposition at Buenos Ayres to occur from May to November of next year.

La Construction Moderne publishes (July 31) the Rockefeller Institute Building in New York; an interesting fencing-school in Paris by M. J. Farcy (August 7) which we reprint; and, on August 14, several new structures for housing dirigible balloons—so far as we know, the first architectural illustration of so "advanced" a type of building construction!

Entrance Front, "Beacon Wood," Lickey Hills, Worcestershire.
Cossins, Peacock & Bewlay, Architects.

Southwest Elevation, House on the Lickey Hills, Worcestershire.
Cossins, Peacock & Bewlay, Architects.

(From "The Architect," London.)

The Architectural Review

Volume XVI   October, 1909   Number 10

Exterior Plaster Construction, V.

Metal and Concrete Framing

By Frank Chouteau Brown

BESIDES the methods for constructing the plaster and fireproof house already considered in these articles, and those types of more strictly concrete buildings that are generally known, there are in more or less general use in different localities several variations from better known forms of construction, the two basic principles of which have been experimentally utilized in different ways. In one, a light form of wall-construction of iron or steel embedded in concrete is employed. In the other, a lighter forms of bars of structural supporting shapes of iron, such as channel, T and I sections, are been adapted to rapid assembling for house-construction.

While each of these methods originated in an attempt in some way to alter the cheaper forms of existing constructive systems, or to reduce the cost of those more expensive, in an endeavor to obtain a more permanent form of house-construction; yet, as a matter of fact, no one of them has yet achieved such general employment as to prove both its general practicability and inexpense. It in each case it must be confessed that the failure materially to reduce expense of employment is probably due in no small part to the peculiarity of the construction and the comparative novelty of the method. It follows that these schemes have been usually used so seldom it becomes particularly difficult to gather very definite or even approximately exact data of costs or of results. This is the more particularly true as each system has as yet come into use only in that locality where it first had its inception, and where, consequently, local circumstances are probably most favorable to its employment at a low cost. If attempted in another locality it might work out with considerably different results.

In that system based altogether on the use of a light iron stud framework for walls and partitions, and a light form of I-beam of the same material for floors, the partitions and ceilings are plastered on wire lath in the ordinary way, and the entire structure may be rapidly erected and thoroughly tied together within itself;

although from the metal framework used and the lightness of the construction employed, it would seem that the separate parts of such a dwelling would not be thoroughly insulated against sound and, if of any considerable size, that the expansion and contraction of so rigid a framework as this might be sufficient to occasion annoying cracks in both exterior and interior plaster surfaces. The metal stud running through the partition from face to face would, too, on account of its greater susceptibility, be likely to conduct sounds from room to room much more readily than in a wooden construction.

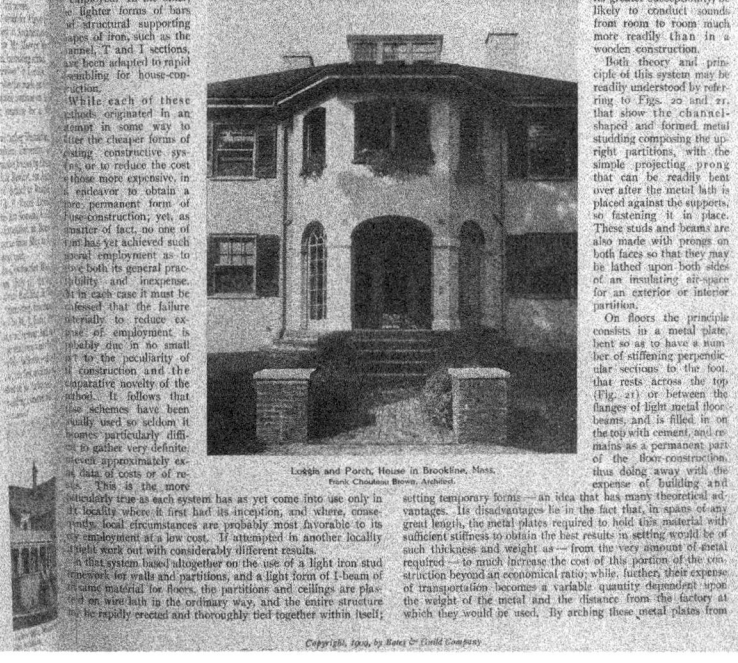

Both theory and principle of this system may be readily understood by referring to Figs. 20 and 21, that show the channel-shaped and formed metal studding composing the upright partitions, with the simple projecting prong that can be readily bent over after the metal lath is placed against the supports, so fastening it in place. These studs and beams are also made with prongs on both faces so that they may be lathed upon both sides of an insulating air-space for an exterior or interior partition.

On floors, the principle consists in a metal plate, bent so as to have a number of stiffening perpendicular sections to the foot, that rests across the top (Fig. 21) or between the flanges of light metal floor beams, and is filled in on the top with cement, and remains as a permanent part of the floor-construction, thus doing away with the expense of building and setting temporary forms — an idea that has many theoretical advantages. Its disadvantages lie in the fact that, in spans of any great length, the metal plates required to hold this material with sufficient stiffness to obtain the best results in setting would be of such thickness and weight as — from the very amount of metal required — to much increase the cost of this portion of the construction beyond an economical ratio; while, further, their expense of transportation becomes a variable quantity dependent upon the weight of the metal and the distance from the factory at which they would be used. By arching these metal plates from

Loggia and Porch, House in Brookline, Mass.
Frank Chouteau Brown, Architect

Copyright, 1909, by Bates & Guild Company

flange to flange (Fig. 22) a lighter section may be used or a stronger floor may be obtained; but the extra weight of concrete added in the haunches of the arch then requires still heavier supporting floor-beams.

While the manufacturers of this system claim that a house at Tuxedo, figured to cost $7,500 in wood, was constructed by this means at a cost of $6,500, still, figuring from their own prices, this could not be a typical instance, as the floor-cost, for the reinforcement alone, up to spans ten feet long, is $.16 to the square foot. The lath and clips would amount to $.03 or $.04, and adding the cost of four inches of concrete and the plastered ceiling, with the labor of installing the necessary ironwork and furrings, it is readily seen that their installation, ready for flooring, would run well above the cost of ordinary methods of floor-construction; while partition work figures out — for the construction alone — on thin interior metal partitions to be plastered both sides, to about $.30 a yard, and on heavier exterior or bearing partitions to about $.50 a yard — both somewhat prohibitive figures, and — adding wire lath, labor, and plastering both sides —very much higher than wooden construction would be in most localities.

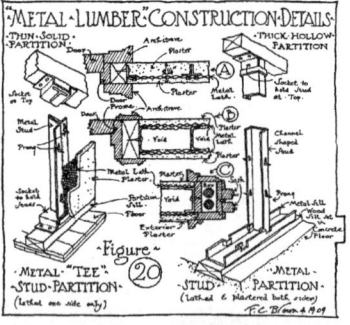

In adapting the other principle of construction, the intention is in each case to avoid the use of temporary wall-forms or centering; and the ironwork, both iron studs and iron lath, is so devised as to itself take the place of this centering and form work, the placing and removal of which is conceded to be a considerable part of the expense of cast concrete construction. So far, experiments have been directed toward using this combination in two different ways. In the first, where substantially a concrete form of construction is desired, the studs could be of much lighter material than in the other; while the lath used against the outer and inner face of these studs is some form of expanded metal or herringbone of sufficiently small mesh, or with a comparatively small number of openings, so that the space between the lath and studs can be poured full of a very fluid mixture of concrete (Fig. 23) without allowing too much of it to escape through these meshes. When hardened, this gives substantially a concrete wall, with rough and uneven lathed outer and inner faces; which can then be plastered and finished in any way desired.

Such a form of construction carries with it all the disadvantages of a solid concrete wall, especially so far as the transmission of moisture is concerned, and would therefore better be water-proofed on its outer or inner face (preferably the former) with some form of hydrolithic or Medusa treatment before the surface finish is applied. Of course, the surface upon which this water-proofing compound must go is excessively rough, and any paint put on with a brush is not likely to cover with a complete and unbroken coat. For that reason possibly a very fluid Medusa mixture applied with a whitewash brush and well worked in would better answer the purposes of waterproofing this form of construction than any of the easier applied water-proof paints. Medusa, too, gives a better bond for holding the surface plastering than some forms of water-proofing that, under certain conditions, have occasionally appeared to be a factor in the peeling off of the surface cement coatings applied upon their face.

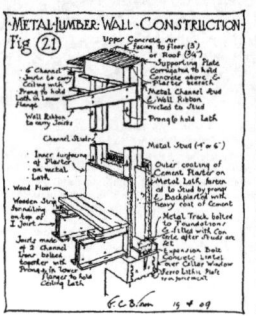

The advantages of this system lie, obviously, in the elimination of carpenters' labor in the placing, fitting, and taking down of wooden forms. It has, too, advantages of quick handling of the original material that should effect a further saving in time of construction. On the other hand, where a form — and much of the material used in making forms — can be used over and over again on the same house, or even upon a number of houses (and, in all, only a comparatively small amount of form lumber may be required for constructing walls and floors of a large dwelling), yet here both faces of the wall have to be entirely covered with an expensive material which becomes a permanent part of the wall and cannot be used again — although it is true it performs its important part as a reinforcement that permits of a thinner wall than the ordinary cement construction. There should also be a further proportionate saving in the cost of stock and labor in mixing of concrete. For instance, where a wall of concrete might have to be eight inches thick, a six-inch or even possibly a five-inch wall of this form of construction would be sufficiently strong for the ordinary dwelling.

The other method of utilizing this same general constructive method is to erect the iron studs and metal lath in exactly the same way as for the system first considered; except that, as more dependence is here placed upon the ironwork for support, the studding would have to be heavier and placed more closely together. Upon each side of this studding, as before, the expanded metal — which may now, however, be correspondingly lighter in weight and more open in mesh — is placed, and given one heavy rough coat of concrete plaster upon its outer faces on both sides of the wall. When thoroughly hard, this first rough plaster coat becomes at one and the same time a form capable of holding any cement pouring that may be placed *inside* the wall for purposes of securing additional strength at weak points, at the same time as it acts as the first coat for the plaster surfacing, both inside and out of the dwelling. The use of any additional poured concrete reinforcement, provided the first metal construction be heavy enough in the first place, can of course be considerably restricted, and need only be used at the sides of large wall-openings, at the corners of the house, or under those points where considerable weight is concentrated from floor or roof loads; so that the amount of concrete actually used is reduced to a minimum, while at the same time the person living in the house possesses the advantages undoubtedly found in a form of outside wall-construction where a permanent and certain air-space is obtained.

It should also be noted that, while in both the cases just described the use of iron or metal studding has been taken for granted, yet the use of such metal studding is not an absolute necessity. In either construction, a wood stud (Fig. 23) could be used with equal ease — so far as the immediate structural necessities are concerned. It gives sufficient support for the metal lath placed upon either side; and if it should happen to later rot out from dampness in the wall surrounding it, in the first instance it would not much matter, inasmuch as an air-space would then be supplied at this point in the wall, which would by that time be amply strong to stand of itself. In the second case it would, of course, be more considerable of a defect; as, unless the poured concrete reinforcements were placed at frequent intervals in the wall, the elimination of the studwork would cause sagging and other deteriorations in the dwelling. On the other hand, the wood studs in this second instance would be much less liable to rot, on account of the conditions being almost precisely the same as they would be in any wooden dwelling, except at those points where additional support of poured concrete had been necessitated, and then it would but seldom be the case that the stud would be surrounded on both sides and completely enclosed in the concrete, and the poured portion would be liable to affect only one side of the wood.

In all three of these methods of construction it should be remembered that, with studs spaced more than ten inches apart, only an expanded metal or sheet iron, or a reinforced wire lath, can be used applied directly on studs or joints. If iron furring-strips are added to obtain smaller spacings for wire-lath supports a considerable addition is made to the cost of the construction.

When it comes to actual floor-construction, neither of the last two treatments has been worked out so as to be wholly satisfactory as yet. In the first variation, a metal beam of eight-inch depth, or thereabouts, is sufficient to carry floor-spans up to 15′ 0″, provided a special additional tension reinforcement is placed in the spaces between the beams before the concrete is run into place. Then it would seem that the strength first required in the I-beams to carry the rough concrete until it sets is wasted after that time; inasmuch as practically a self-supporting concrete floor is individually laid between and around these metal beams. This construction possesses, too, all the disadvantages of the solid concrete type, especially in the transmission of noise, and the reverberation likely to result when no air-spaces are provided. Of course, the finished floor-surface can be attached to screeds laid in cement; or clear of the cement floor-construction, so as to obtain an air-space at this point; and an air-space can be provided in all partitions, bearing or non-bearing, but both means of insulation are only to be obtained at a still further increase in cost.

In the case of the second system, the floor is individually supported on joists or beams of either metal or wood; with metal lathing fastened to their bottom surfaces for, if spaced too far apart, on cross-furrings) and plastered to provide the ceiling, quite as would be the case in ordinary house-construction. As no advantage is to be obtained from the extra weight imposed by filling in with concrete the spaces between the beams (the floor-beams themselves being necessarily of sufficient strength to carry the floor and its imposed weight), the floors are generally laid directly across the top of these joists (Fig. 21), with the air-space in between that helps to prevent the transmission of noise; but this space provides the customary conveniences for

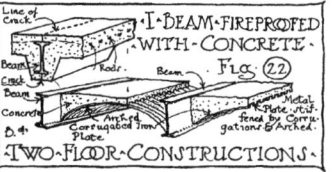

vermin, dirt, and fire. Of course the substitution of wood joists or studs for metal at once detracts from what fire-proof qualities might exist in this combination of metal and concrete.

And right here enters a serious consideration. In no one of these forms of construction is the metal adequately and properly protected on its surfaces from attack by fire, and in a frame containing so much iron it would require but little heat to start expansion in such a way as would seriously rack the entire framework of the house and most certainly crack plastering or concrete. Despite the statements of theorists to the contrary, the use of metal in the form of beams in conjunction with concrete *does* detract from the latter's permanence. Even the amount of expansion occasioned by the heat of the sun, through a long-continued spell of dry weather, transmitted by so good a conductor as concrete, will cause a movement in a body of metal such as composes an I-beam to an extent that will inevitably crack through the surface of a body of concrete several inches thick, both above and below the beam (Fig. 22), when thoroughly encased in the material. When exposed on either surface the metal is even more peculiarly susceptible to extremes of heat and cold. Unprotected iron is more easily injured by fire than unprotected wood, and this fact perfectly applies to its use under the above conditions.

Other ingenious inventions have been made and exploited, among them being concrete floor-joists; a structural framework of standard pipe sizes; canvas on supporting wire instead of wood or metal forms for floors; and numerous others; but writing at the present time, it hardly seems possible that any of the above types of construction are going to be of permanent interest and value to the community. Dangerous as is the assumption of the rôle of prophet, it yet seems obvious enough that, both in practical advantages and in cost, the terra-cotta constructed dwelling is undoubtedly superior and cheaper, while at the same time providing a supporting-wall perfectly adapted to carrying a fire-proof floor; which is *not* true of the iron constructions unless additional expense is added by the amount of metal employed, or by its additional reinforcement or strengthening by means of poured concrete, or concrete piers.

For certain portions of the building some of these treatments may hereafter, with further experiment and use, become better available. As a fire-resisting and inexpensive roof-construction, for instance, some one of the several methods just mentioned would seem to offer possibilities of development that would allow a roof of some one of the types indicated to be used in combination with concrete floors and terra-cotta walls with the greatest economy of cost and weight, and with the most beneficial results. Interior non-supporting partitions, it would seem, could also be readily and quickly constructed of the metal stud, and, where lathed and plastered on both sides, would probably be sufficiently fire-resisting for all ordinary purposes. They could, further, be easily made soundproof (such as by some form of mineral wool or other insulating filling) if it became advisable so to do. As a complete form of house-construction, however, it is doubtful if any one of the above methods is to be widely commended at the present time; while it has been extremely difficult, as has before been stated, to get sufficiently exact costs and comparative figures on these constructions to enable the architect to compare them advantageously with the other systems before, or hereafter to be, considered.

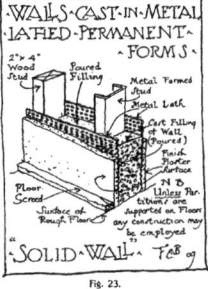

Fig. 23.

There remain to be considered two other forms of construction — presenting, at the least, distinct theoretical advantages — that are hardly to be classified under any of the ordinary cement methods of building. These schemes are also still in an experimental stage (patents on both being pending); but they would seem to promise — in certain cases — to be possibly inexpensive and advantageous ways of constructing dwellings; especially those small in size and not too involved in horizontal or perpendicular outline.

As was the case with the constructions above considered, both had their inception in the endeavor to avoid loss of labor and material in the use of forms; only, instead of avoiding forms by incorporating some other substitute as a permanent part of the construction, the endeavor here has been to adopt some one unit capable of becoming a "type" form which could be used over and over again. The inventors have also realized that the least expensive way of running and surfacing concrete is upon a horizontal plane; and the system first considered is therefore adapted to the construction of a building, both walls and floors, altogether in this way; the walls being afterward "raised," set in place, and held by reinforcement at the angles. This scheme, too, requires a minimum amount of material, both of cement and its various aggregates; so that, in these directions, it is more economical than most methods for the use of concrete in building construction. The difficulty in applying this method to actual work comes, however, in the fact that a number of angles in the wall, or a number of openings, add greatly to the complexity of the problem and to the additional labor of construction. This is, of course, true of any concrete or masonry wall; but, in the present case, the difficulty is greater in proportion to the cost of the system itself, which is essentially simple and, if used upon a simply planned dwelling, is particularly available for rapid and inexpensive progress.

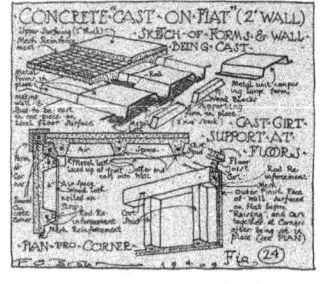

In brief, this method may be described as follows: As soon as the foundations are brought up to the level of the first floor this floor is laid, in any desired form of construction, that may be adopted. Upon this floor the walls of the house are separately cast in sections, these sections being as long as the wall is unbroken by an angle — up to distances of about forty feet. A series of metal forms of uniform size and section, arranged so that each can be laid inside of and overlapping the other units, on short supporting blocks placed upon the floor to support the raised surfaces of the sections, shown in Fig. 24, enables the entire wall to be laid out easily and rapidly once its outside dimensions have been determined and laid down upon the floor. In height this wall would extend up to the bottom of the second-story floor. The forms once in place, rod reinforcements are inserted in the stud spaces and the concrete poured over the entire surface of the form, filling completely the places left for the studs and covering the shallow portions to the uniform depth of an inch, or thereabouts — depending on the desired strength of the wall (Fig. 26). After this concrete is poured, a second reinforcement composed of any cheap form of wire mesh — even chicken-fencing is sufficient — is spread entirely over the cement, and over this again is run a further cement coat of any required thickness; — which can also be of a different formation and aggregate, when it is desirable to obtain a texture or color-effect upon the finished surface. This upper coat can then be surfaced while upon the floor (Fig. 27), at the greatest possible saving of expense, either by washing with acid or by some textural treatment such as hammering or scouring, or whatever has been adopted for the final surface treatment of the building. After the various sections comprising the wall of the building are cast and surfaced, they are "raised" into place (see below) by means of a special derrick and then firmly held until the spaces coming at the corner angles are enclosed by boards inside and out and run with a fluid mixture of concrete around iron-rod reinforcements put in place from above, so thoroughly tying the house together at the angles — and giving in this "corner-board" treatment, as well, a different surface effect on the outside angle, that may be made a decorative element of the house-design. Of course, all openings for doors and windows are blocked out before this wall is run — either by placing the frames of windows and doors upon the floor in the exact positions they will occupy in the house; or a furring may be substituted, when such is more desirable. After the walls of the house have been raised, a story the second floor is put in place (if of concrete, it can even be run upon the same forms as were set for the first floor) and the second-story walls are made and raised from the level of the second floor in the same way as were those of the first. Upon the attic floor, in turn, the roof may be made, provided that it is to be of concrete construction (and this is, by the way, the cheapest method of forming roof-construction yet invented for cement). For this purpose the rougher aggregates are used and left exposed, the cement being cleaned from the surface, thus allowing the waterproof covering of tar, pitch, — or whatever it may be — to have an opportunity to combine firmly and permanently with the structural portion of the roof.

The matter of lathing and plastering upon the inside of these walls is taken care of in two ways. If metal lath is used the lath is set into the form before the stud portion of the wall is run, in such a way that it is locked firmly on one edge, the other edge being loose. When the wall is raised into place this loose edge is laced by wire, or nailed by staples or otherwise, into the firmly fastened edge of the next adjoining strip, and the inner plaster coating then applied on the wire, just as in any house-plastering. This wall then provides the air-space generally considered desirable in the best forms of concrete dwelling construction. It is also possible to place a wooden furring-strip or screed along the bottom of the form

Fig. 26. Forms in Place and First Pouring Under Way.    Raising Section of Wall with Special Derrick.    Fig. 27. Surfacing Cast Wall on Floor before Raising.

at the inner or lower edge of the stud before pouring the concrete, so obtaining a nailing to which wire lath may be afterward stapled or wooden lath nailed.

This method of construction does not lend itself to actual work as easily as it is theoretically explained. There arise a number of minor difficulties in its application to actual construction that have either to be foreseen by the contractor or otherwise taken care of as they come up; but where so many of the problems having to do with the construction and design of the concrete house are so ingeniously solved, it would be comparatively easy to work out these necessary further details of construction as they might arise.

In this form of cement construction the matter of expense depends — as always — almost wholly on the arrangement and design of the house. As holds true of any concrete house, the grouping of the windows, the elimination of unnecessary angles and projecting bays, the adoption of uniform lines for floors, eaves, and roof slopes, all tend toward simplifying and keeping down the cost of construction. The house shown on page 138 was actually estimated — the exterior wall-constructions only — with a wooden frame, furred and fire-lathed with Clinton cloth, plastered outside and lathed in, to cost $1,075.00. The same exterior wall in vitrified glazed terra-cotta, plastered outside, amounted to $1,475.00; and the estimate in the form of construction just described was $1,590.00, or $515 above the cost in wood; showing how the figures for these three forms of plastered house-construction would compare in this definite case. (With both the last two named figures, by the way, $50 for "box" window-frames should be added to the cost of carpenter-work on the house.) The house used as an example is shown herewith (in Plates LXXX, LXXXI, and LXXXII), so that each reader may come to his own conclusions as to the comparative application to his own practice of the estimates given. It was neither unduly simple nor very complex, but was indeed designed as inexpensively as was deemed advisable when contemplating its construction in salt-glazed, or vitrified, terra-cotta tile.

In the above figures neither the construction of floors nor of interior partitions was taken into account; therefore a wholly fireproof house would *not* have been obtained for this slight additional cost. Attention was here directed solely toward securing a permanent wall to carry the exterior stucco surface. Given concrete floors, however (which, if surfaced with wood, would cost about thirty-five per cent more than wooden floor joist construction), the interior partitions could be constructed in various ways which would provide fire-resisting partitions at a cost substantially little different from a partition built of wood — in which case a house substantially "fire-proof" has been obtained, (the ordinary American understands the term so to mean could have been obtained.)

Another most ingenious and likewise inexpensive way of forming a hollow concrete wall is also intended to avoid the use of expensive forms and at the same time cheapen the cost of making the hollow concrete block which, except in the dry-tamped form, has not inexpensive; and then neither so strong nor so impervious to moisture as the block made from a wet mixture. This scheme briefly consists in making, either in the factory or on the building-site, a number of separate slabs, 1¼ or 2 inches thick, reinforced by poultry-netting, through which run two or three lengths of heavy wire projecting a considerable distance beyond the ends — depending on the thickness of wall desired. In practice, these slabs are often made one on top of the other, in bottomless boxes of the

determined thickness of the slab required (Fig. 25), with a sheet of building-paper laid across the boxes to keep the slabs separate one from the other. The top surface of each slab is "struck off" with a straight-edge, and, the blocks being always made face up, this surface can be troweled, floated, or faced with a coating of marble dust or other material to give any granular texture or color desired. The top of the slab may afterward be surface finished by washing with acid or otherwise, treating it just as in the system of making walls above described. After a number of slabs have been made the wall is constructed by placing a slab on the outside and a slab on the inside of the wall, bringing the wires sticking from the ends together and twisting them as is shown in the sketch (Fig. 25). The horizontal joints are spread with mortar, then the next portion is laid, and the wires locked together, precisely as just described. These joints and twisted wires come directly over each other in every alternate course and, by placing the two wooden forms two, three, or four inches apart, on each side of this joint and between the slabs of concrete, the distance between the latter is regulated and a form is made in which the stud may be poured, thus completely enclosing the wires and locking both faces of the wall absolutely together. The short board studs — made in two wedge-shaped portions for convenience in removing — composing the forms at each side of the cast stud can be used over and over again. To obtain a horizontal tie between the courses only a short length of the stud is poured at a time. By this means the pouring may be made to include the lower wire of the uppermost course and extend part way down the course below (in order to catch the top bond wires in the same pouring as the lower wires in the course imposed above it). The joists may be placed so as to carry the floor-load directly — by arranging a joist to come upon each stud; or, by setting up a shallow form and pouring a solid girt all around the building, so connecting the top of the studs together, any form of floor-construction may be carried on in the ordinary fashion.

With this system the greatest freedom in handling is possible, as any thickness of wall or size of stud may be used with equal ease and rapidity, it being necessary only to widen the space between the wooden forms used in casting the stud in case greater strength is required at any one place. The wall-spaces between the studs may also be poured full of fluid concrete with the greatest ease. The size and thickness of the blocks may easily be varied to suit the purposes of the building. As a rule the wall-slab is made about 1¼" thick, about 2' 0" high and 3' 0" or 3' 6" long. It can be made with a finished surface both inside or out; or left a rougher texture to afterward receive a plaster coating. This method requires a very small amount of concrete and of form-construction, the latter particularly being so simple that a sufficient quantity to run slabs for an entire house may be made in a few hours. It is also possible — by pouring the studs in a three-sided box — to use slabs only upon the *outer* face of the wall, and lath and plaster on the inner face by the same methods as are shown in plan section in Fig. 24.

These various methods of house-construction are here described for what suggestive values they may possess. Almost all of them as yet remain in an experimental stage, and while further investigation and experiment may succeed in cheapening and bettering any one of them, or all, it will probably require some years more of experience before definite results can be known as to their permanence, fire-proof and weather-resisting qualities, inexpense of maintenance, and adaptability to the purposes of American house-design.

HOUSE, CORNER AMORY AND FREEMAN STREETS, BROOKLINE, MASS.
FRANK CHOUTEAU BROWN, ARCHITECT.

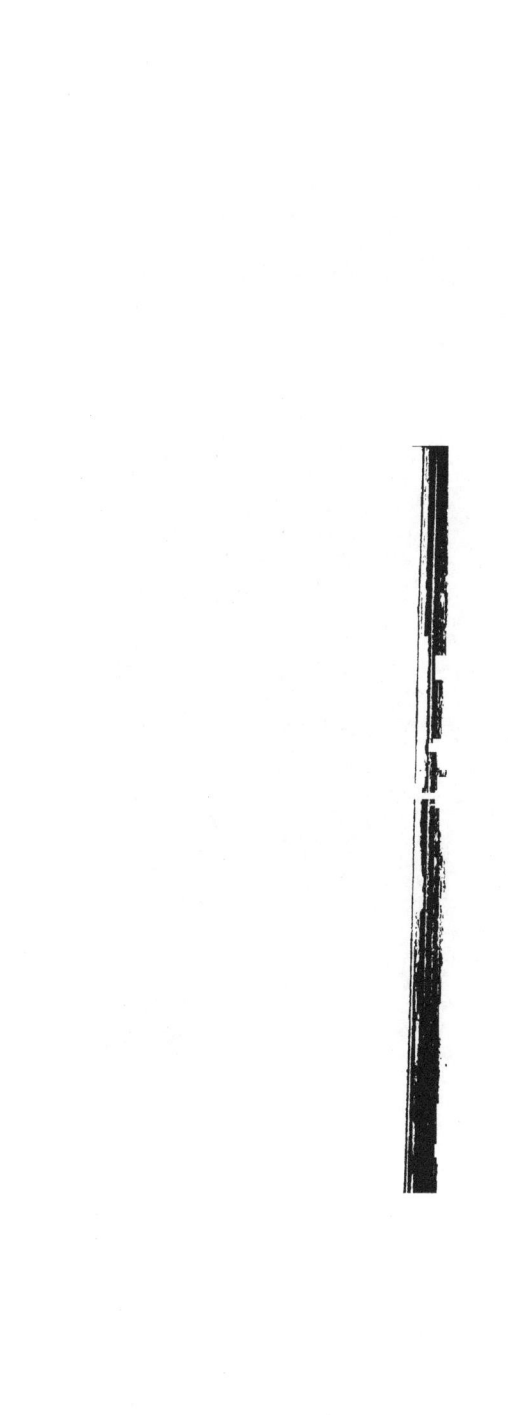

MODERN ENGLISH COUNTRY HOUSES

PARISH CHURCH OF ST. HELENA, BOERNE, TEXAS.
CRAM, GOODHUE & FERGUSON, ARCHITECTS.

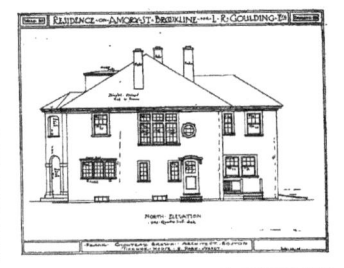

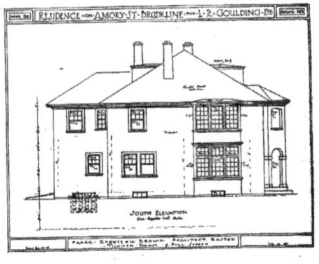

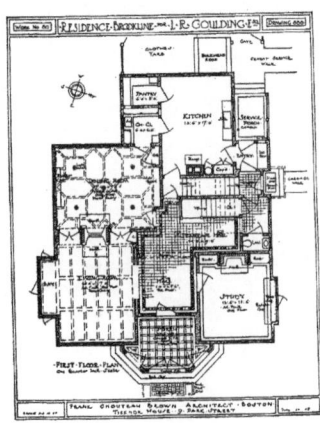

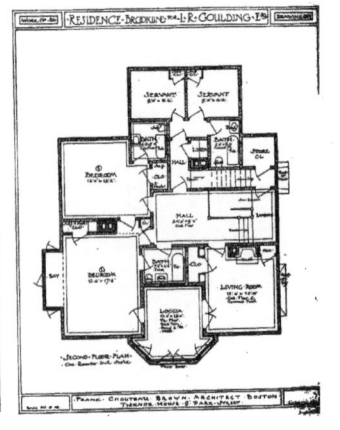

PLANS AND ELEVATIONS, HOUSE ON AMORY STREET, BROOKLINE, MASS.
FRANK CHOUTEAU BROWN, ARCHITECT.

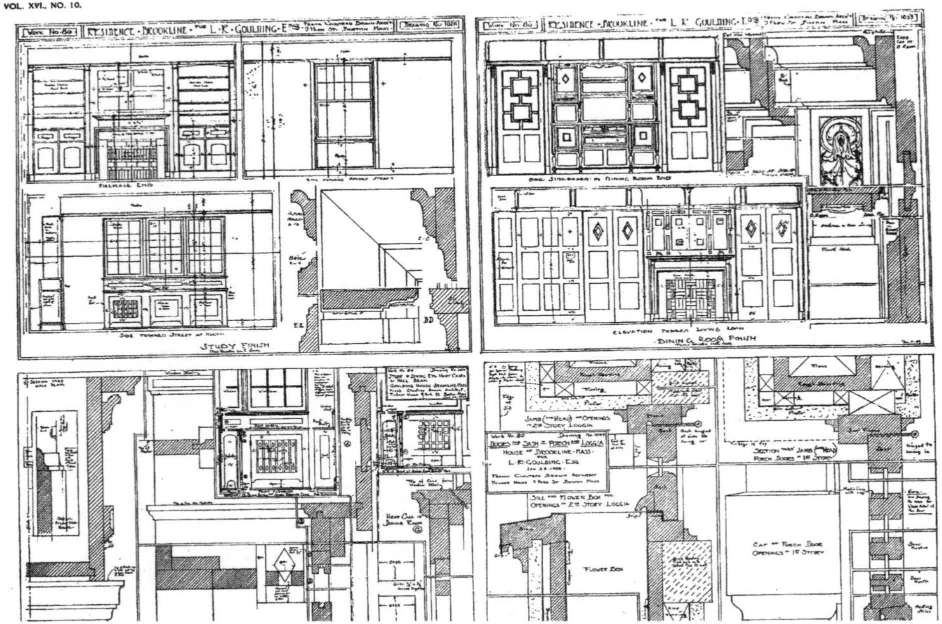
RESIDENCE · BROOKLINE · FOR L · R · GOULDING · ESQ
FIREPLACE END
STUDY FINISH
SIDE TOWARD STREET AT NORTH
OAK SIDEBOARD IN DINING ROOM END
ELEVATION TOWARD LIVING ROOM
DINING ROOM FINISH
JAMB (AND HEAD) OF OPENINGS IN 2ND STORY LOGGIA
DOORS AND SASH OF PORCH AND LOGGIA
HOUSE AT BROOKLINE · MASS ·
L · R · GOULDING · ESQ
SILL AND FLOWER BOX FOR OPENINGS IN 2ND STORY LOGGIA
FLOWER BOX
SECTION THRO' JAMB (AND HEAD) PORCH DOORS IN 1ST STORY
CAP OF PORCH DOOR OPENINGS IN 1ST STORY
HEAD CASE IN DINING ROOM

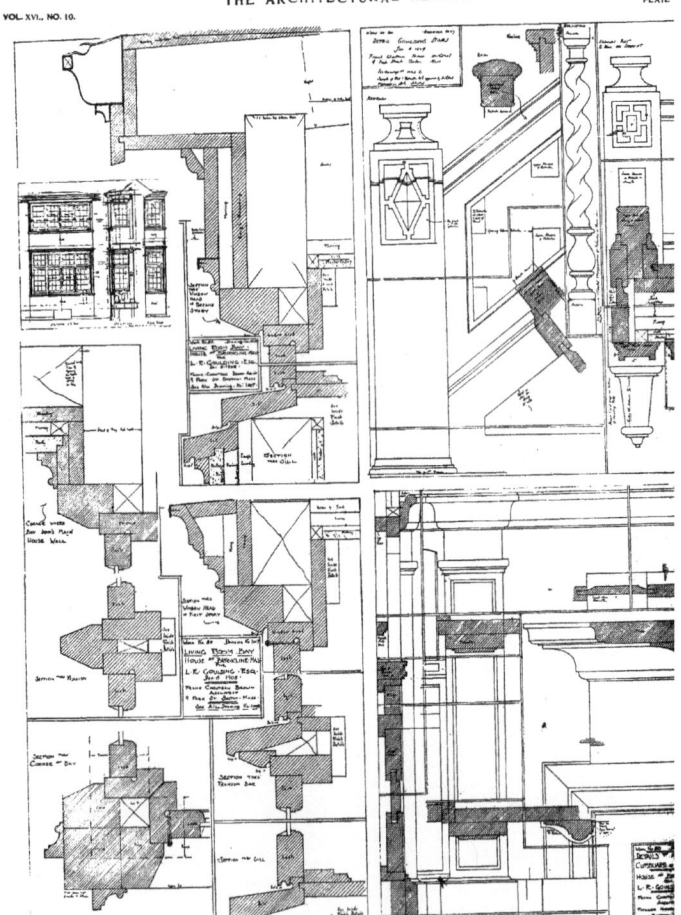

EXTERIOR AND INTERIOR DETAILS, HOUSE ON AMORY STREET, BROOKLINE, MASS.
FRANK CHOUTEAU BROWN, ARCHITECT.

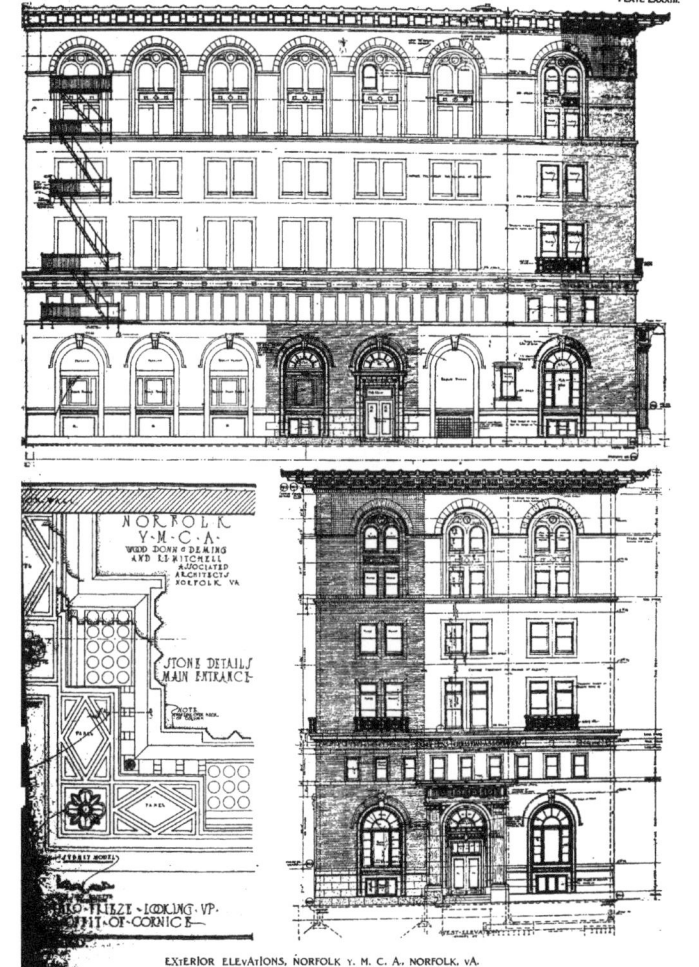

EXTERIOR ELEVATIONS, NORFOLK Y. M. C. A., NORFOLK, VA.
WOOD, DONN & DEMING AND R. E. MITCHELL, ASSOCIATE ARCHITECTS.

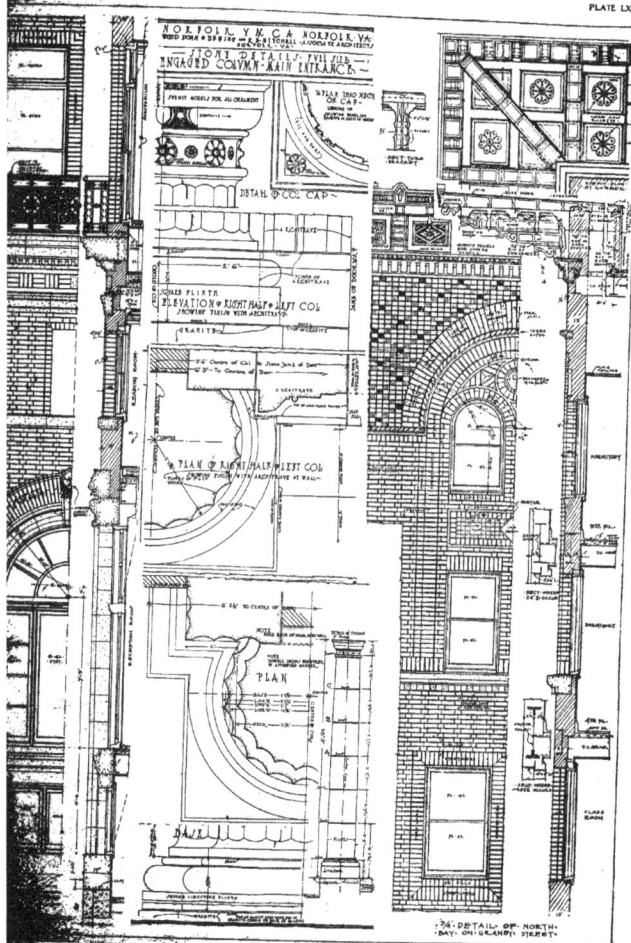

SCALE DRAWINGS AND DETAILS, NORFOLK Y. M. C. A., NORFOLK, VA.
WOOD, DONN & DEMING AND R. E. MITCHELL, ASSOCIATE ARCHITECTS.

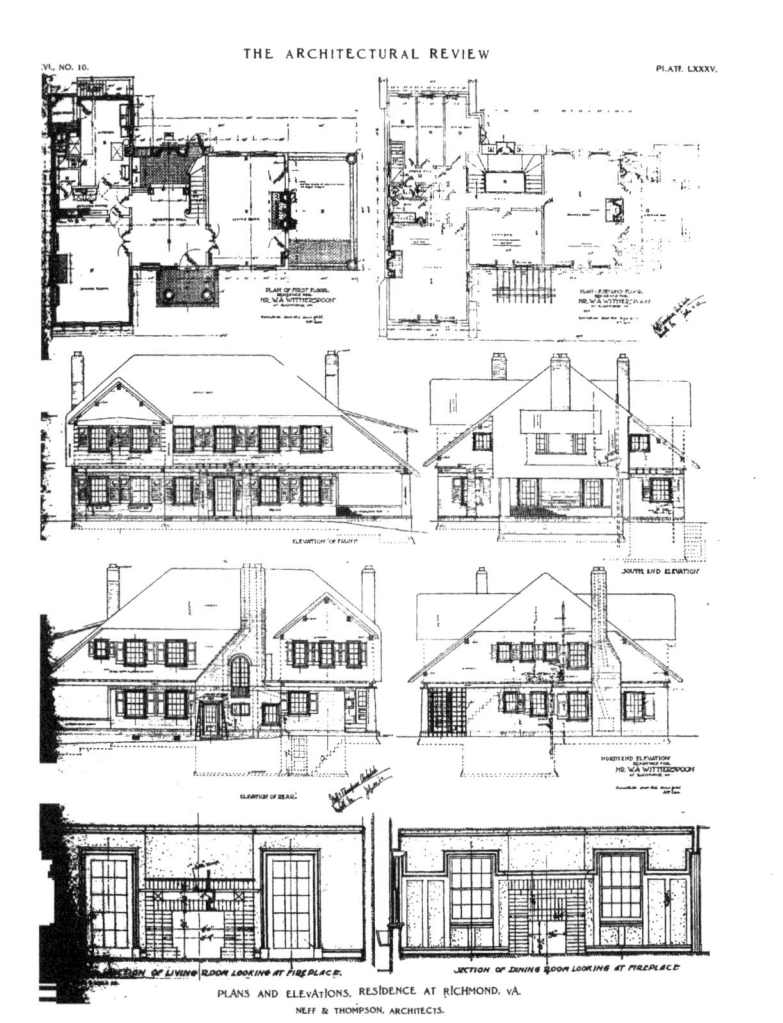

PLANS AND ELEVATIONS, RESIDENCE AT RICHMOND, VA.
NEFF & THOMPSON, ARCHITECTS.

CHURCH OF THE ASCENSION, MONTGOMERY, ALABAMA.
CRAM, GOODHUE & FERGUSON, ARCHITECTS.

DINING-ROOM, LUCKLEY, WOKINGHAM, BERKSHIRE, ENGLAND.
ERNEST NEWTON, ARCHITECT.

PLATE XII.

PLAN, CHURCH OF THE ASCENSION, MONTGOMERY, ALA.

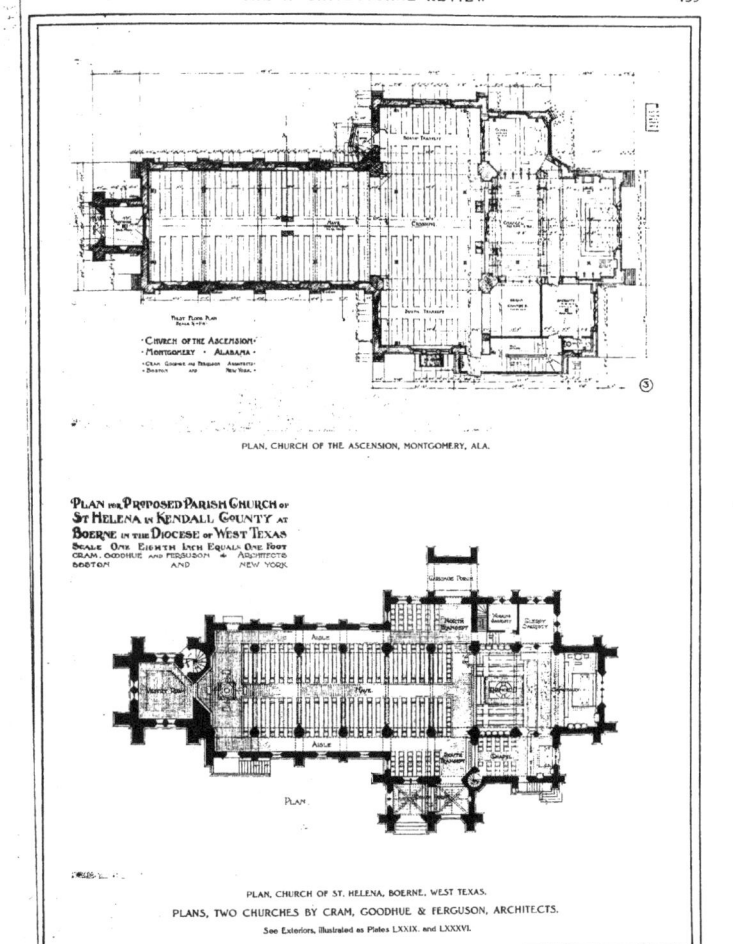

PLAN, CHURCH OF ST. HELENA, BOERNE, WEST TEXAS.
PLANS, TWO CHURCHES BY CRAM, GOODHUE & FERGUSON, ARCHITECTS.
See Exteriors, illustrated as Plates LXXIX. and LXXXVI.

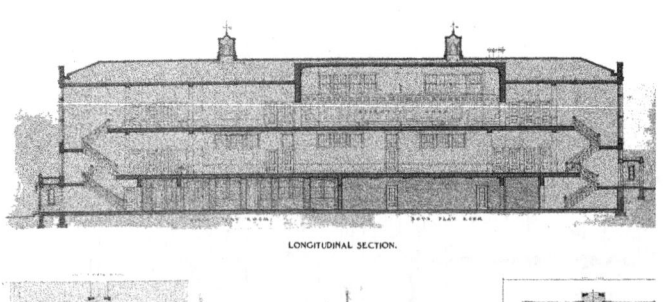

LONGITUDINAL SECTION.

FRONT ELEVATION.

PUBLIC SCHOOL, NO. 10,
MT. VERNON, N. Y.
ALBRO & LINDEBERG, ARCHITECTS.
THOMAS R. JOHNSON, ASSOCIATE.

GROUND FLOOR PLAN

FIRST FLOOR PLAN

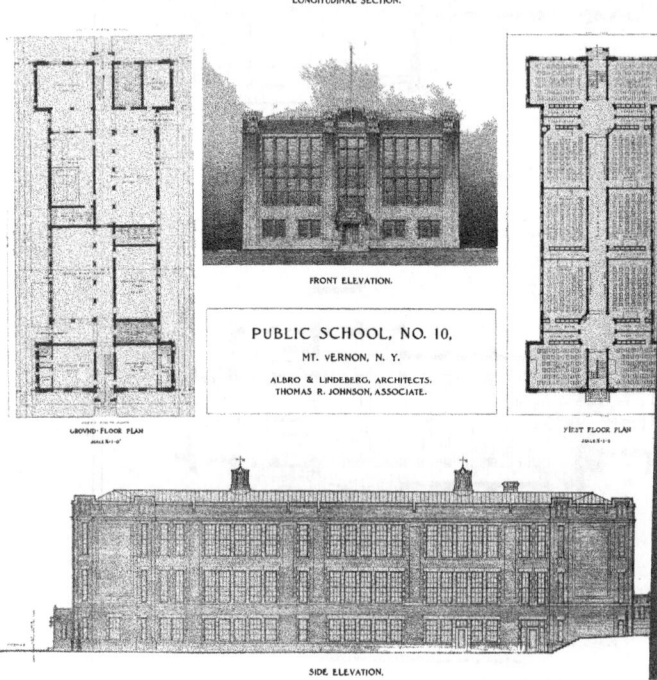

SIDE ELEVATION.

The Architectural Review

VOLUME XVI. NUMBER 10

OCTOBER, 1909

BATES & GUILD COMPANY, Publishers
144 Congress Street, Boston
NEW YORK OFFICE, PARK ROW BUILDING

PLATES

PLATE LXXIX.— Church of St. Helena, Boerne, West Texas (Photographic View) — Cram, Goodhue & Ferguson, Architects.

Plates LXXX — LXXXII — House at Brookline, Mass. (Plans, Elevations, and Details) — Frank Chouteau Brown, Architect.

Plates LXXXIII.— LXXXIV.— Norfolk Y. M. C. A., Norfolk, Va. (Elevations and Details) — Wood, Donn & Deming and Rossel Edward Mitchell, Associate Architects.

Plate LXXXV.— Residence at Richmond, Va. (Elevations and Plans) — Neff & Thompson, Architects.

Plate LXXXVI.— Church of the Ascension, Montgomery, Ala. (Photographic View) — Cram, Goodhue & Ferguson, Architects.

It is an interesting and anomalous fact that while in the field of science, mechanics, and engineering the American genius is proverbially and characteristically original, resourceful, and daring; in the matter of architectural design it is conventional, timid, and conservative compared with the European, notwithstanding the fact that from the very nature of the case it is less subject to solicitation to follow in those well-worn paths whose milestones are the architectural masterpieces of preceding generations more richly dowered with the æsthetic sense than is our own. The American architect, for some mysterious reason, has an ear as sensitive and attuned to the modern note than his European contemporary. Even the uninitiated and for the most part unobservant tourist can scarcely escape (whether for liking or abhorrence) the appeal of the "New Art," in some of its various manifestations, in such cities as Paris, Berlin, Munich, and Stockholm; yet he will look in vain for anything even remotely of its kind or conceived in similar spirit in the streets of New York, Philadelphia, or Boston — Chicago is perhaps an exception. The Middle Ages, the Fifteenth Century, the Eighteenth, find representation in any and varied presentments reminiscent of the architecture of these periods, but the spirit of the Twentieth Century speaks nowhere except in works of sheer engineering; and these are often figleaved from the old and consecrated architectural vine.

What is the reason of "this thinness"? It is not be that though not lacking in assurance of our competence in all practical fields, of the æsthetic side we are still so uncertain of ourselves that we hasten to take refuge in "the all right thing," which in architecture, we conceive to be nothing other than the imported article, tried by time and hallowed by tradition? Nor differently, a member of our nouveau riche class, with full confidence in his ability but mistrustful of his antecedents, provides himself with a collection of family portraits, a coat of arms, and a family tree with which to face the world, instead of standing squarely on his achievements and his personality.

The comparison, further developed, may have in it a useful lesson. The parvenu's course is admittedly foolish, and is apt to defeat its own end. May not we architects — by following precedents which are not ours, and which the European architects whose they are, are themselves abandoning as inadequate and inexpressive — be making a similar mistake, and missing, at the same time, a golden, a never-to-be-recovered opportunity: that of imaging the Zeit-geist in a manner beautiful, rational, and new?

In this country we are in our beginnings, all along the line. Only on this hypothesis is our civilization comprehensible; only so is it tolerable. Why, then, concern ourselves so much with architectural finalities? Why not be content to be beginners in architecture, too?

THE above editorial, first intended for our November issue two years ago, was put aside in favor of some more pressing and timely topic. Yet so rapid is our progress as a nation — even in the comparatively quiet backwaters of the port of Boston — that it may not now be printed without qualifying at least one statement that it incidentally contains. The Art Nouveau — it is with regret that we confess the fact before the world — has at last come, even unto Boston. Already one margin of the Sacred Street of the Cowpath carries a tall façade largely composed of flowing outlines, circular forms, smiling, mask-like faces, and rare and exotic vegetable growths; while a half dozen "picture theaters" have even more latterly blossomed out with smiling leprous fronts in the most eviscerated plastications of the "Philadelphia Lubinesque!"

But — the shame presses still deeper and nearer to Boston's most holy of holies — other hoardings on Washington Street, since removed, expose to the irreverent gaze of staid Bostonians and ribald Western visitors alike, nestling close under the shadow of that *sacrosanct* Museum, the Old South Church, two "Vomitories" of cast cement, in a shape and design exactly like unto the one pictured below, photographed a couple of short blocks further along this same street, in Adams Square.

Shades of the Pilgrim Fathers, how did this come to be?

ONE of the prevailing defects in the present-day dwelling architecture of this country is its lack of simplicity. In color, in design, in plan, in detail, its absence is felt throughout. In color it tends to the use of many materials and — especially in brick — of odd or bizarre tones. In design it tends to the use of complex and conventional compositions that do not suit the material in which they are constructed any more than they are likely to suit the site where they are placed. The detail, too, often runs to foreign motives, and conventional or hackneyed designs. In plan, a needless multiplicity of rooms increases the expense of building, and running the household; while it is also largely responsible for the "servant question" that is now so omnipresent!

Why is it necessary that we clothe the exterior of our buildings with consciously borrowed and derived historic trappings, till we come, unblushingly, to ask "Was such a house done in the François Premier' style?" nor experience no surprise at the answer, "No, that was the one before; this is a 'Cement Mission' design"? Just think how much architecture in America would be improved if we could but clean off all this extraneous and foreign ornament and decoration, that now confuse our designs and muss up our drawings of façades until the eye is perverted from its intent of analyzing and correcting proportions of outline and opening, and led into a trackless maze of applied and unnecessary detail. Much better no detail at all than so bastard, false, and inexpressive a lot as is now the current architectural coin!

Simplify the plan, and difficulties of housekeeping and expense of construction will both be reduced. Eliminate yet more complexity — as of finish — and who knows but they may vanish altogether!

Current Periodicals
A Review of the Recent American And Foreign Architectural Publications

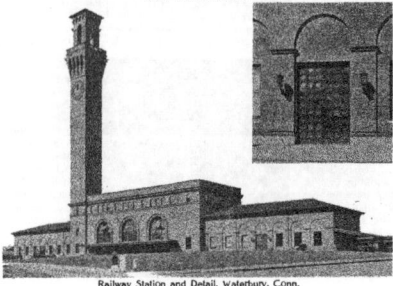

Dwelling-house, Berlin.
The Late Alfred Messel, Architect.

New Salesian Church, Bologna, Italy.
Edoardo Collamarini, Architect.
(From "The Brickbuilder.")

Church of St. Paul, Philadelphia, Pa.
Thomas, Churchman & Molitor, Architects.
(From "The Brickbuilder.")

Railway Station and Detail, Waterbury, Conn.
McKim, Mead & White, Architects.

School Administration Building, Berlin.
Ludwig Hoffmann, Architect.

PLACES of honor are given this month to Germany and Italy, those countries having produced the best of the architecture published in the September American magazines. Rivalled only by the Waterbury Station; the Salesian Church and Institute at Bologna is so unexpected a continuance of local material and precedent that it well deserves reproduction at the head of these columns; while the Berlin School Administration Building might actually have come from the very hand of Brunelleschi, or — more probably — Sanmichelli himself!

Undoubtedly the most interesting contribution to the September *Architectural Record* is Mr. Granger's article on "Modern German Architecture," which, for the last half-dozen years, has swept far and away beyond the conventional architectural output of France; being indeed the single continental country where architecture is to-day a live and vital art. For a number of years those few architects in England and America who have had the freedom of mind that enabled them to appreciate the best designs of the German and Austrian schools, at the same time as they recognized and disregarded its eccentricities and extremes, have made much profit and progress by the lessons there learned. A very considerable part of the movement for simplicity in architectural design, the use of color and the emphasis of beautiful contours and outline rather than conventional ornamentation, has resulted from the lessons taught by modern German architects — although absorbed oftentimes at second, third, or fourth hand! It is greatly to be regretted that Prof. Alfred Messel, whose work is of principal interest among the illustrations shown, and whose masterpiece, the Wertheim Warehouse, was illustrated on our own pages in July, 1906, should have recently died — as his death is a loss not only to art development in Germany, but to the entire progress of modern architecture.

Next in interest is a short article with illustrations of some sixteenth and seventeenth century Parisian mansions. While some are of familiar work, they yet make an interesting group — and a few, such as the Hôtel D'Aumont and the Hôtel de Châlons, are worthy of the most careful study and consideration. Articles on "Architecture of the Business Northwest" and "The Work of William Appleton Potter" compare rather unfavorably with the modern German work, both commercial and otherwise. Of Mr. Potter's reproduced designs, the Library at Princeton University is certainly the best.

Architecture for September publishes a number of illustrations of the Metropolitan Life Tower interiors, upon the bad taste of which we have already remarked. The interiors of a New York residence also fail narrowly but completely, from that refinement that is coming to be demanded as the standard of modern taste. Mr. Horace Trumbauer's country house at Lansdowne, Penn., that we reprint, is as distinctively a type of good Colonial architecture as the "Colonial Club" at Princeton is of bad. Win[low] & Bigelow's new well-known Garland House at Hamilton (published in THE REVIEW April, 1905) also appears. The most interesting single building is the new brick church

THE ARCHITECTURAL REVIEW 143

(From "The American Architect.") 
House at "Bayberry Point," Islip, L. I.
Grosvenor Atterbury, Architect

Detail of Entrance, "Bayberry Point,"
Grosvenor Atterbury, Architect

(From "The American Architect.") 
Pergola and Landing, "Bayberry Point," Islip, L. I.
Grosvenor Atterbury, Architect

Bologna, illustrated by a general view and detail, the former of which we reprint. This is as excellent an example of the intelligent use of material as can be provided in this country, and quite in accord with the most modern treatments anywhere in vogue. Indeed, we doubt if the expression of detail in brickwork can be carried much further than has here been done.

For articles, the September *Brickbuilder* contains the fifth instalments of "The Housing Problem" and "Warming and Ventilating of Hospitals;" and another dealing with the work of Jules Guerin — the illustrations of which, for some reason or other, express much less character and texture than is generally to be found in this artist's work. The exteriors, too, by the way, are uniformly better than his interiors, principally because better suited to the monotone brick or moonlight treatments that he affects, and in the expression of which his work appears always to the best advantage.

The plates this month are considerably more interesting than usual. A number reproduce modern treatments of brick of varied color and rough texture set in extra wide mortar joints, and include Trowbridge & Livingston's dispensary in New York; St. Mary's Church, by Carrère & Hastings & T. E. Blake; Louis Boynton's stores and apartments at Cedarhurst, L. I., and a well-conceived and conservative Colonial design for

a Washington home by Marsh & Peter. Four plates — including two of consistent interiors — are devoted to MacLaren & Thomas's home at Broadmoor, Col., a reworking (in terra-cotta) of the well-known Trianon motif. Thomas, Churchman & Molitor's Church of St. Paul at Philadelphia is along the best line of modern English design, and is here selected for reproduction.

The McKim, Mead & White railroad station at Waterbury is a most delicate and refined (possibly, too refined) treatment of a station problem, incorporating the now conventionally accepted triple-arch motive in a somewhat unhackneyed fashion. The Campanile is particularly refined *Italianate*. The texture of the brickwork shows only in the photographs of smaller details.

The Western Architect for September contains two proposed civic improvement schemes, — one at Baltimore, in the region immediately south of the present City Hall; the other for the City of Milwaukee. A number of small dwellings are illustrated, as well as a characteristic design by Mr. Ittner for the Rose Fanning School at St. Louis.

The New York Architect for August is devoted to the work of Grosvenor Atterbury and his associates. Most of it is, to a considerable extent, already well known to the profession. Still other illustrations are of old and unimportant work. A number of the best show the houses at Bayberry Point (also reproduced in

(From "Architecture.")
Country House at Lansdowne, Pa.
Horace Trumbauer, Architect.
(From "The American Architect.")

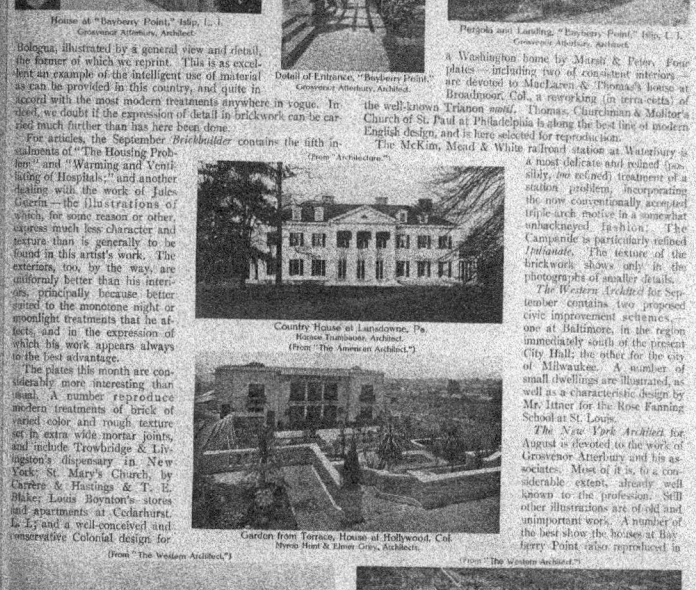

Garden from Terrace, House at Hollywood, Cal.
Myron Hunt & Elmer Grey, Architects.

(From "The Western Architect.") 
Proposed Civic Development Plan for Baltimore, Md.
J. B. Carrère & A. W. Brunner, Archts. Frederick Law Olmsted, Landscape Archt.

(From "The Western Architect.") 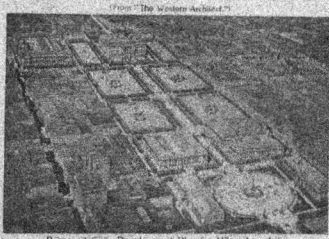
Proposed Civic Development Plan for Milwaukee, Wis.
Alfred W. Clas, Architect.

United Counties Bank, Walsall.
Cossins, Peacock & Bewley, Architects.
(From "The Architect," London.)

United Counties Bank, Dudley.
Cossins, Peacock & Bewley, Archts.
(From "The Architect," London.)

Façade in Kingsway, London.
Edwin L. Lutyens, Architect.
(From "The Architect," London.)

Small Hotel, Rue de la Faisanderie, Paris
M. Blanche, Architect.
(From "La Construction Moderne.")

The American Architect for September 8. The details of the Governor's room are valuable and distinctive. The hallway of the Bessemer Building has carried out the suggestion of the name by treating the walls and ceiling with structural ironwork — albeit rather after the style of the American engineer than the French architect! One or two new city houses; as many — and more interesting — commercial buildings, and two or three pseudo-picturesque and older-fashioned dwellings conclude the issue.

The American Architect for September 1 contains "Notes from Europe," and illustrates an attractive California garden at Hollywood by Myron Hunt & Elmer Grey (of which we reprint a general view) and a number of unusually attractive illustrations of English garden bits, from photographs by Thomas W. Sears.

September 8 appear the second article on the Goodyear series of "Refinements," illustrations of a hotel at San Antonio, and more pictures of the same stucco houses at "Bayberry Point" reproduced in *The New York Architect*. We reprint several details, giving a general idea of the treatment of the entire property.

September 15 the plates are entirely given to a stodgy and underdone court-house at Wilkes Barre, Penn., that contains, nevertheless, some excellent mural decorations.

September 22 the article deals with "The Lighting of Churches," a most particular problem that is generally, in this country, very poorly done. The illustrations hardly show types suitable to typical American church problems. The plates illustrate a number of small and attractive dwellings by Aymar Embury, 11.

Drawings for an Institution for the Blind at St. Augustine, by Edwards & Walter, are published September 20, along with some other Southern work, and a house of rather unusual

New West Wing, Temple Dinsley, Herts.
Edwin L. Lutyens, F.R.I.B.A., Architect.
(From "The Architect," London.)

"Great Roke," Witley, Surrey.

Buckland & Haywood-Farmer, Architects.
(From "The Builder's Journal," London.)

plan arrangement at St. Charles, Ill. We are pleased to note that several of this month's frontispieces are of current American work.

The September English *Architectural Review* contains interesting drawings for a restoration of the courtyard of the Morosini Palace at Venice, and the completion of the articles on "Public Buildings in the Sicilian Earthquake." The department of "Current Architecture" illustrates some additions at Chertsey by Ronald P. Jones, some changes for a Piano Warerooms in London by Walter Cave, and some views of the new Birmingham University Buildings by E. Aston Webb and E. Ingress Bell. While this pretentious group is hardly in the best commendable style, yet the details are of distinctly modern English type and treatment.

The Builder publishes competitive drawings for various municipal buildings and town halls, including Stoke-upon-Trent, Burslem, Grimsby, and Reading; and, September 18, a picturesque chapel at Fresham, Surrey, by W. Curtis Green.

The Architect prints a number of business premises, as well as one or two of the town hall competitions already mentioned, and, September 24, an article on "Town Planning." We reprint two designs by Mr. Lutyens, and a couple of bank façades by Cossins, Peacock & Bewley, one of which, to the American mind, rather more suggests a dignified moving-picture show than a banking institution.

The Builder's Journal writes of two American architects, — George B. Post (September 8) and Charles F. McKim (September 29), — and reproduces representative work. On September 15 they print a house at Witley, Surrey, by Herbert Buckland and Haywood-Farmer.

La Construction Moderne prints a modern hotel by M. Blanche, a typically bizarre French villa, and reproductions of the buildings for the Nancy Exposition.

The Architectural Review

Volume XVI   November, 1909   Number 11

Montebello, Maryland

By Lawrence Hall Fowler

With Photographs by Julian A. Buckly

ONE of the chief charms of an old dwelling is the power it has of picturing for us customs and manners that belong irrevocably to the past. Yet however strong its suggestiveness, if it be but another example of a local type it lacks a certain tantalizing quality possessed by a house which, like the one we are considering, is unique even in its own neighborhood.

Montebello, when built, was about two and a half miles northeast of Baltimore Town. Still further north was Hampton, the estate of the Ridgelys, with its many acres and its imposing mansion. To the south, nearer the town, stood Belvedere, the hospitable home of Col. John Eager Howard; and, but a short distance to the west, was Homewood, that beautiful house which Charles Carroll of Carrollton built for his son soon after his marriage to Mrs. Howard's sister, in 1800.

Hampton, Belvedere, and Homewood, though built after the Revolution, carry on to the beginning of the nineteenth century the Colonial tradition of large landed estates. Differing as they do from one another, yet they belong to the same general type, having in common a central building connected by one-story passages to lower wings on each side. Montebello not only breaks with this traditional plan, but is the product of rather different social conditions.

About the middle of the eighteenth century many families of Scotch and North Irish descent settled in Baltimore. Among these was the family of General Samuel Smith, the builder of Montebello. By the year 1776 Samuel Smith's father had become one of the wealthiest merchants of the town. Samuel, then twenty-four years of age, enlisted in Smallwood's Regiment as a Captain; was finally promoted to Lieutenant-Colonel and voted a sword by Congress for his gallant defense of Fort Mifflin.

But war had put a stop to commerce; and when Samuel Smith returned to his father's counting-house — having resigned in 1779 or 1780 — we can thenceforth follow his steady advance in wealth and influence, and even obtain occasional glimpses of his efforts to provide himself with homes suitable to his position.

The declaration of peace in 1783 was followed by a period of great prosperity for the merchants of Baltimore, and its population increased from 13,503 in 1790 to 26,514 in 1800. In 1790 Samuel Smith is found among the incorporators of the Bank of Maryland, which was in the habit of declaring "exorbitant dividends." In 1792 James McHenry wrote to Alexander Hamilton that Smith was "largely in the iron works, a man of great wealth, without skill in public affairs." In this same year he bought the first tract of the estate afterwards named Montebello. Other tracts, parts of old grants known as "Gosnel's Folly," "Sheridan's Discovery," "Broad's Improvement," "Hosier's Choice," "Merryman's Chance," "Loveleve's Addition," and "Orange" were added at various times up to 1800, ma-

A Corner of the Portico

Montebello from the South

Copyright, 1909, by Bates & Guild Company

Entrance Front, from the South.

Looking in to the Entrance.

king a total of more than 520 acres.

From Griffith's "Annals of Baltimore" we learn that, in 1796, ' The home of General Smith on the north side of Water Street was erected on a plan furnished by himself and executed by Messrs. John Scroggs, Robert Steuart, and James Mosher, Builders." While this town house was being built General Smith bought the particular piece of land on which his country house was to stand. Although it is hardly probable he was erecting two such important homes at the same time, yet the one in the country seems to have been started within a few years after the purchase of this land.

In the summers of 1797, 1799, and 1800 there were serious epidemics of yellow fever in Baltimore, which drove many from the town to build homes on the hills to the north. Doubtless during one of these years General Smith began his country house; indeed, there is a tradition that it was being built when the French, under Marshal Lannes, defeated the Austrians at Montebello, in June, 1800, and that the General, a great admirer of the French, named his place in honor of this victory.

We have a delightful picture of the neighborhood of Montebello as it appeared to William Wirt in 1822. Writing from Baltimore to his daughter in Washington, he describes a walk he took early one morning "two and a half miles out to Mr. Thompson's to breakfast.... After walking about a mile, I came to the summit of a hill that overlooks the city, and there I stopped a moment to take breath and look back on it.... After feasting my eye for some time on the rich, diversified and. boundless landscape that lay before me, meditating on the future grandeur of this city, and the rising glories of the nation, I turned round my face to resume my walk into the country, when all its soft beauties burst by surprise upon me. For while I had been looking back on town, bay, and

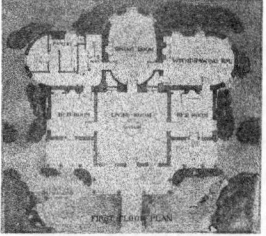

Scale Drawing, Entrance and Porch.

fort, the sun had risen and was now so high that its light was pouring full upon hill and valley, field and forest, blazing in bright reflection from all the eastern windows of the hundreds of country houses that crowned the heights around me, and dancing on all the leaves that waved and wantoned in the morning breeze.... The sites of the houses are well selected — always upon some eminence, embosomed amid beautiful trees, from which their white fronts peep out enchantingly; for the houses are all white, which adds much to the cheerfulness and grace of this unrivaled scenery."

Thus William Wirt brings us to the very gate of Montebello, for General Smith lived just across the Harford Road from Mr. Thompson. The house, facing southwest, was on high land with a fine view over the city and harbor. In front the ground sloped gradually for about two hundred feet to a terrace, but at the back it fell more abruptly, and had been scooped out, amphitheatrical fashion, to give light and air to the rear of the basement. Except the terrace mentioned above and a small one immediately in front of the house, there seems to have been no formal treatment of the grounds. To-day there is a stately grove of oaks at the rear, and on the lawn in front are evergreens and other ornamental trees.

In plan, the house was in two nearly equal parts. The front half, but one story above the ground, had a columned porch extending across the front; from the marble pavement of which, only a few inches above grade, you entered, in the center, a large square drawing-room and, on each side, a smaller room. The rear half, two stories and a basement above ground, was trefoil in plan, and contained, on the first floor, an oval dining room on the center axis, a large semi-circular ended room on the right, and on the left, a similar space occupied by the stairway, pantry, and, in a mezzanine story, the bath and housekee

The Front in the Late Fall. Western End

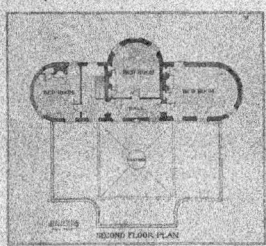

Second Floor Plan

Detail, Entrance and Porch Finish.

quarters. In the second story there are three bedrooms and a hallway, and in the basement, which extended under the entire house except the porch, there was a kitchen and laundry in the rear and, in front, storerooms, a wine cellar, and the entrance to a mysterious, inclined, vaulted tunnel that extended to a considerable distance from the house.

The oval dining-room had a low panelled wainscot, the openings framed with architrave, pilaster-strips and cornice, and at the ceiling a simple cornice with dentils. Formerly there was a fine marble mantel from Italy, and on the walls two handsome Stuart portraits of General Smith and his wife. This room, more elaborately finished than the others, when possessed of its original furniture, much of it from France and of exceptional workmanship, must have presented a very dignified appearance. Except the drawing-room, with its built-in glazed bookcases and its ceiling slightly bowed to an odd circular lantern in the center, the interiors were not remarkable; while the staircase, unimportant in plan, was treated very plainly. A graceful hallway arch, springing from oval fluted columns, was the principal decorative feature of the second story.

The detail, both exterior and interior, was extremely minute in scale. The interior cornices, especially, departed far from the classic tradition; even as allowed at Annapolis, not so many years before. The resemblance between the detail of this house and that of Homewood, not only in the scale and character of the mouldings, but even in the design of individual features, is very close — indeed, much closer than can be entirely explained by the fact that they were contemporaries. It seems almost certain that the same man must have "executed" the work in both places.

With its unusual mass, its white walls, its long stretches of fine balustrade, and its oddly curved porch, level with the ground, and more extensive than usual at that time, Montebello must certainly have produced a much gayer and more villa-like effect than its refined and stately neighbor, Homewood. Some of this villa character is no doubt due to tastes formed by Samuel Smith when, as a young man, he spent four years in Europe, traveling not only in England and France but also most extensively in Italy, Spain, and Portugal. In this connection it is interesting to note that at Strabane, Ireland, the birthplace of General Smith's father, there is a villa which, as shown in an old eighteenth-century architectural book now in the library of the Maryland Historical Society, quite decidedly resembles Montebello — certainly a striking coincidence, if nothing more.

About 1793 Samuel Smith began to take a more prominent part in the affairs of his city and State, as well as of the nation — no longer deserving McHenry's description as "without skill in public affairs." For forty years in Congress he was a close friend and firm supporter of Jefferson, Madison, and Monroe, and was one of the last of the Revolutionary stock in the Senate. During this period he and his wife Margaret Spear, "a beautiful and imperious woman," extended their hospitality to many of the most distinguished men of the day. From France came Lafayette, the Duc de Montebello, son of Marshal Lannes, and Prince Achille Murat; and among Americans there were Madison, Monroe, John Quincy Adams, and Andrew Jackson.

When eighty-three years old General Smith was called from Montebello, by the citizens of Baltimore, to put down the serious Bank Riot of 1835. The mob suppressed, he was unanimously chosen Mayor, which office he held to within a short time of his death, in 1839. A contemporary manuscript life of the General closes with the couplet:

"Washington saved the country;
General Smith, his city."

148 THE ARCHITECTURAL REVIEW

General view from the West.

Detail of Entrance.

A Detail of the Porch.

Corner of Porch Entablature and Balustrade.

Entrance, General View.

Corner of Porch and House.

Detail, Porch Roof Balustrade.

Detail of Niche and Cornice.

HOUSE FOR J. DAVENPORT CHENEY, ESQ., SOUTH MANCHESTER, CONN.
CHARLES A. PLATT, ARCHITECT.

MODERN ENGLISH COUNTRY HOUSES

PLATE XIII.

SOUTHWEST VIEW, WEST CHART, LIMPSFIELD, SURREY, ENGLAND.
C. FORSYTH DOUSLE, ARCHITECT

THE ARCHITECTURAL REVIEW

PLATE XXXVIII

ADMINISTRATION BUILDING, CARNEGIE INSTITUTION OF WASHINGTON, WASHINGTON, D. C.
CARRÈRE & HASTINGS, ARCHITECTS

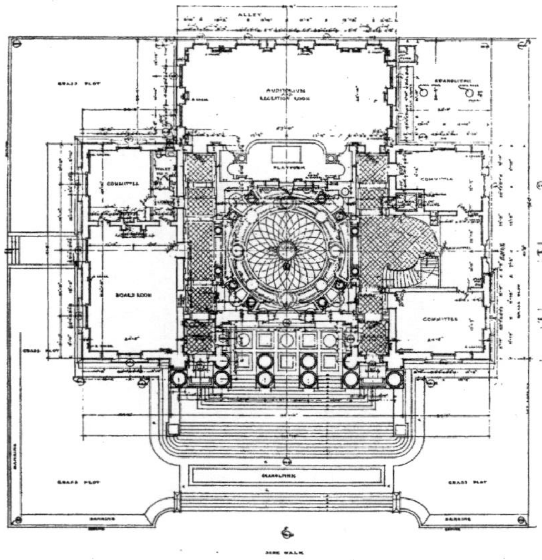

FIRST FLOOR PLAN

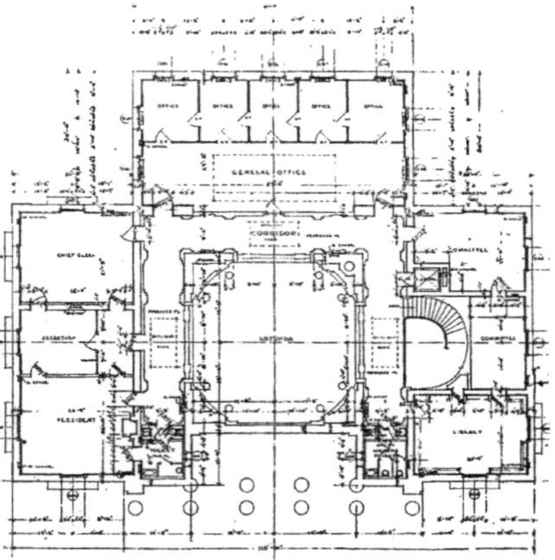

SECOND FLOOR PLAN

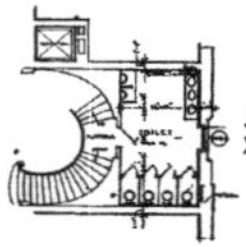

MEZZANINE

· NORTH · ELEVATION ·
· SCALE ⅛" = ONE FOOT ·

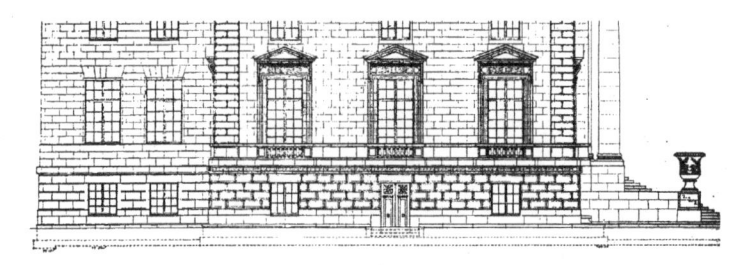

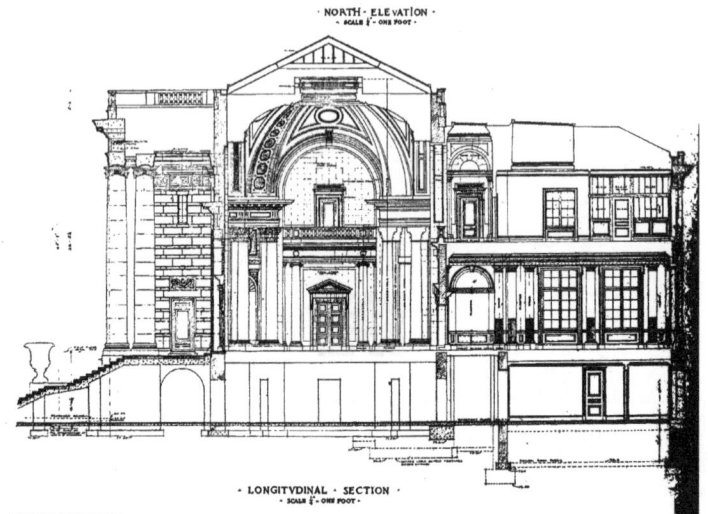

· LONGITVDINAL · SECTION ·
· SCALE ⅛" = ONE FOOT ·

ELEVATION AND SECTION, CARNEGIE INSTITUTION OF WASHINGTON, WASHINGTON, D. C.
CARRÈRE & HASTINGS, ARCHITECTS.

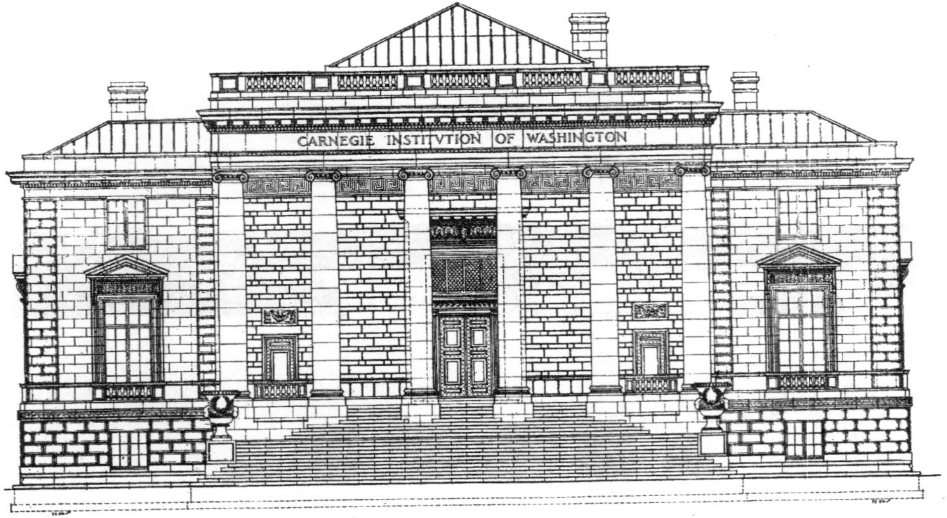

FRONT ELEVATION, CARNEGIE INSTITUTION OF WASHINGTON, WASHINGTON, D. C.

SCALE DETAIL, CARNEGIE INSTITUTION OF WASHINGTON, WASHINGTON, D. C.
CARRÈRE & HASTINGS, ARCHITECTS.

THIRD FLOOR.

FIRST FLOOR.

BASEMENT.

FLOOR PLANS. RELIEF STATION OF THE BOSTON CITY HOSPITAL, PORTER STREET, EAST BOSTON, MASS.
EDWARD PERCY DANA, ARCHITECT.

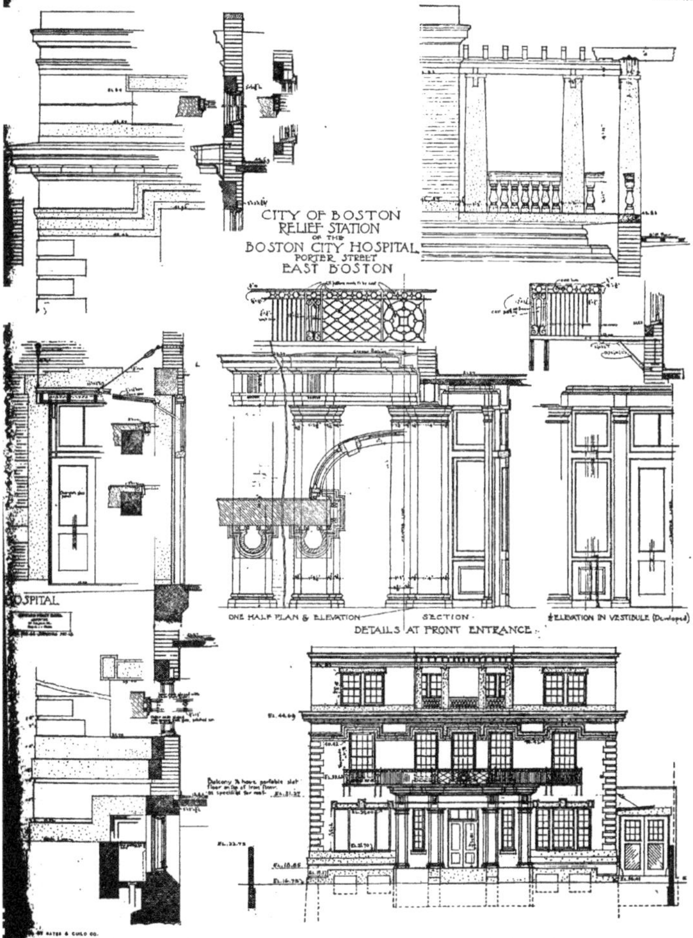

ELEVATION AND DETAILS, RELIEF STATION OF THE BOSTON CITY HOSPITAL, PORTER STREET, EAST BOSTON, MASS.

EDWARD PERCY DANA, ARCHITECT.

RELIEF STATION OF THE BOSTON CITY HOSPITAL, PORTER STREET, EAST BOSTON, MASS.
EDWARD PERCY BAXA, ARCHITECT

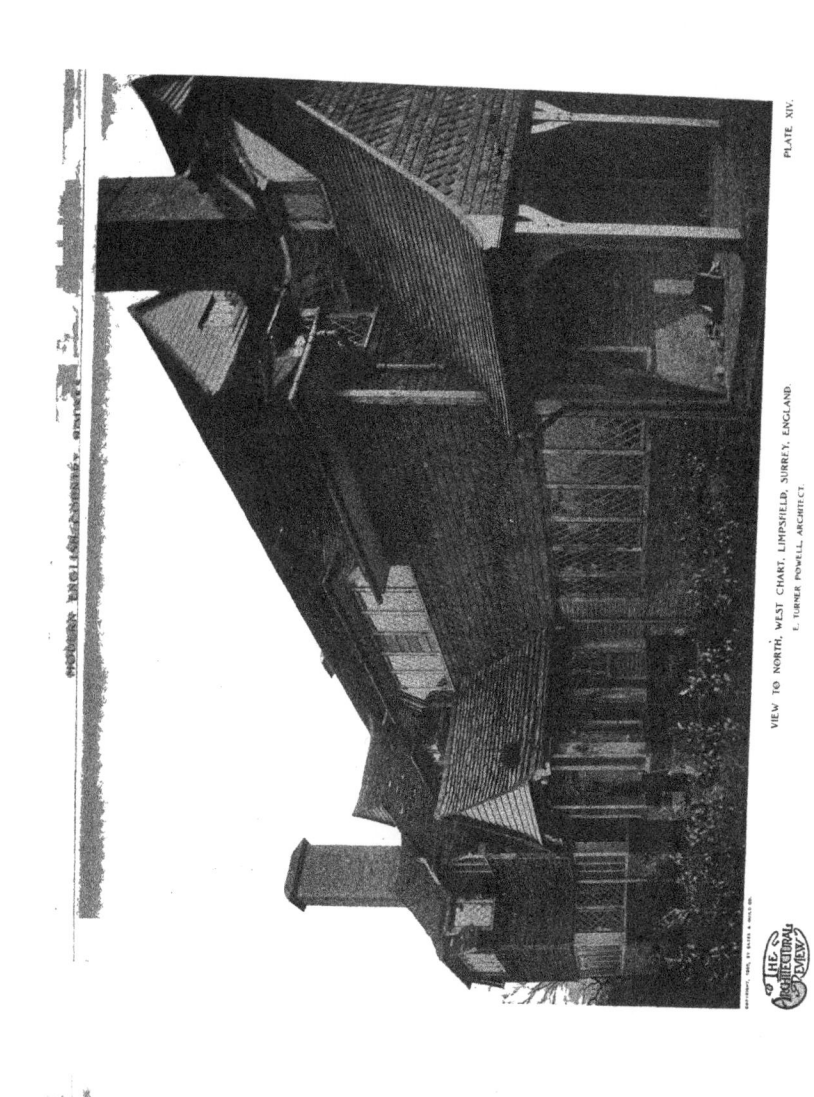

VIEW TO NORTH, WEST CHART, LIMPSFIELD, SURREY, ENGLAND.
E. TURNER POWELL, ARCHITECT.

PLATE XIV.

HOUSE AT NEWPORT, LIVING SIDE.

HOUSE AT BROOKLINE, FROM THE GARDEN.

HOUSE AT AUBURN, ENTRANCE FRONT.

HOUSE AT CHESTNUT HILL, FROM THE STREET.

THREE PLASTER HOUSES. A. LOVELL LITTLE, JR., ARCHITECT.

RESIDENCE FOR
EDWIN S. MACK
MILWAUKEE, WIS.
BRUST & PHILIPP, ARCHITECTS

The Architectural Review

VOLUME XVI. NUMBER 11

NOVEMBER, 1909

BATES & GUILD COMPANY, Publishers
144 Congress Street, Boston
NEW YORK OFFICE, PARK ROW BUILDING

Published monthly. Price, mailed flat to any address in the United States or Canada, five dollars per annum, in advance; to any foreign address, six dollars per annum, in advance. Subscriptions begin with the issue *following* their receipt. Single copies, fifty cents. Special numbers, two dollars. Entered as second-class mail-matter at the Post-office, Boston, Massachusetts, November 27, 1891.

PLATES

PLATES LXXXVII.—XCI.—CARNEGIE INSTITUTION OF WASHINGTON, WASHINGTON, D. C. (PHOTOGRAPHIC VIEW, PLANS, ELEVATIONS, SECTION, AND DETAIL) — CARRÈRE & HASTINGS, ARCHITECTS.

PLATES XCII.—XCIV.—RELIEF STATION OF THE CITY OF BOSTON, PORTER STREET, EAST BOSTON, MASS. (PLANS, ELEVATIONS, DETAIL, AND PHOTOGRAPHIC VIEW)—EDWARD PERCY DANA, ARCHITECT.

WE have frequently occasion to cavil at the way architecture is treated in the popular magazines. An instance occurs — and, most unfortunately, in rather a more authoritative quarter than usual! — in a recent issue of *Scribner's;* where an article dealing with "The Evolution of the Sky-Scraper" contains a number of illustrations that, from the point of view of the architect, most inadequately present the case.

Difficult as it would seem to be to select a dozen structures that would definitively illustrate this subject, yet Mr. Claude Bragdon (as recently as the August number of *The Architectural Record*) has made precisely the best showing of American office buildings it would be possible to select; provided one were restricted to the number (12) there reproduced. The illustrations in the popular monthly above referred to, however, woefully misrepresent the standard of design holding in this country at the present day. Most of all we quarrel with the titling of a picture of the now antiquated and old-fashioned Singer Building, at 561 Broadway, as "The Logical Sky-Scraper"— a most misleading caption, and one calculated to give a particularly unpleasant and wrong impression by suggesting this structure to be an ideal solution of the problem! The single virtue — if such it can be called — of this design is that it frankly recognizes the use of a steel framework, employed in much the way half-timber was first used in France, filling the spaces between the supporting framework with another structural material, generally brick. Yet it has been recognized now for some years that the employment of exposed and unprotected steelwork is as false and artificial a construction as any of the old and historic shams — for steel must be protected from both fire and weather in order to endure! Certainly neither the designers of this building nor any one else in the profession would consider it worthy — in this present day and generation — of being set up as the ultimate standard of "sky-scraper" design!

Yet in even casually glancing over the illustrations the general reader would — from this most misleading title — naturally come to just such a conclusion; and so has a notable injustice been done to the profession, placing it at a distinct disadvantage before the readers of this magazine. The editor doubtless relied entirely upon the reputation of the writer of this article; and in accepting his personal preferences or predilections has done his small, but responsible, part in postponing by that much the longer the artistic coming-of-age of the American people!

Apparently, if we are ever to progress as a nation beyond the nursery stage of our artistic development, not only is a Bureau of Fine Arts a necessity, but we need, as well, a Bureau to Censor the Public Press! Otherwise there is little hope of ever raising the standards of the public to such a point that they will recognize, and appreciate, good, reputable, and spontaneously direct architectural design and construction.

IN all things connected with the education of the public it is increasingly important that those attempting to deal with these subjects should be so carefully selected and properly supervised that they have no opportunity to exploit bad taste rather than good! At times, even people of reputation, through failure to understand their audiences; a neglect of those elementary things that they themselves assume as being taken for granted, but of which their hearers may happen to be ignorant; or from a wider eclecticism in taste, fail in setting standards that will be accepted by those they are endeavoring to instruct, thus sometimes ending by doing more effective harm than good.

Of the general inadequacy of the public press to deal with this subject we have given above a fairly representative example. Even those papers professing to most authoritatively instruct the public do so in the most happenstance manner, without proper editorial supervision; their editors rarely having had the architectural training and experience necessary to enable them to act as public censors — and in what other capacity *do* they act! — of American art. How can anything be expected from the present state of affairs? Should not the architects make it their business, as individuals and as a body, to see that proper advisory boards are instituted, to whom the editors of these popular magazines could turn with confidence when considering the publication of architectural subjects, with some certainty of obtaining authoritative and unbiased criticism, by means of which they might help towards the betterment of our public artistic morals!

A DOZEN years ago, or thereabouts, a draughtsman employed in a Baltimore office had his curiosity so aroused by rumors of an unknown but interesting house existing upon the outskirts of the town, as to devote a Sunday afternoon to following up the elusive trail. Eventually he found the building — at that time already abandoned and fast falling into ruin. His enthusiasm brought the entire office force the following Sunday in a pilgrimage to view the structure, which none of them had before known. On that occasion they divided among themselves the task of measuring and photographing the dwelling; while later one of their number undertook to find out what was to be discovered about the building, and its history.

The result of that picnic jaunt appears in this number as our leading article; and causes us to wonder if there do not exist in other localities houses of as much interest, and dwellings as little known. Could not some of our younger draughtsmen much benefit themselves, as well as perform work of actual value to the profession, by seeking out and preserving, by photographs and measured drawings, examples of the early architecture of this country that would otherwise be lost to posterity? It is not even necessary that such pilgrimages should be undertaken by any definite organization. An informal sketch club composed of members of an office, or a group of friends, could do the work as well; and undoubtedly would undertake it once they were assured the fruits of their energy would be preserved as a record of their local architecture in some permanent form. Could the Architectural League itself do better than undertake so important a work, making a yearly or occasional publication of the material collected, in portfolio or other convenient form; such publication possibly taking the place of their fragmentary year-book, now defunct?

The Architectural Sketch Association of England make their annual tours in just this informal picnicing way; and yearly return laden with architectural plunder of novel interest and undoubted value, which they afterwards publish. "The Committee for the Survey of the Memorials of Greater London" is making a thorough canvass of that entire vicinity, under the systematic control of individuals responsible for certain sections, thus keeping track of all historic buildings and reporting any contemplated changes that endanger them; so that, if it is impossible to preserve the structure itself, it may be thoroughly photographed and measured before being torn down, or otherwise injured by permanent alterations or emendations. We are firmly convinced there is equal need and opportunity in America. It remains only for our developing architects to look about them, each in his own neighborhood, and observe what awaits his hand to be done.

Current Periodicals
A Review of the Recent American And Foreign Architectural Publications

(From "The American Architect.")

Detail, House of W. N. Steigerwalt, Merion, Pa.
Horace Trumbauer, Architect.

(From "The American Architect.")

Two New York Towers.

(From "The Western Architect.")

Mural Decoration by Kenyon Cox, Luzerne County Court-House, Wilkes-Barre, Pa.
McCormick & French, Architects.

(From "The American Architect.")

House of W. H. Crowell, Esq., Glenridge, N. J.
Davis, McGrath & Kiessling, Architects.

(From "The American Architect.")

Side Door, Country House, Radnor, Pa.
Cope & Stewardson, Architects.

OCTOBER 6 *The American Architect* describes the Metropolitan Tower. Further comment is unnecessary, but we reproduce one plate for its picturesque grouping of old and new American city architecture — as well as for its exact illustration of the right and wrong way (in towers) for architects to avail themselves of foreign motives as precedent.

October 13 appears an article, by Oswald C. Hering, reproducing an attractive design by the author for a house at Garden City, as well as the month's instalment of "The Current Architectural Press." From the plates we reproduce Davis, McGrath & Kiessling's Crowell House at Glenridge, which, with Mr. William Bates's now well-known Lawrence Park House and Mr. Trumbauer's stone and half-timber house at Merion, are illustrated in this issue. The latter, by the way, contains an extremely charming entrance detail, much more intimate and domestic than the larger composition itself.

October 20 Mr. Swales's "Notes from Europe" illustrates two attractive houses by Mr. Macartney, while the plates are devoted to one of the worst American Gothic (?) church designs we ever remember having seen, whose real demerits are obvious despite the editorial care in publishing views wherein the "hifaluting" tower is rendered as inconspicuous as possible. It appears in all its dazzling magnificence in the plates of working drawings! A classic church, by C. P. Huntington, and Mr. Emile Weil's Touro Synagogue at New Orleans, which was published in *The Brickbuilder* for August, complete the issue.

October 27 contains the third paper of Mr. Goodyear's series; and a house near Radnor, Penn., by Cope & Stewardson — of which one side, that toward the garden, is considerably the simpler and more attractive. We reproduce an entrance detail. Eames & Young's new Washington Hotel at Seattle appears, in the exterior view reproduced, rather too bare and bald of interest. In skyscraper office buildings simplicity *can* sometimes become a fault.

Architecture for October prints sketches for a Country Club at Rumson, N. J., and a Borough Hall at Roselle, N. J., the latter by Squires & Wynkoop. Bliss & Faville's Bank of California at San Francisco has been previously illustrated by drawings and studies, where it appeared to rather better advantage than in the unpleasantly square form in which it has here been realized. An attractive country house of Spanish suggestion, by Oswald C. Hering, and some studies of novel types for a one-story house (Thank Heavens, it is *not* a "bungalow") by the "B. N." Design

Whitney Central Bank, New Orleans, La.
Linton & Russell, Architects. Emile Weil, Associate Architect.
(From "The New York Architect.")

Artillery Stables, Military Academy, West Point.
Cram, Goodhue & Ferguson, Architects.
(From "The Brickbuilder.")

Royal Insurance Building, San Francisco, Cal.
Howells & Stokes, Architects.
(From "Architecture.")

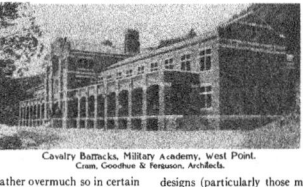

Cavalry Barracks, Military Academy, West Point.
Cram, Goodhue & Ferguson, Architects.
(From "The Brickbuilder.")

Country House, Daniel Bacon, Esq., Ardsley, N. Y.
Oswald C. Hering, Architect.
(From "The Western Architect.")

New Franklin School, St. Louis, Mo.
William B. Ittner, Architect.

ng Club, are also to be noted. Mr. Trumbauer's residence for George Gould, corner Fifth Avenue and 67th Street, New York, is classically and uninterestingly formal and cold, partly because of the monotony of the material — neither of which criticisms could be applied to Howell & Stokes's Royal Insurance Building at San Francisco (which we reproduce). Although equally formal and classic in scheme, both color-treatment and handling add interest and variety; in fact, rather overmuch so in certain of the details, which might have been better handled with more restraint. The primly formal city house by Taylor & Levi with its "stepped" gable rather strongly suggests Dutch Renaissance precedent — an unworked field that, from this attempt, would appear to have much better still in sterile.

The *Brickbuilder* for October contains an article dealing with the actual attempt to provide modern working men's houses at low cost in Philadelphia; Part I of "The Warming and Ventilating of Hospitals;" an article on "The Character and Construction of Terra-Cotta," the latter in part illustrated with cuts taken from the Catalogue of the Northwestern Terra-Cotta Company; and a report of the Jury of Award of the brick house competition, accompanied by reproductions of one of the premiated and mentioned designs.

From these results, it would appear that rather more attention had been paid by the contestants to the limit of cost than was the case with the last competition; although — despite the optimistic statement contained in the opening paragraph of the Jury's report — it is *extremely* doubtful if more than two or three of the designs reproduced could possibly built for $10,000! Setting aside this purely practical and commercial consideration, a number of the designs reproduced are aesthetically attractive and commendable; particularly that given first place. It is suggested that one or two of the others are more nearly suited to exterior treatment in plaster or concrete than in brick, the perspective of the third-prize design — and the elevation of the one placed second — being even so rendered.

While several of these house designs (particularly those most evidencing English influence) indicate a feeling for and study of textural treatments of brickwork, it is to be questioned whether, on a small house, too much patterning in this material — particularly when panels or closures of concrete form a part of the design — does not detract from its simplicity and restfulness, just as they help save a larger structure from monotony. There also comes into the question a very serious consideration of expense, inasmuch as anything out of the ordinary materially increases the labor necessary in constructing the work, and this — in a $10,000 house — would prove to be a very important consideration.

The plates illustrate Cram, Goodhue & Ferguson's Artillery and Cavalry Stables at West Point, along with two of the new officers' quarters and the Cavalry and Artillery Barracks; a brick church at Denver, Col., by the same architects, shown with some of the working drawings; the office building and library for the College of Physicians at Philadelphia, by Cope & Stewardson; and Albert Randolph Ross' Fairmount College Library at Wichita, Kan. Of these the stables and officers' quarters, West Point, are the most pleasing and simple uses of English precedent, better suited to the material than the classic columns of the last,

(From "La Construction Moderne.") *(From "The Architectural Review," London.)* *(From "The Architect," London.)*

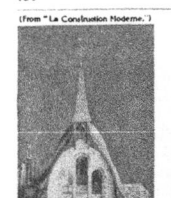

Model of Chapel in Normandy.
M. Storez, Architect.

Entrance Front, Coldicote, Warwickshire.
E. Guy Dawber, Architect.

Addition to St. Chads Church.
J. Gibbons & Son, Architects.

and nervous window-treatment of the next to last structure named.

The Western Architect for October publishes the Luzerne County Court-house at Wilkes Barre, Penn. (illustrated in *The American Architect* last month). For reproduction we have preferably selected one of the mural decorations; the building being — architecturally — a most disappointing use of tedious conventional precedent. The new Franklin School at St. Louis, the perspective of which we reprint, shows a modern variant from the ordinary type of school plan; and a couple of houses in Cleveland by Frank B. Meade, a house at Baltimore by Ellicott & Emmart (credit not given), another dwelling in Seattle, and a couple of business blocks, complete the publication of United States work. The residence and theater in Chili are of interest as showing what our South American contemporaries are doing.

The Architectural Record for October has for its principal article a description of the architecture of Harvard College, with a number of illustrations, on barely half of which are the names of the architects given. A French theater in concrete is illustrated and described, and some California work by Lewis P. Hobart, of which the majority appears of a uniformly high grade — and interesting, besides, from the unusual character of a number of the problems. We regret that the poor quality of the illustrations makes it impossible for us to reproduce any of the buildings shown. The pages of "Notes and Comments" contain some illustrations of a "bottling-house," by Henry C. Hengels, of direct and rational concrete construction and design.

The September *New York Architect* is devoted to commercial buildings (and the Jersey City Hospital) by Clinton & Russell, of which the best known is the Hudson Terminal. We reprint a study for a bank building at New Orleans, frankly inspired by such excellent precedent as the Gorham and Knickerbocker

(From "The Architect," London.)

Fulham Central Library.
Henry T. Hare, F.R.I.B.A., Architect.

Buildings in New York. The number is prefaced by three views of M. Laloux' Hôtel de Ville at Tours.

The October English *Architectural Review* has two articles treating of distinguished architects, — Sir Christopher Wren and Charles Follen McKim, — the latter being illustrated by a great number of photographs of work of the firm, that show evidence of having been gathered somewhat hastily together. Certainly the Tiffany House and the Rhode Island State Capitol are not to be considered as among their masterpieces! "Current Architecture" illustrates one of Mr. Guy Dawber's picturesque English stone houses. Except the somewhat disturbing lack of expressed support over the mullioned window-openings, the building is thoroughly domestic, successful, and attractive.

The Builder's Journal for October 6 prints an article on D. H. Burnham and his work, accompanied by illustrations of the latter; and, on October 27, three buildings for a "Village in the Elan Valley for the City of Birmingham Water Department," by Messrs. Buckland and Haywood-Farmer.

The Architect publishes premiated designs for the County Council Offices at Reading and, October 22, the new Fulham Central Library, by Henry T. Hare — that we reproduce — along with the new vestry and chancel for St. Chads Church near Leeds; and, on October 29, views of Selby Abbey and some work of the Liverpool School of Architecture.

The Builder continues to print designs in the Glamorgan County Hall and the County Council Offices for Cornwall and Berkshire Competitions. October 16 Mr. Temple Moore's new nave for Hexham Abbey is published.

La Construction Moderne is more interesting this month than usual, as it provides us with the two reproduced illustrations of a "Pavilion" for W. K. Vanderbilt, by M. Guillaume, and the model of the little Normandy chapel by M. Storez.

(From "The Builder's Journal," London.) *(From "La Construction Moderne.")* *(From "The Builder's Journal," London.)*

Dwelling, Elan Valley Village.
Buckland and Haywood-Farmer, Architects.

"Pavilion," W. K. Vanderbilt.
M. Henri Guillaume, Architect.

Double Cottage, Elan Valley.
Buckland and Haywood-Farmer, Architects.

The Architectural Review

Volume XVI   December, 1909   Number 12

The Preparation of Working Drawings

PART I.

H. Van Buren Magonigle

THE Editor of THE REVIEW is of the opinion that a series of articles treating of the preparation of working drawings and details would be of interest and value; he seems convinced, from the number that pass through his hands in his editorial capacity, that both practitioners and draughtsmen might find in such a series suggestions profitable to them. In the pages that follow it will often be difficult to avoid the didactic tone and the careful explanation of the apparently obvious; but the skilful man will remember that it is not to him the fruits of experience are offered. In the course of years one picks up so many ideas from so many men that it is impossible now to remember whence they all came and give due credit to the proper source; so my friends must grant me absolution from any intention of stealing their thunder, and they are invited to claim their own again when they find it here, with my thanks for its use and help. My greatest debt is to my friend and former chief assistant, Mr. Frank M. Snyder, the author of the remarkable series of plates now appearing under the title "Building Details." We differ on many points on this subject, but we are agreed in the main; and after giving his methods a full trial variants have been developed which seem to me somewhat better adapted to the practical conditions of office work.

Let it be borne in mind from the outset that the point of view here taken is that of a practising architect who believes in a high standard of draughtsmanship in the office; not for the sake of draughtsmanship itself, but *because it is easier to build from a clear, well made, and correct set of drawings than from a sloppy one.* Sloppy drawings are the natural products of sloppy minds. Justification for the unjustifiable is often offered in the familiar phrases, "*We* care for the executed work, not for the drawings;" or, "Drawings are only a means to an end;" and, judging from some of the ends, the means were probably good enough. But to be perfectly plain, such excuses are simple "rot." The best executed work is almost invariably the product of those offices where draughtsmanship is respected as a good means to a good end. Motives of false economy are the frequent source of poor draughtsmanship,—"Get it done!" or "Rush it through!" is the *mot d'ordre* in many offices. Sufficient time is not allowed to study carefully, draw clearly, figure lucidly. Stuff is thrown on a sheet any old way; when the contractor makes a mistake because of ill-digested and careless drawings, let him make it good, or give him an extra!

If half the time spent in most offices looking for lost drawings because of slipshod methods of making and filing them, and half the time consumed in drawing work over twice because "there was no time" was first expended in doing the work right once and for all, and then filing it properly, the "get-it-done" and "rush-it-through" offices would very quickly where the economy so dear to their souls really lies.

An immense amount of time is lost and the running expenses immensely increased in many offices by doing things over and over again, because either the chief or the managing assistant does not get down to business and settle every uncertain or debatable point before the drawings are permitted to go out. *Every drawing should be finished, with every point settled and covered, before it leaves the office.*

As to the draughtsman, the first lesson he has to learn is that his business is to *draw* — not with his hands alone, but also with his head; and if he is too lazy or careless or top-lofty to draw just as well as he possibly can, and then some, and pants for the time when he may drop draughtsmanship and be a real architect, the sooner he becomes an honest butcher the better perhaps for both professions. A friend in need of a draughtsman received a visit from an applicant for the position, who said, "I am a better architect than I am a draughtsman!" My friend was somewhat puzzled — he happened to be an architect himself. Of course the man meant that his judgment and taste and his knowledge of the thing depicted exceeded his ability in depicting the thing. The anecdote serves to emphasize the point that a draughtsman's job is to *draw*, and that is what he is usually hired for; and the further point that he must also draw from the point of view of the practising architect; at the same time as, to a very large extent, he must also work from the point of view of the contractor who is to use the drawings.

Every architect wants a draughtsman to be something more than a mere hewer of pencils and a drawer of lines. The more of an architect a draughtsman is the better draughtsman he must be, and vice versa; and although there have been and are many excellent architects who cannot draw a decent line, it is my firm conviction that they would nevertheless be better architects if they were better able to draw; for unless a man is able to express his ideas himself, with his own hand, the result cannot be truly personal. The personality of the draughtsman is what gets itself executed. It is said of Garnier that he drew the full-size details of every part of the Paris Opera himself; and, whether one likes it or not, it is Garnier and no one else. This is not possible under the usual conditions of practice to-day and in this country — but every architect ought to be *able* to do it; if he is not, his work cannot properly express his own personality. If the eye is not sensitive to the relations of whites, grays, and blacks in a drawing, and the hand not trained to their delicate adjustment on paper, one may hardly expect to see them properly related in the executed work of a man whose eye and hand are not so trained.

The drawing should mean the executed work, of course; but the executed work is first seen in the drawing, and *that* is where it has first to be studied. Draughtsmanship is a man's job and not to be sniffed at. And by draughtsmanship I do not mean the ability to compose and draw charming ornament alone, nor to produce a line of exquisite quality alone, nor precision and clear arrangement and presentation alone, nor legible figuring and lettering alone, nor a knowledge of what the builder needs alone; but a combination of all of these qualities — and more — directed from the heart and brain, not from the eye that watches the clock.

In order that I may not be misunderstood, let me say that I consider the best draughtsman to be the man who can, in the most direct, clear, and simple way, and with the minimum of fuss and turmoil, convey to the builder all the information that is required for a given piece of work,— no more and no less. If his line is good, so much the better; personally, I prefer a good head. Draughtsmen are architects in the making; and if some draughtsmen would only try to remember that besides working for another man they are working for themselves and for their own present increase in knowledge and usefulness and their own future welfare; remember that, in the self-discipline of to-day, they are pre-

Copyright, 1909, by Bates & Guild Company

paring themselves for the worthy practice of the most splendid profession on this earth to-morrow. Your horizon may seem to be restricted; it is not. It is as wide as you make it; and you can't widen it enough in the seven or eight working hours of the office day: there is too much to learn. Put in three or four more hours every day, and see what a year of that will do for you! An interest in your work is presupposed. If you have no interest in it, for God's sake quit! for you'll never become an architect worthy of the name.

There is no high road to success, and the way most of us go is a tough road to travel. My sympathies are all with the man who has never been able to go to a technical school, but plugs along in the office doing his utmost to learn. We'll never learn it all, and that is the joy of it; and it is up to the practising architect to descend from his pedestal once in a while, condescend to give a reason, explain things to a thirsty youngster, and help him to realize that drawings mean architecture; and architecture — what does it not mean?

The term "working drawing" as used herein means not only the small-scale general drawings, but those of larger scale as well, including full-size details. A working drawing is neither a picture nor a sketch, but a serious scientific document in which ambiguities have no place: it should present the information to be conveyed to the builder in the clearest and simplest possible form; it should be complete in every essential detail so far as it is determined to make the drawing go; it should be as condensed as may be consistent with absolute readability; and avoid the repetition of parts already shown or elsewhere given. Each individual drawing should be planned as carefully to effect these things as the building itself; and to do this properly is to know what, for example, in the case of a plan, is to go on that plan and prepare for it beforehand; and not to find — after spending hours figuring it — that some symbol that has been forgotten, indicating lights or switches or whatever, should go just where some figure or line that will confuse it occurs.

The essential and the non-essential, what to show and what to leave out, — this takes experience or good teaching to discover; but *when in doubt don't leave out anything!* Better a dozen repetitions than a solitary omission of an essential. There are very few full-size details that cannot be so condensed with a little thought and by squeezing the essential parts together that they will occupy but a fraction of the area usually given to them. The lazy or careless draughtsman will often give his chief or the superintendent endless trouble and annoyance because he has been too indolent to look up some point or to show something with the exact workings of which he is unfamiliar, and so slurs it over or puts in anything. *It takes less time to do a thing properly in the first place than to correct resulting mistakes.* And it is to be remembered that if contractors and workmen make errors, even when using drawings prepared with the utmost care, the chance of more mistakes in using sloppy drawings is increased in a direct ratio to the extent of their sloppiness.

It is, on the other hand, easy to push virtue to a point where it becomes a fault and the non-essential is given as much importance and emphasis as the essential. This is the common fault of the would-be careful man who has lost his sense of proportion and cares so much for the drawing *as* a drawing that he has lost sight of what it is, or rather should be; a clear, graphic representation of something that is to be built, not a picture nor a heaven-sent opportunity to show his chief how beautifully he can draw exactly the same kind of thing over and over again on the same sheet — and forget to put on an important dimension! In fact, some men seem to think that figures, notes, and similar prosaic practical information spoil a drawing, and hate to put them on.

In the opinion of the writer, a working drawing, and especially a detail, should be so complete that reference to the specifications is unnecessary; frequently quotations from the specifications as to the finish of materials or some special point of construction impracticable to indicate graphically should be considered as essential parts of a complete drawing; and the text of explanatory notes should be carefully considered, so that they really explain and are not confusing to the builder.

No man can make a really good working drawing unless he is familiar with actual building-operations. There are hundreds of draughtsmen who never get a chance to visit a job, a mill, or a yard and see their work in execution, and in three dimensions. Theory, not practice, controls them. They are told by the chief to "make it bigger," and they make it bigger; to "make it smaller," and they make it smaller — often without reason asked or given. They do not visualize because they are neither taught nor helped to visualize.

It would be to the interest of every practising architect to give all his men (and the younger the man the more important that he should have the opportunity) a chance, not necessarily to "superintend," but to see how the stuff they have been drawing works out in execution. A boy will learn more about making framing plans in an hour spent at the building, seeing the beams he has drawn, in place, than he would in six months at a drawing-board being told what to do, instead of doing it for himself because he then knows from his own observation what is right. The boy is helped to become more valuable, and the "boss" is that much better off. (A demand for a raise will ultimately follow, of course, but that is a necessary evil to be met with such courage as one may command.) A man who does not see what his work looks like when executed more than once a year or so can hardly be blamed if he continues to make the same mistakes year after year in scale, or in the relations of various projections to each other, or in the profiles of moldings. Of course it is difficult to arrange in a busy office, but it would pay in the end.

The first point about working drawings to be considered here is convenience in filing for daily reference in the office; and their use in the field, which includes not only the building, but the contractor's office, his shop, and the offices and shops of the subcontractors.

All the drawings — general, large-scale, and full-size — for each building should be made on sheets of tracing cloth or paper of a uniform size; as may be established for that building. This solves once and for all the vexed question of filing drawings and, as will be seen, of finding a drawing when it is wanted. In practice, an office-copy print should be made of every drawing as soon as it is finished; and, each drawing being numbered consecutively, *the last-made print is bound in with the others in its proper numerical order, and stays there.* This set of prints is used for office reference, and the originals are placed, also in their numerical order, in a manila folder in the bottom of the drawer; and kept fresh and in good condition for further prints as they may be needed. By this method there is no excuse for losing a drawing, nor for not finding it in an instant; it is bound in with the others and can't get away.

This system also eliminates card indexes, and all the other cumbersome systems of keeping track of drawings; one is no longer at the mercy of the office-boy or the filing-clerk; all *he* has to do is to bind each office copy as it comes back from the printers into the file set, and that ends it.

When a small revision has to be made in a hurry it is often hard to resist the temptation to make it on a scrap of paper or cloth — but it is just these scraps that are always being lost, and they are nearly always, from a business point of view, very important, as showing, perhaps, an extra or an allowance. It can usually, however, be placed on a standard sheet, and other later revisions can be put on that same sheet; this naturally takes some head work on the part of the man in charge of the job, but it has been proven possible in practice.

More often than not, one must consult more than one drawing (and sometimes two, three, or four) to get at all the conditions governing some point that is to be decided. Instead of calling for "the first-floor plan, the front elevation, the ¾" detail of the central bay, and the full sizes of the entrance doorway," which are found probably only after a long delay, intense excitement, pulling out all the drawers in the case to see if one of the drawings wanted has not "slipped down behind," threats of discharge, and the final discovery of a missing drawing in the wrong drawer; you find you need still another drawing — more excitement, more lost time, more threats. Instead of this daily or hourly upheaval, you have only to say, "Give me the Jones house drawings" or "The State Capitol set," and there they are, all together, every drawing in its place in the set; and you can turn over from one drawing to the other, refer back, look at a third;—all peace, all quiet, and the hunted look leaves the eye of the office-boy. This method is recommended to irritable temperaments. After adopting it, every lapse brings swift retribution in the old confusion, the old chaos, the old irritation.

For a very large piece of work it is well to divide the set into two or more parts, to keep it from being unwieldy. When a job is finished the drawings are filed flat, just as they are, in a complete set — general drawings, scale details, and full sizes — and any one of them can then be found years afterward at a moment's notice.

Rolling drawings is a primitive, space-wasting, and maddening way to file them, or to keep them during the progress of the work. A drawing of any sort for office use should never be rolled; and when prints or drawings are to be sent or taken out they should be rolled *face out*, so that they will lie flat when opened and laid right side up. For daily reference, the drawings for a job in course of construction, or of which the general drawings are finished and detailing is in progress, are in many offices placed in a contrivance similar to a newspaper file and hung on a rack in the draughting-room; and in one of the largest offices in the country, for very large work where many men need to refer to the general drawings constantly, half a dozen reference sets are printed and made available for their use.

As to the contractor; he may keep the drawings as he pleases, except at the building; but he receives as many prints of each drawing as he requires — one for his office, one for use on the work, and one for each of the sub-contractors in the different branches of the work covered by the drawing. Each print is thus to all intents and purposes an original drawing. Not so very long ago it was the custom (and it still exists here and there) for architects to maintain a corps of draughtsmen, haughty creatures who scorned tracing-cloth, and a body of wretched beings called tracers. The draughtsmen made the "originals" on manila or similar paper, which was turned over to the tracers to make the copy from which the print that went into the hands of the builder was made. The original may or may not have been correct—if the copy was, it was more good luck than good management! In the case of full-size details the original on manila was sent out, and a copy on tracing-paper was made for office use and reference. Somebody had either to "take a chance," and let the original go out without a proper scrutiny of the copy; or else, if he were really conscientious, had to look over it once to discover omissions and mistakes, again to see if they had all been corrected, and then repeat the wearisome process until he could be sure that, when the copy was referred to later, it would be found complete and accurate. Let any head draughtsman who has done or is doing this sort of thing, and any practising architect who was trained in an office, look back to the years when they were boys tracing lines to them absolutely meaningless, try to recall the dense fog in which their minds then worked, try to realize the ignorance (not the lack of intelligence) of the average boy; and then ask themselves whether it is fair to the client, to himself, or to the boy to continue such a practice.

Also, the detail copies usually become torn and worthless in a very short time, if they do not get lost or misplaced. Further, instead of the architect providing the builder with a number of absolutely accurate copies of the original for the necessary distribution among sub-contractors, he is left to make his own copies, with as many chances for more mistakes as a builder's draughtsman is worse than an architect's, multiplied by the number of copies made. It is perfectly true that many drawings that come from an architect's office have to be drawn over by the contractor and made into a "shop drawing" better adapted to the intelligence of the workmen who are to get out the work (especially in the case of cabinet-makers); but it is also perfectly true that it is better for the contractor's draughtsman to work from an accurate original than from an inaccurate copy. *The fewer hands intervening between the architect himself and the executed work the better* — and the less possibility of mistakes of intention intervening; and to entrust inexperienced boys with the production of the document that goes into the hands of the builder is an entirely reprehensible practice.

I wonder whether the old custom of coloring prints by hand still exists anywhere; if it does, the man who keeps it up is respectfully referred to a future chapter on "Indications of Materials." The junior draughtsmen in progressive offices to-day can have no idea of the horrible drudgery of coloring fifteen or twenty sets of ten or twelve prints each. It is small wonder that in those old bad days we sometimes used to make them different, just to vary the hideous monotony!

What has been written above is meant to clear the ground; to define a working drawing, and draughtsmanship as applied to working drawings; to plead for a more sympathetic relation between the practitioner and his draughtsmen; and, perhaps, to indulge a little in that propensity for preaching so difficult to resist when one is made free of the pulpit. In future chapters processes, methods, and systems will be discussed, and illustrated with examples drawn from various sources.

Plaster House at Bronxville, New York.
Delano & Aldrich, Architects.

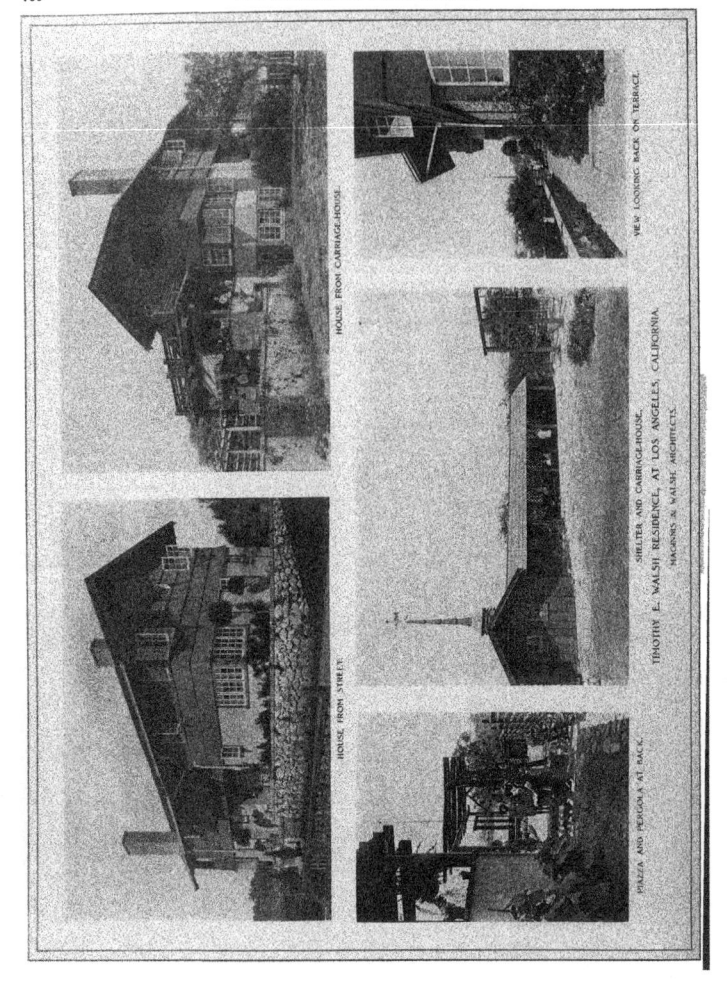

160 THE ARCHITECTURAL REVIEW

HOUSE FROM CARRIAGE-HOUSE.

VIEW LOOKING BACK ON TERRACE.

HOUSE FROM STREET.

SHELTER AND CARRIAGE-HOUSE.

TIMOTHY E. WALSH RESIDENCE, AT LOS ANGELES, CALIFORNIA.

HAGGARD & WALSH, ARCHITECTS.

PIAZZA AND PERGOLA AT BACK.

BEDROOM

DINING ROOM

HALL AND STAIRCASE

LIVING ROOM

TIMOTHY E. WALSH RESIDENCE, AT LOS ANGELES, CALIFORNIA
HUNT & WALSH, ARCHITECTS

DETAIL OF EAST LOGGIA, RESIDENCE FOR MR. WILLIAM MAXWELL, ROCKVILLE, CONN.
CHARLES A. PLATT, ARCHITECT

MODERN ENGLISH COUNTRY HOUSES

ENTRANCE FRONT, CLIVE HOUSE, ROEHAMPTON, ENGLAND.
C. H. B. QUENNELL, ARCHITECT.

ENTRANCE FRONT, RESIDENCE FOR MR. WILLIAM MAXWELL, ROCKVILLE, CONN.
CHARLES A. PLATT, ARCHITECT.

DOORWAY. RESIDENCE FOR MR. WILLIAM MAXWELL, ROCKVILLE, CONN.
CHARLES A. PLATT, ARCHITECT.

THIRD FLOOR PLAN.

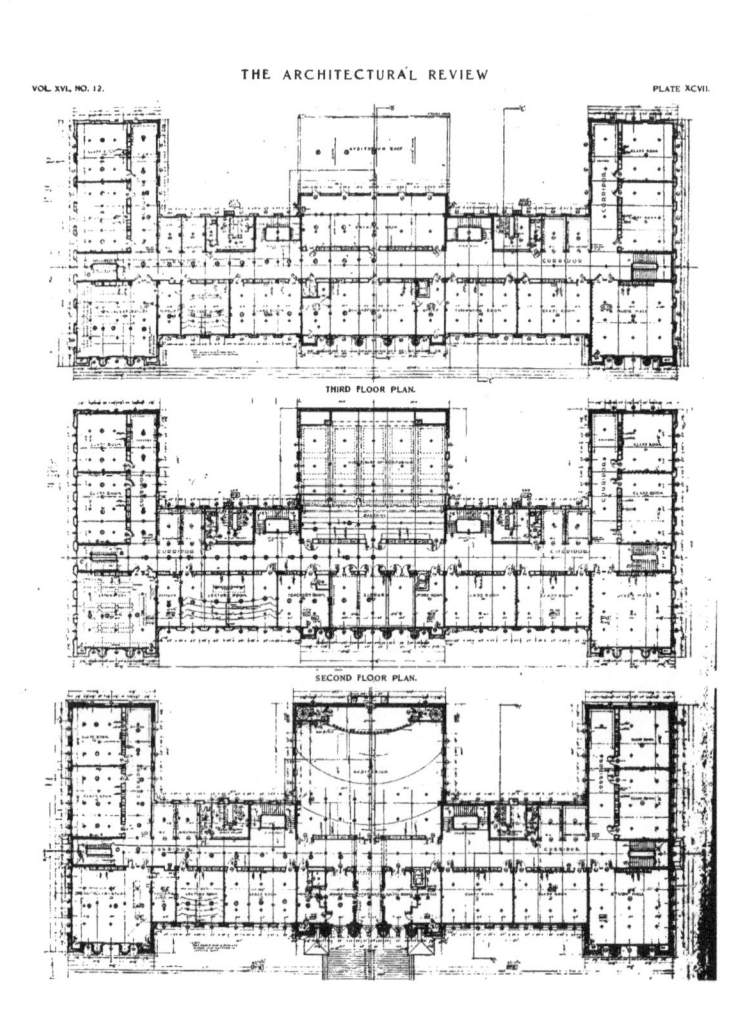

SECOND FLOOR PLAN.

VOL. XVI., NO. 12.

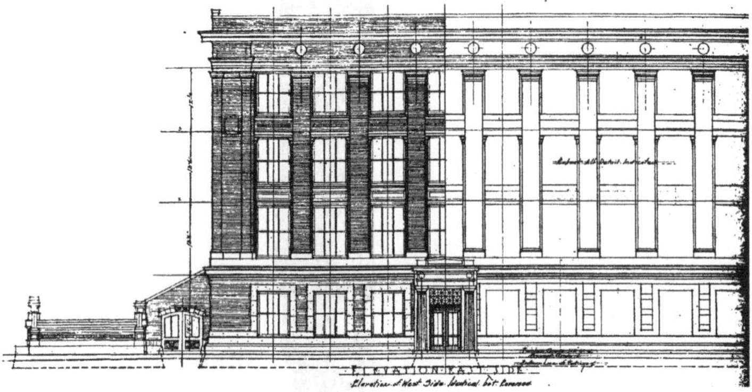

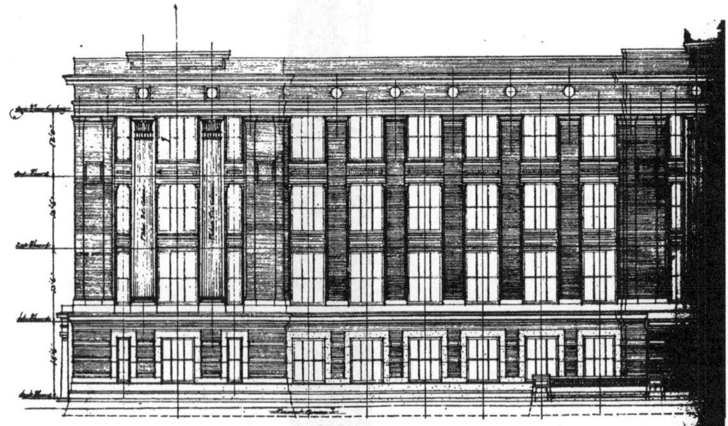

ELEVATIONS AN

E VIEW.

PLATES XCVIII, XCIX.

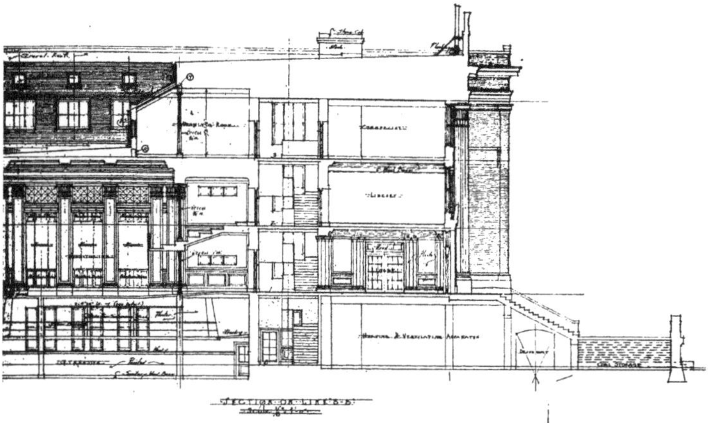

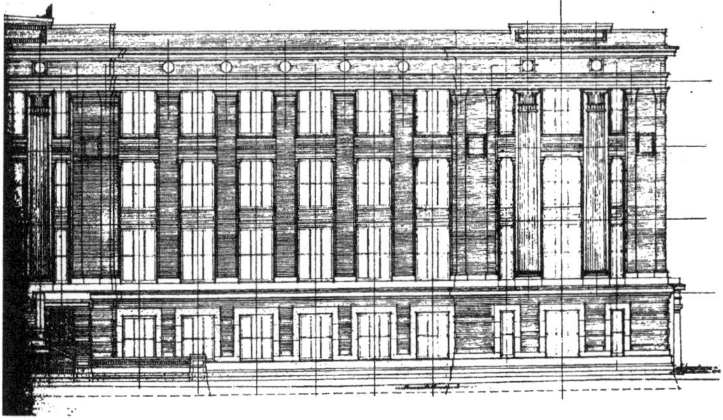

NORFOLK, VA.

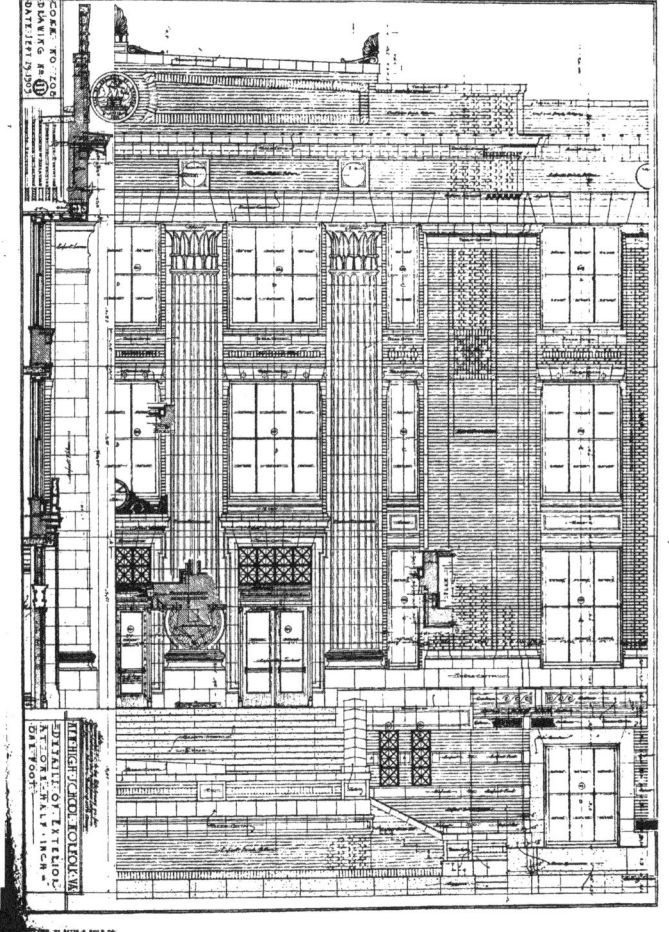

EXTERIOR DETAILS, NORFOLK HIGH SCHOOL, NORFOLK, VA.
NEFF & THOMPSON, ARCHITECTS.

DETAIL RESIDENCE FOR MR. WILLIAM MAXWELL, ROCKVILLE, CONN.
CHARLES A. PLATT, ARCHITECT.

GARDEN FRONT, RESIDENCE FOR MR. WILLIAM MAXWELL, ROCKVILLE, CONN.
CHARLES A. PLATT, ARCHITECT.

MODERN ENGLISH COUNTRY HOUSES

GARDEN FRONT, CLIVE HOUSE, ROEHAMPTON, ENGLAND.
C. H. B. QUENNELL, ARCHITECT.

PLATE XVI.

MODERN ENGLISH COUNTRY HOUSES

GARDEN FRONT, CLIVE HOUSE, ROEHAMPTON, ENGLAND.
C. H. B. QUENNELL, ARCHITECT.

PLATE XVI.

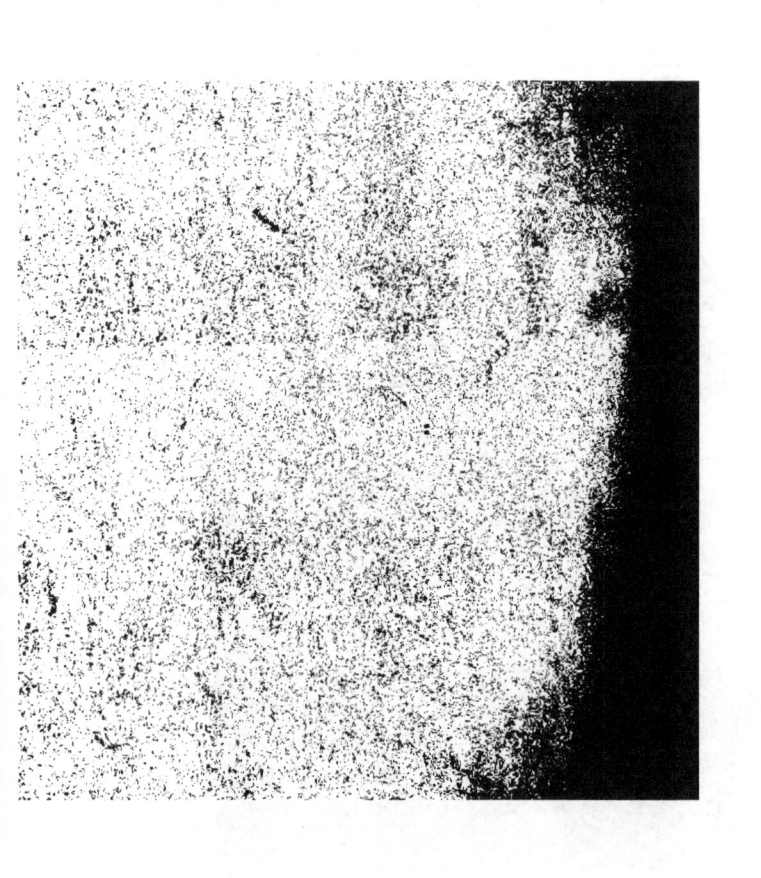

ENTRANCE CORRIDOR. WINDOW ON STAIRS.

VISTA FROM DRAWING-ROOM THROUGH MUSIC-ROOM TO DINING-ROOM.
INTERIORS, CLIVE HOUSE, ROEHAMPTON, ENGLAND.   C. H. B. QUENNELL, ARCHITECT.

164 THE ARCHITECTURAL REVIEW

ENTRANCE FRONT, ROBERT TODD LINCOLN RESIDENCE.

RESIDENCE OF ROBERT TODD LINCOLN AT MANCHESTER, VT.

EDWARD S. GREW RESIDENCE, MANCHESTER, MASS.

SUMMERFIELD HAGGERTY HOUSE AT CLIFTON, MASS.

THREE PLASTER DWELLINGS BY SHEPLEY, RUTAN & COOLIDGE, ARCHITECTS.

The Architectural Review

VOLUME XVI. NUMBER 12

DECEMBER, 1909

BATES & GUILD COMPANY, Publishers
144 Congress Street, Boston
NEW YORK OFFICE, PARK ROW BUILDING

Published monthly. Price, mailed flat to any address in the United States or Canada, five dollars per annum, in advance; to any foreign address, six dollars per annum, in advance. Subscriptions begin with the issue following their receipt. Single copies, fifty cents. Special numbers, two dollars. Entered as second-class mail-matter at the Post-office, Boston, Massachusetts, November 27, 1891.

PLATES

PLATES XCV.— XCVI.— RESIDENCE FOR WILLIAM MAXWELL, ROCKVILLE, CONN. (PHOTOGRAPHIC VIEWS) — CHARLES A. PLATT, ARCHITECT.

PLATES XCVII.— C.— HIGH SCHOOL, NORFOLK, VA. (PLANS, ELEVATIONS, AND DETAILS) — NEFF & THOMPSON, ARCHITECTS.

PLATES CI.— CII.— RESIDENCE FOR WILLIAM MAXWELL, ROCKVILLE, CONN. (PHOTOGRAPHIC VIEWS) — CHARLES A. PLATT, ARCHITECT.

ONE of the matters now before the Institute of Architects (as well as a number of the individual chapters composing the national body), and most demanding an immediate settlement, is concerned with the relationship to exist between the younger men, who at present naturally compose the League, or the Architectural Clubs — where such exist — and the older body, largely composed of practising members of the profession.

We would direct attention toward the necessity, under which the Institute — and, in even greater degree, every separate chapter, as well — now lies, for its own preservation, to incorporate into its membership in some way or other the younger men; and so benefit by an infusion of younger blood. Among those matters brought up at the last convention, this was certainly not the least important; and upon its successful solution depends the future growth and development of the American Institute of Architects.

At present the Institute — along with many of its chapters — is unprogressive; largely because of the dominance exercised by older members, that rarely places any of the younger men in positions of importance. The chapters — and the Institute — include among their membership less than ten per cent of the available number of younger architectural practitioners! The last reports of the Committee on Junior Membership unfortunately were not calculated to help toward a solution of the problem, their suggestions being too complicated and, in some ways, too radical to meet with the approval of the Institute as a whole. Yet this should not prevent the subject being given the most careful consideration. There is no reason that, instead of — or supplementary to — the present procedure of obtaining membership in the Institute of Architects, membership in that body could not be made one of a series of progressive steps that — once initiated — would progress almost automatically. For instance, a graduate of an architectural school, or a draughtsman of a certain number of years' experience, becomes eligible for membership in an architectural club — such club being either a junior department of the local chapter of the American Institute or, through its affiliation with the Architectural League, under their patronage and partial control; especially so far as concerns the system of educational classes, which now constitutes a large part of the architectural clubs' interest and work. A certain number of years' membership in the club would perhaps make the member eligible for junior membership in the local chapter of the Institute and, after one or two more years, he might become eligible to full or regular membership, *carrying along with it* membership in the American Institute, the grade of Fellow being retained as an honorary title and bestowed much as it is at present.

While this does not solve all the difficulties of the situation, it would at least offer a working basis of more simplicity of interrelation than was suggested by the committee who last dealt with this problem. That the Institute should exercise a control over the education of the draughtsman, there can be no doubt; that a proper relation between the two would be mutually helpful to both, there can also be no question. It merely remains to provide the necessary machinery that will cause the relation to be fruitful to both parties; and this is, after all, a matter of not unsurmountable difficulty. The relation to be borne by the Institute to the League need not of necessity enter into the matter. The League could well remain, as at present, a collection of the younger clubs having for its laudable purpose the matter of the general education of their members; and the yearly issuance of a book, or other publication, representative of their ambitions or ideals.

SOME such action as this would, at least, do away with the present undignified and confusing state of affairs — existing, as it appears, only by sufferance as a survival from a period when conditions were altogether different from what they are at present. A person in full and regular membership in a chapter of the Institute should, *ipso facto*, become a member of the American Institute. If acceptable to the chapter, he ought certainly to be eligible to the Institute; and it would save much confusion if, in this one matter alone, Institute membership could be standardized.

Some few chapters of the Institute already possess a class of members known as Juniors. As a rule, the junior members are the older men in the architectural clubs: either those starting practice for themselves, or those having active charge of offices for the larger firms. It is from this class that the Institute, as well as the chapter, must draw its future membership — just as the junior class is yearly reinforced by men from the architectural schools and clubs below it. Their interests are identical; while it is obvious that both organizations would benefit from a closer relationship.

The officers of the Architectural League are at present fully impressed with the importance of obtaining some working agreement by which they may perform more effective work in the profession, and their members ultimately be taken into the Institute. The League possesses the more enthusiasm and initiative, but the less authority. Offered the proper incentive and recognition, its members would undoubtedly work to better purpose. It remains merely for the Institute to proffer this recognition and take advantage, in what ways it can, of the spirit now ruling in the Architectural League.

CERTAIN remarks made by Senator Elihu Root at the formation of the American Federation of Arts were most illuminative as to the demand for such an organization and the specific objects for which it was formed. These included encouragement of private artists and exhibitions for the benefit and education of the public; encouragement of the study of art in the public schools; provision for the appointment of proper commissions, municipal and otherwise, to supervise public art and architecture, to improve the standards of private architecture, the arrangement of buildings, monuments and other improvements in our cities and at our national Capitol; to assist in preserving from destruction our natural scenery and forests, and to preserve all our remaining historic and natural landmarks; to support the movement for the organization of a Bureau of Fine Arts; to support and advance the project for a National Gallery of Art, and to obtain the erection of an appropriate building for this purpose at Washington.

From this brief enumeration, it can be seen how wide the field is to be bettered by the work of such an organization — provided only that it is properly directed. Besides those general suggestions advocated in Senator Root's speech, he expressed a specific promise of official support for the movement for a Bureau of Fine Arts that was last year inaugurated by the Institute of Architects.

Senator Root was followed by Senator Newlands, who promised, as well, to bring before Congress in the immediate future a bill for the Council of Fine Arts recently dissolved by President Taft; while he prophesied that the Government would soon encourage and support schools of Fine Arts and Architecture — in the same way that they already foster schools of Agriculture and the Mechanic Arts!

Current Periodicals
A Review of the Recent American And Foreign Architectural Publications

(From "The American Architect.")

Liberty School, Englewood, N. J.
Davis, McGrath & Kiessling, Architects.

THE November *Brickbuilder* is largely devoted to the showing of schoolhouses: two for Boston, three in Chicago, one in Mt. Vernon, and another in Washington being illustrated and described. Of all the number, only the Bishop Cheverus School in Boston has the separately located first-floor auditorium that appears to be the coming custom, albeit it is at the rear rather than the front of the building and does not appear to have the separate public entrances that are its most important requisite. Albro & Lindeberg's Mt. Vernon School (published in last month's REVIEW) is here shown completed. Chicago seems momentarily to have ceased experimenting in the most modern of American architectural styles and has cast back into historic archæology for the principal motives of the three schools reproduced, all being atavistic in tendency. One suggests a buttressed type of early Gothic; another is perhaps Egyptian in the expression of its cornice and general form; while the third is — possibly — Assyrian, although its most prominent architectural motive appears based upon the Cleopatra needle. Of them all, we should select Marsh & Peter's Washington School as being most sanely modern and architecturally commendable in style.

Coolidge & Carlson's small Squash Court at North Easton is unusually dashing and attractive — although hardly satisfactory as regards scale; the very small dentils and refined moldings of the wooden entablature not consorting with the large brick and stone members. Also, why the cusped or circular topped door-panels? An elaborate garden and house at Cleveland by C. F. Schweinfurth are shown, the former being especially interesting. A brick Colonial house by Newman &

(From "The Brickbuilder.")

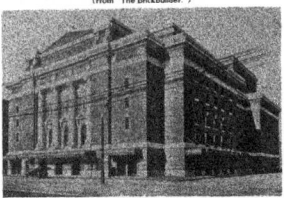

Boston Opera-House, Boston, Mass.
Wheelwright & Haven, Architects.

(From "The American Architect.")

Orient Life Insurance Building, Hartford, Conn.
Davis & Brooks, Architects.

(From "The American Architect.")

Dining-Hall and Dormitory, Auburn, Ala.
Warren & Welton, Architects.

(From "The American Architect.")

High School, Simsbury, Conn.
E. F. Hapgood, Architect.

Harris is rather disappointing — principally from the undue number of bays and porches added to an otherwise dignified central motive — the modern amendments being quite irreconcilable with the simplicity necessary to the Georgian style of dwelling.

Finally, Wheelwright & Haven's Boston Opera-House is illustrated by exterior and interior views. Satisfactory as this building is in meeting the general requirements of its purpose, it is, architecturally, regretfully to be classed as another of Boston's lost architectural opportunities. On the interior, the contrast between the over-simple surfaces and light coloring of the walls and the over-dark and rich material of the draperies should certainly have been avoided. The moldings around the proscenium arch are also too many and too retiring, and one wonders how the treatment adopted for the proscenium boxes above the balcony tier could ever have been carried through into execution. Despite the great height of the auditorium (emphasized by the columns between these boxes), the requirements of an audience interested more in the stage than in their neighbors have been exceptionally well satisfied. Exteriorly, of course, the location is most to be regretted. Hardly any city other than musical Boston would for a moment have contemplated disposing their principal Opera-House in a storage-warehouse district. It consequently naturally follows that the façade must be unpretentious, almost to the point of being commonplace.

In view of the reception accorded the MacMonnies Bacchante in Boston, the observer is curious to see how long it will take that same city to awaken to the joke played on them in Bela Pratt's panel of "The Dance," where a figure surprisingly

(From "The Brickbuilder.")

Bernhard Moos School, Chicago, Ill.
Dwight H. Perkins, Architect.

Laboratory Building, Chicago, Ill.
Hill & Wollersdorf, Architects.

Tilton School, Chicago, Ill.
Dwight H. Perkins, Architect.

THE ARCHITECTURAL REVIEW

(From "The Brickbuilder.")

Squash Court, North Easton, Mass.
Coolidge & Carlson, Architects.

(From "The Brickbuilder.")

Henry D. Cooke School, Washington, D. C.
Marsh & Peter, Architects.

(From "The Brickbuilder.")

Garden at Cleveland, Ohio.
C. F. Schweinfurth, Architect.

(From "The Architectural Record.")

William G. Mather House, Cleveland, Ohio.
Charles A. Platt, Architect.

like unto the statue prim and prudish Boston has already scorned is prominently displayed! We also note that, in reproducing these three panels, credit is given both to the Atlantic Terra-Cotta Company and to the architects — but that the modest sculptor has been entirely overlooked!

The Architectural Record for November is issued as a "Country House Number," and numerously illustrates recent suburban American domestic architecture. Mr. Platt's Mather house at Cleveland — as far as may be seen from the reproductions attempted in this magazine — gives opportunity for a garden lay-out such as he has not had since the two gardens of Weld and Faulkner Farm) The garden is, on the whole, Italian in spirit — considerably more so than the house itself, which, nearly white in color, is rather pompous Georgian of that type of which the city of Bath and vicinity has given us several historic examples.

Among the other houses reproduced, several are already familiar from previous publication, including Bosworth & Holden's very attractive house at Oceanic, N. J. (illustrated in these columns last May), Marshall & Fox's Miller house at Barrington, Ill. (which we reproduced last March), the Norton house at Lake Forest, Ill., by Richard E. Schmidt, Garden & Martin (published in our last Februray number), and Horace Trumbauer's classic Scott house at Lansdowne (which we reproduced and mentioned last October). One of the most effective portions of the issue is devoted to the recent work of Howard Shaw, of which the Fernald house — a treatment based on wholly domestic and charming Colonial forms — is, so far as appears in the illustrations, the most distinctive. Among the most attractive illustrations are two smaller houses by Charles Barton Keen (not forgetting a delightful spring-house!) on the estate of Mr. Sharples at West Chester, Penn., which we prefer to the larger manor house itself — despite a charming use of ledge stone, such as we seem unable to obtain elsewhere than

(From "The Architectural Record.")

The Dale House, Winnetka, Ill.
Perkins & Hamilton, Architects.

(From "The Architectural Record.")

in the vicinity of Philadelphia. Mr. Thompson's house at Hamilton, O., is disappointing, particularly upon the interior. Mr. Wallis' additions to the Dixon house somewhat overweight the original building; and his Earle residence, while an interesting essay in suiting a distinctive English type of design to American conditions, does not yet solve that problem. Frost & Granger's Dangler residence at Lake Forest is exteriorly more successful, although hardly anything worse than the library mantelpiece is to be found in recent American architecture. A group of Western designs illustrates attractive houses by Perkins & Hamilton, Pond & Pond, Spencer & Powers, Bohnard & Parsson, W. A. Otis, and Myron Hunt & Elmer Grey.

The American Architect for November 3 has an article of direct practical value — rather the exception for this magazine — treating of "The Essentials of Fireplace Construction." Messrs. Davis & Brooks's Orient Insurance Company Building at Hartford, Conn., and the First National Banks of Hoboken, N. J., and Lynchburg, Va., by Kenneth Murchison and P. Thorton Marye, respectively, are shown. We select a view of the first named for reproduction.

November 10 some interesting factories by Hill & Woltersdorf are illustrated and described. The one at Chicago we have already reproduced in these columns. Warren & Welton's dining-hall at the Polytechnic Institute at Auburn, Ala., is a simple and commendable modernization of Southern brick Colonial motives — much better than most of the Southern work this magazine has published during the last half-dozen months.

November 17 is a "special number" on schoolhouses, with a very haphazard selection of reproductions made from completed buildings and of sketches for others proposed. Several of the best have already been illustrated, including Carrère & Hastings' Ely School at Greenwich and Mr. Magonigle's school at Briar Cliff Manor. As a rule, the buildings conform to those types that have now become

Bishop House, Sharples Estate, West Chester, Pa.
Charles Barton Keen, Architect.

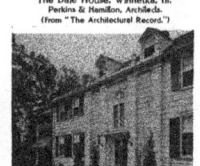

Entrance, Chas. Fernald House, Lake Forest, Ill.
Howard Shaw, Architect.

Spring-house, Sharples Estate, West Chester, Pa.
Charles Barton Keen, Architect.

pretty well established in our more advanced communities. Because of their picturesque elements — a characteristic rather rarely appearing in this class of building design — we have selected for reproduction Davis, McGrath & Kiessling's school at Englewood and E. F. Hapgood's building at Simsbury, Conn.

November 24 contains Mr. Swales's "Notes from Europe" and, for plates, drawings of a brick school of Industrial Arts at Trenton, by Cass Gilbert, and a Club-House at York Harbor, by James Purdon.

The November *Western Architect* illustrates hotels for Chicago and Buffalo, the latter, by Esenwein & Johnson, having interiors of a decided Art Nouveau tendency. Two residences at Lake Forest by George W. Maher are also "Art Nouveau," but a bit more in "the Chicago style." A Kansas City school by Charles A. Smith and a New York house façade by J. H. Freedlander are both interesting — the latter rather surprisingly restrained and simple, the only questionable detail being the very temporary appearance of the brick vestibule attached to the stone house front. The best bit of monumental architecture is The Pacific Mutual Life Insurance Building at Los Angeles, quite evidently inspired by the Knickerbocker Trust.

Architecture for November shows an attractive study for a Society building at Yale University, by Donn Barber, and photographs from Lord & Hewlett's model for a Soldiers' and Sailors' Memorial at Albany, N. Y. Several residences of varying degrees of attraction by W. B. Tubby, Milton See & Son, and Mellor & Meigs are also reproduced. The most remarkable part of this number, however, is the plate section — entirely devoted to showing interiors of a Masonic Temple in New York, dignified by such euphonistic and pretentious titles as "the Renaissance room," "the Colonial room," "the Grecian-Ionic room," "the Gothic room," "the Grecian-Doric room," etc., *ad infinitum!* A careful regard for the artistic sensibilities of our subscribers prevents us from here reproducing

(From "Architecture.")

Homœopathic Cottage Hospital, Southport, Eng.
H. P. Adams and Charles Holden, Architects.
(From "The Builder," London.)

House at Bishopthorpe, York, Eng.
Walter H. Brierley, F.S.A., Architect.
(From "The Architectural Review," London.)

Canadian Bank of Commerce, Montreal, Can.
Frank Darling, Architect.
(From "The Architect," London.)

any one of the interiors named.

The English *Architectural Review* for November is particularly valuable for the English Renaissance exterior and interior details contained in its "Practical Exemplar" and for the article on Ebberston Lodge in Yorkshire. Some Paris buildings by Charles Mèwes are illustrated, and, in "Current Architecture," Darling & Pearson's Bank of Commerce at Montreal. Mr. Macartney's Pump-house, Seddlescombe, Sussex, is particularly charming, and a Crematorium with a chimney disguised as a tower is both doubtful architecture and poor art.

The Builder's Journal for November 3 contains some work by Lanchester & Rickards and, November 24, an article by Mr. Triggs on "Planning and Laying Out the Public Places."

The Builder, for November 13, shows a small house by Walter Brierley and a garden pavilion by Frank Atkinson. On November 20 it publishes the selected set of drawings for the proposed training-college at Hull — Crouch, Butler & Savage, architects— which, unfortunately, it is impossible to reproduce.

The Architect for November 12 publishes competitive drawings for several town halls, and a small house by A. Jessop Hardwick. November 19 a couple of competitive drawings for the Berkshire County Council Offices are illustrated, along with Skipper & Skipper's scheme for the Hull Training-College, again unsuited to reproduction; and a rather out-of-the-usual classic church design by F. A. Walters, portraying more than a suggestion of the "Art Nouveau" influence. November 26 appear two other schemes for the training-college at Hull, a somewhat belated design for the Glamorgan County Offices, and a design for the Northern Assurance Company's Offices in London, that is rather simpler than they are wont to do in that metropolis.

La Construction Moderne for October 30 contains M. Tony Garnier's comprehensive scheme for a new abbatoir at Lyon; and on November 13 is shown a new building for the Minstère des Postes et Telegraphes at Martignac.

(From "The Architect," London.)

House at Kingston Hill.
A. Jessop Hardwick, F.R.I.B.A., Architect.

Church of SS. Anselm and Cecilia, London.
F. A. Walters, A.R.I.B.A., Architect.

(From "The Architect," London.)

Northern Assurance Company's Offices, London.
The Late E. A. Gruning, and E. W. Mountford, FF.R.I.B.A., Archts.